T0267373

Information Security:
Principles and Practices

Information Security: Principles and Practices

Edited by
Miles Carr

Larsen & Keller
www.larsen-keller.com

Information Security: Principles and Practices
Edited by Miles Carr
ISBN: 978-1-63549-151-7 (Hardback)

© 2017 Larsen & Keller

Larsen & Keller

Published by Larsen and Keller Education,
5 Penn Plaza,
19th Floor,
New York, NY 10001, USA

Cataloging-in-Publication Data

Information security : principles and practices / edited by Miles Carr.
    p. cm.
Includes bibliographical references and index.
ISBN 978-1-63549-151-7
1. Information technology--Security measures. 2. Computer networks--Security measures. 3. Computer security.
4. Cryptography. 5. Data encryption (Computer science). I. Carr, Miles.

TK5105.59 .I54 2017
005.8--dc23

The publisher's policy is to use permanent paper from mills that operate a sustainable forestry policy. Furthermore, the publisher ensures that the text paper and cover boards used have met acceptable environmental accreditation standards.

Printed and bound in the United States of America.

For more information regarding Larsen and Keller Education and its products, please visit the publisher's website www.larsen-keller.com

Table of Contents

Preface

This book elucidates the concepts and innovative models around prospective developments with respect to information security. It talks in detail about the various methods and applications of this subject. Information security refers to the practice of safeguarding the information from theft, unauthorized use, modification, distortion, inspection, destruction, etc. It consists of IT security and information assurance. The aim of this text is to provide the readers with topics which are crucial and of utmost importance. While understanding the long-term perspectives of the topics, the book makes an effort in highlighting their impact as a modern tool for the growth of the discipline. It will serve as a valuable source of reference for those interested in this field.

A short introduction to every chapter is written below to provide an overview of the content of the book:

Chapter 1 In this age of information technology the need to ensure the safety of data has become a paramount concern for companies and organizations across the world. Information security refers to the protection of data from unapproved access, use, deletion while preserving confidentiality. It is a term used regardless of the form of data i.e. physical or electronic; **Chapter 2** - This chapter elucidates the various approaches to information security like data-centric security, bottom-up, top-down etc. The chapter also talks about the various techniques that help in the implementation of these approaches like data masking, cyber security standards, global surveillance etc.; **Chapter 3** Sometimes referred to as IT security, computer security indicates the security involved in the protection of technology. Information systems are prone to attacks by hackers who steal sensitive data or try and disrupt the functioning of businesses. IT security ensures that the systems are protected on a real-time basis. This chapter describes the various methods of protection of information systems; **Chapter 4** - Organizations are becoming largely dependent on information and its processing hence there is always a potential to risk and this can unfold in the manner of a security incident or event. To mitigate this, there are several IT risk laws and regulations in place. This chapter provides an insight into these areas and provides valuable information about the various challenges and threats to computer technology; **Chapter 5** - Encryption ensures that only the person meant to receive the data can make sense of it. Cryptography studies the techniques used for secure data communication. This chapter provides an in-depth study of the discipline while delving into topics like copyright infringement, enterprise information security architecture, network security, digital rights management etc.; **Chapter 6** - Cryptography as a discipline is extensive and this chapter focuses on its various aspects and forms. Confidentiality, authentication, data integrity and non-repudiation are some of the aspects of cryptography explored in this chapter. Based on the type of key used, the forms of cryptography can be broadly divided into symmetric-key algorithm and public-key algorithm, both of which have been studied in detail. Also this chapter scrutinizes topics like Cryptanalysis, Network Security Services, data security etc.

Finally, I would like to thank my fellow scholars who gave constructive feedback and my family members who supported me at every step.

Editor

Information Security: An Introduction

In this age of information technology the need to ensure the safety of data has become a paramount concern for companies and organizations across the world. Information security refers to the protection of data from unapproved access, use, deletion while preserving confidentiality. It is a term used regardless of the form of data i.e. physical or electronic.

Information security, sometimes shortened to InfoSec, is the practice of defending information from unauthorized access, use, disclosure, disruption, modification, perusal, inspection, recording or destruction. It is a general term that can be used regardless of the form the data may take (e.g. electronic, physical).

Overview

IT Security

Sometimes referred to as computer security, information technology security is information security applied to technology (most often some form of computer system). It is worthwhile to note that a computer does not necessarily mean a home desktop. A computer is any device with a processor and some memory. Such devices can range from non-networked standalone devices as simple as calculators, to networked mobile computing devices such as smartphones and tablet computers. IT security specialists are almost always found in any major enterprise/establishment due to the nature and value of the data within larger businesses. They are responsible for keeping all of the technology within the company secure from malicious cyber attacks that often attempt to breach into critical private information or gain control of the internal systems.

Information Assurance

The act of providing trust of the information, that the Confidentiality, Integrity and Availability (CIA) of the information are not violated. E.g., ensuring that data is not lost when critical issues arise. These issues include, but are not limited to: natural disasters, computer/server malfunction, physical theft, or any other instance where data has the potential of being lost. Since most information is stored on computers in our modern era, information assurance is typically dealt with by IT security specialists. A common method of providing information assurance is to have an off-site backup of the data in case one of the mentioned issues arise.

Threats

Computer system threats come in many different forms. Some of the most common threats today are software attacks, theft of intellectual property, identity theft, theft of equipment or information, sabotage, and information extortion. Most people have experienced software attacks of some sort. Viruses, worms, phishing attacks, and Trojan horses are a few common examples of software attacks. The theft of intellectual property has also been an extensive issue for many businesses in the IT field. Intellectual property is the ownership of property usually consisting of some form of protection. Theft of software is probably the most common in IT businesses today. Identity theft is the attempt to act as someone else usually to obtain that person's personal information or to take advantage of their access to vital information. Theft of equipment or information is becoming more prevalent today due to the fact that most devices today are mobile. Cell phones are prone to theft and have also become far more desirable as the amount of data capacity increases. Sabotage usually consists of the destruction of an organization's website in an attempt to cause loss of confidence to its customers. Information extortion consists of theft of a company's property or information as an attempt to receive a payment in exchange for returning the information or property back to its owner. There are many ways to help protect yourself from some of these attacks but one of the most functional precautions is user carefulness.

Governments, military, corporations, financial institutions, hospitals and private businesses amass a great deal of confidential information about their employees, customers, products, research and financial status. Most of this information is now collected, processed and stored on electronic computers and transmitted across networks to other computers.

Should confidential information about a business' customers or finances or new product line fall into the hands of a competitor or a black hat hacker, a business and its customers could suffer widespread, irreparable financial loss, as well as damage to the company's reputation. Protecting confidential information is a business requirement and in many cases also an ethical and legal requirement. Hence a key concern for organizations today is to derive the optimal information security investment. The renowned Gordon-Loeb Model actually provides a powerful mathematical economic approach for addressing this critical concern.

For the individual, information security has a significant effect on privacy, which is viewed very differently in different cultures.

The field of information security has grown and evolved significantly in recent years. There are many ways of gaining entry into the field as a career. It offers many areas for specialization including securing network(s) and allied infrastructure, securing applications and databases, security testing, information systems auditing, business continuity planning and digital forensics.

History

Since the early days of communication, diplomats and military commanders understood that it was necessary to provide some mechanism to protect the confidentiality of correspondence and to have some means of detecting tampering. Julius Caesar is credited with the invention of the Caesar cipher c. 50 B.C., which was created in order to prevent his secret messages from being read should a message fall into the wrong hands, but for the most part protection was achieved through the application of procedural handling controls. Sensitive information was marked up to indicate that it should be protected and transported by trusted persons, guarded and stored in a secure environment or strong box. As postal services expanded, governments created official organizations to intercept, decipher, read and reseal letters (e.g. the UK Secret Office and Deciphering Branch in 1653).

In the mid-19th century more complex classification systems were developed to allow governments to manage their information according to the degree of sensitivity. The British Government codified this, to some extent, with the publication of the Official Secrets Act in 1889. By the time of the First World War, multi-tier classification systems were used to communicate information to and from various fronts, which encouraged greater use of code making and breaking sections in diplomatic and military headquarters. In the United Kingdom this led to the creation of the Government Code and Cypher School in 1919. Encoding became more sophisticated between the wars as machines were employed to scramble and unscramble information. The volume of information shared by the Allied countries during the Second World War necessitated formal alignment of classification systems and procedural controls. An arcane range of markings evolved to indicate who could handle documents (usually officers rather than men) and where they should be stored as increasingly complex safes and storage facilities were developed. Procedures evolved to ensure documents were destroyed properly and it was the failure to follow these procedures which led to some of the greatest intelligence coups of the war (e.g. U-570).

The end of the 20th century and early years of the 21st century saw rapid advancements in telecommunications, computing hardware and software, and data encryption. The availability of smaller, more powerful and less expensive computing equipment made electronic data processing within the reach of small business and the home user. These computers quickly became interconnected through the Internet.

The rapid growth and widespread use of electronic data processing and electronic business conducted through the Internet, along with numerous occurrences of international terrorism, fueled the need for better methods of protecting the computers and the information they store, process and transmit. The academic disciplines of computer security and information assurance emerged along with numerous professional organizations – all sharing the common goals of ensuring the security and reliability of information systems.

Definitions

Information Security Attributes: or qualities, i.e., Confidentiality, Integrity and Availability (CIA). Information Systems are composed in three main portions, hardware, software and communications with the purpose to help identify and apply information security industry standards, as mechanisms of protection and prevention, at three levels or layers: physical, personal and organizational. Essentially, procedures or policies are implemented to tell people (administrators, users and operators) how to use products to ensure information security within the organizations.

The definitions of InfoSec suggested in different sources are summarized below (adopted from).

1. "Preservation of confidentiality, integrity and availability of information. Note: In addition, other properties, such as authenticity, accountability, non-repudiation and reliability can also be involved." (ISO/IEC 27000:2009)

2. "The protection of information and information systems from unauthorized access, use, disclosure, disruption, modification, or destruction in order to provide confidentiality, integrity, and availability." (CNSS, 2010)

3. "Ensures that only authorized users (confidentiality) have access to accurate and complete information (integrity) when required (availability)." (ISACA, 2008)

4. "Information Security is the process of protecting the intellectual property of an organisation." (Pipkin, 2000)

5. "...information security is a risk management discipline, whose job is to manage the cost of information risk to the business." (McDermott and Geer, 2001)

6. "A well-informed sense of assurance that information risks and controls are in balance." (Anderson, J., 2003)

7. "Information security is the protection of information and minimises the risk of exposing information to unauthorised parties." (Venter and Eloff, 2003)

8. "Information Security is a multidisciplinary area of study and professional activity which is concerned with the development and implementation of security mechanisms of all available types (technical, organisational, human-oriented and legal) in order to keep information in all its locations (within and outside the organisation's perimeter) and, consequently, information systems, where information is created, processed, stored, transmitted and destroyed, free from threats.

Threats to information and information systems may be categorised and a corresponding security goal may be defined for each category of threats. A set of security goals, identified as a result of a threat analysis, should be revised periodically to ensure its adequacy and conformance with the evolving environment. The currently relevant set of security goals may include: *confidentiality, integrity, availability, privacy, authenticity & trustworthiness, non-repudiation, accountability and auditability.*" (Cherdantseva and Hilton, 2013)

Profession

Information security is a stable and growing profession. Information security professionals are very stable in their employment; more than 80 percent had no change in employer or employment in the past year, and the number of professionals is projected to continuously grow more than 11 percent annually from 2014 to 2019.

Basic Principles

Key Concepts

The CIA triad of confidentiality, integrity, and availability is at the heart of information security. (The members of the classic InfoSec triad — confidentiality, integrity and availability — are interchangeably referred to in the literature as security attributes, properties, security goals, fundamental aspects, information criteria, critical information characteristics and basic building blocks.) There is continuous debate about extending this classic trio. Other principles such as Accountability have sometimes been proposed for addition – it has been pointed out that issues such as non-repudiation do not fit well within the three core concepts.

In 1992 and revised in 2002, the OECD's *Guidelines for the Security of Information Systems and Networks* proposed the nine generally accepted principles: awareness, responsibility, response, ethics, democracy, risk assessment, security design and implementation, security management, and reassessment. Building upon those, in 2004 the NIST's *Engineering Principles for Information Technology Security* proposed 33 principles. From each of these derived guidelines and practices.

In 2002, Donn Parker proposed an alternative model for the classic CIA triad that he called the six atomic elements of information. The elements are confidentiality, possession, integrity, authenticity, availability, and utility. The merits of the Parkerian Hexad are a subject of debate amongst security professionals.

In 2011, The Open Group published the information security management standard O-ISM3. This standard proposed an operational definition of the key concepts of security, with elements called "security objectives", related to access control (9), availability (3), data quality (1),compliance and technical (4). This model is not currently widely adopted.

In 2013, based on a thorough analysis of Information Assurance and Security (IAS) literature, the IAS-octave was proposed as an extension of the CIA-triad. The IAS-octave includes Confidentiality, Integrity, Availability, Accountability, Auditability, Authenticity/Trustworthiness, Non-repudiation and Privacy. The completeness and accuracy of the IAS-octave was evaluated via a series of interviews with IAS academics and experts. The IAS-octave is one of the dimensions of a Reference Model of Information Assurance and Security (RMIAS), which summarizes the IAS knowledge in one all-encompassing model.

Confidentiality

In information security, confidentiality "is the property, that information is not made available or disclosed to unauthorized individuals, entities, or processes" (Except ISO27000).

Integrity

In information security, data integrity means maintaining and assuring the accuracy and completeness of data over its entire life-cycle. This means that data cannot be modified in an unauthorized or undetected manner. This is not the same thing as referential integrity in databases, although it can be viewed as a special case of consistency as understood in the classic ACID model of transaction processing. Information security systems typically provide message integrity in addition to data confidentiality.

Availability

For any information system to serve its purpose, the information must be available when it is needed. This means that the computing systems used to store and process the information, the security controls used to protect it, and the communication channels used to access it must be functioning correctly. High availability systems aim to remain available at all times, preventing service disruptions due to power outages, hardware failures, and system upgrades. Ensuring availability also involves preventing denial-of-service attacks, such as a flood of incoming messages to the target system essentially forcing it to shut down.

Non-repudiation

In law, non-repudiation implies one's intention to fulfill their obligations to a contract. It also implies that one party of a transaction cannot deny having received a transaction nor can the other party deny having sent a transaction. Note: This is also regarded as part of Integrity.

It is important to note that while technology such as cryptographic systems can assist in non-repudiation efforts, the concept is at its core a legal concept transcending the realm of technology. It is not, for instance, sufficient to show that the message matches a digital signature signed with the sender's private key, and thus only the sender could have sent the message and nobody else could have altered it in transit. The alleged sender could in return demonstrate that the digital signature algorithm is vulnerable or flawed, or allege or prove that his signing key has been compromised. The fault for these violations may or may not lie with the sender himself, and such assertions may or may not relieve the sender of liability, but the assertion would invalidate the claim that the signature necessarily proves authenticity and integrity and thus prevents repudiation.

Risk Management

The *Certified Information Systems Auditor (CISA) Review Manual 2006* provides the following definition of risk management: "Risk management is the process of identifying vulnerabilities and threats to the information resources used by an organization in achieving business objectives, and deciding what countermeasures, if any, to take in reducing risk to an acceptable level, based on the value of the information resource to the organization."

There are two things in this definition that may need some clarification. First, the *process* of risk management is an ongoing, iterative process. It must be repeated indefinitely. The business environment is constantly changing and new threats and vulnerabilities emerge every day. Second, the choice of countermeasures (controls) used to manage risks must strike a balance between productivity, cost, effectiveness of the countermeasure, and the value of the informational asset being protected.

Risk analysis and risk evaluation processes have their limitations since, when security incidents occur, they emerge in a context, and their rarity and even their uniqueness give rise to unpredictable threats. The analysis of these phenomena which are characterized by breakdowns, surprises and side-effects, requires a theoretical approach which is able to examine and interpret subjectively the detail of each incident.

Risk is the likelihood that something bad will happen that causes harm to an informational asset (or the loss of the asset). A vulnerability is a weakness that could be used to endanger or cause harm to an informational asset. A threat is anything (man-made or act of nature) that has the potential to cause harm.

The likelihood that a threat will use a vulnerability to cause harm creates a risk. When a threat does use a vulnerability to inflict harm, it has an impact. In the context of information security, the impact is a loss of availability, integrity, and confidentiality, and possibly other losses (lost income, loss of life, loss of real property). It should be pointed out that it is not possible to identify all risks, nor is it possible to eliminate all risk. The remaining risk is called "residual risk".

A risk assessment is carried out by a team of people who have knowledge of specific areas of the business. Membership of the team may vary over time as different parts of the business are assessed. The assessment may use a subjective qualitative analysis based on informed opinion, or where reliable dollar figures and historical information is available, the analysis may use quantitative analysis.

The research has shown that the most vulnerable point in most information systems is the human user, operator, designer, or other human. The ISO/IEC 27002:2005 Code of practice for information security management recommends the following be examined during a risk assessment:

- security policy,
- organization of information security,
- asset management,
- human resources security,
- physical and environmental security,
- communications and operations management,
- access control,
- information systems acquisition, development and maintenance,
- information security incident management,
- business continuity management, and
- regulatory compliance.

In broad terms, the risk management process consists of:

1. Identification of assets and estimating their value. Include: people, buildings, hardware, software, data (electronic, print, other), supplies.

2. Conduct a threat assessment. Include: Acts of nature, acts of war, accidents, malicious acts

originating from inside or outside the organization.

3. Conduct a vulnerability assessment, and for each vulnerability, calculate the probability that it will be exploited. Evaluate policies, procedures, standards, training, physical security, quality control, technical security.

4. Calculate the impact that each threat would have on each asset. Use qualitative analysis or quantitative analysis.

5. Identify, select and implement appropriate controls. Provide a proportional response. Consider productivity, cost effectiveness, and value of the asset.

6. Evaluate the effectiveness of the control measures. Ensure the controls provide the required cost effective protection without discernible loss of productivity.

For any given risk, management can choose to accept the risk based upon the relative low value of the asset, the relative low frequency of occurrence, and the relative low impact on the business. Or, leadership may choose to mitigate the risk by selecting and implementing appropriate control measures to reduce the risk. In some cases, the risk can be transferred to another business by buying insurance or outsourcing to another business. The reality of some risks may be disputed. In such cases leadership may choose to deny the risk.

Controls

Selecting proper controls and implementing those will initially help an organization to bring down risk to acceptable levels. Control selection should follow and should be based on the risk assessment. Controls can vary in nature but fundamentally they are ways of protecting the confidentiality, integrity or availability of information. ISO/IEC 27001:2005 has defined 133 controls in different areas, but this is not exhaustive. Organizations can implement additional controls according to requirement of the organization. ISO 27001:2013 has cut down the number of controls to 113. From 08.11.2013 the technical standard of information security in place is: ABNT NBR ISO/IEC 27002:2013.

Administrative

Administrative controls (also called procedural controls) consist of approved written policies, procedures, standards and guidelines. Administrative controls form the framework for running the business and managing people. They inform people on how the business is to be run and how day-to-day operations are to be conducted. Laws and regulations created by government bodies are also a type of administrative control because they inform the business. Some industry sectors have policies, procedures, standards and guidelines that must be followed – the Payment Card Industry Data Security Standard (PCI DSS) required by Visa and MasterCard is such an example. Other examples of administrative controls include the corporate security policy, password policy, hiring policies, and disciplinary policies.

Administrative controls form the basis for the selection and implementation of logical and physical controls. Logical and physical controls are manifestations of administrative controls. Administrative controls are of paramount importance.

Logical

Logical controls (also called technical controls) use software and data to monitor and control access to information and computing systems. For example: passwords, network and host-based firewalls, network intrusion detection systems, access control lists, and data encryption are logical controls.

An important logical control that is frequently overlooked is the principle of least privilege. The principle of least privilege requires that an individual, program or system process is not granted any more access privileges than are necessary to perform the task. A blatant example of the failure to adhere to the principle of least privilege is logging into Windows as user Administrator to read email and surf the web. Violations of this principle can also occur when an individual collects additional access privileges over time. This happens when employees' job duties change, or they are promoted to a new position, or they transfer to another department. The access privileges required by their new duties are frequently added onto their already existing access privileges which may no longer be necessary or appropriate.

Physical

Physical controls monitor and control the environment of the work place and computing facilities. They also monitor and control access to and from such facilities. For example: doors, locks, heating and air conditioning, smoke and fire alarms, fire suppression systems, cameras, barricades, fencing, security guards, cable locks, etc. Separating the network and workplace into functional areas are also physical controls.

An important physical control that is frequently overlooked is the separation of duties. Separation of duties ensures that an individual can not complete a critical task by himself. For example: an employee who submits a request for reimbursement should not also be able to authorize payment or print the check. An applications programmer should not also be the server administrator or the database administrator – these roles and responsibilities must be separated from one another.

Defense in Depth

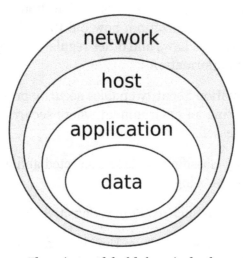

The onion model of defense in depth

Information security must protect information throughout the life span of the information, from the initial creation of the information on through to the final disposal of the information. The information must be protected while in motion and while at rest. During its lifetime, information may pass through many different information processing systems and through many different parts of information processing systems. There are many different ways the information and information systems can be threatened. To fully protect the information during its lifetime, each component of the information processing system must have its own protection mechanisms. The building up, layering on and overlapping of security measures is called defense in depth. In contrast to a metal chain, which is famously only as strong as its weakest link, the defense-in-depth aims at a structure where, should one defensive measure fail, other measures will continue to provide protection.

Recall the earlier discussion about administrative controls, logical controls, and physical controls. The three types of controls can be used to form the basis upon which to build a defense-in-depth strategy. With this approach, defense-in-depth can be conceptualized as three distinct layers or planes laid one on top of the other. Additional insight into defense-in- depth can be gained by thinking of it as forming the layers of an onion, with data at the core of the onion, people the next outer layer of the onion, and network security, host-based security and application security forming the outermost layers of the onion. Both perspectives are equally valid and each provides valuable insight into the implementation of a good defense-in-depth strategy.

Security Classification for Information

An important aspect of information security and risk management is recognizing the value of information and defining appropriate procedures and protection requirements for the information. Not all information is equal and so not all information requires the same degree of protection. This requires information to be assigned a security classification.

The first step in information classification is to identify a member of senior management as the owner of the particular information to be classified. Next, develop a classification policy. The policy should describe the different classification labels, define the criteria for information to be assigned a particular label, and list the required security controls for each classification.

Some factors that influence which classification information should be assigned include how much value that information has to the organization, how old the information is and whether or not the information has become obsolete. Laws and other regulatory requirements are also important considerations when classifying information.

The Business Model for Information Security enables security professionals to examine security from systems perspective, creating an environment where security can be managed holistically, allowing actual risks to be addressed.

The type of information security classification labels selected and used will depend on the nature of the organization, with examples being:

- In the business sector, labels such as: Public, Sensitive, Private, Confidential.

- In the government sector, labels such as: Unclassified, Unofficial, Protected, Confidential, Secret, Top Secret and their non-English equivalents.

- In cross-sectoral formations, the Traffic Light Protocol, which consists of: White, Green, Amber, and Red.

All employees in the organization, as well as business partners, must be trained on the classification schema and understand the required security controls and handling procedures for each classification. The classification of a particular information asset that has been assigned should be reviewed periodically to ensure the classification is still appropriate for the information and to ensure the security controls required by the classification are in place and are followed in their right procedures.

Access Control

Access to protected information must be restricted to people who are authorized to access the information. The computer programs, and in many cases the computers that process the information, must also be authorized. This requires that mechanisms be in place to control the access to protected information. The sophistication of the access control mechanisms should be in parity with the value of the information being protected – the more sensitive or valuable the information the stronger the control mechanisms need to be. The foundation on which access control mechanisms are built start with identification and authentication.

Access control is generally considered in three steps: Identification, Authentication, and Authorization.

Identification

Identification is an assertion of who someone is or what something is. If a person makes the statement "Hello, my name is John Doe" they are making a claim of who they are. However, their claim may or may not be true. Before John Doe can be granted access to protected information it will be necessary to verify that the person claiming to be John Doe really is John Doe. Typically the claim is in the form of a username. By entering that username you are claiming "I am the person the username belongs to".

Authentication

Authentication is the act of verifying a claim of identity. When John Doe goes into a bank to make a withdrawal, he tells the bank teller he is John Doe—a claim of identity. The bank teller asks to see a photo ID, so he hands the teller his driver's license. The bank teller checks the license to make sure it has John Doe printed on it and compares the photograph on the license against the person claiming to be John Doe. If the photo and name match the person, then the teller has authenticated that John Doe is who he claimed to be. Similarly by entering the correct password, the user is providing evidence that they are the person the username belongs to.

There are three different types of information that can be used for authentication:

- Something you know: things such as a PIN, a password, or your mother's maiden name.
- Something you have: a driver's license or a magnetic swipe card.
- Something you are: biometrics, including palm prints, fingerprints, voice prints and retina (eye) scans.

Strong authentication requires providing more than one type of authentication information (two-factor authentication). The username is the most common form of identification on computer systems today and the password is the most common form of authentication. Usernames and passwords have served their purpose but in our modern world they are no longer adequate. Usernames and passwords are slowly being replaced with more sophisticated authentication mechanisms.

Authorization

After a person, program or computer has successfully been identified and authenticated then it must be determined what informational resources they are permitted to access and what actions they will be allowed to perform (run, view, create, delete, or change). This is called authorization. Authorization to access information and other computing services begins with administrative policies and procedures. The policies prescribe what information and computing services can be accessed, by whom, and under what conditions. The access control mechanisms are then configured to enforce these policies. Different computing systems are equipped with different kinds of access control mechanisms—some may even offer a choice of different access control mechanisms. The access control mechanism a system offers will be based upon one of three approaches to access control or it may be derived from a combination of the three approaches.

The non-discretionary approach consolidates all access control under a centralized administration. The access to information and other resources is usually based on the individuals function (role) in the organization or the tasks the individual must perform. The discretionary approach gives the creator or owner of the information resource the ability to control access to those resources. In the Mandatory access control approach, access is granted or denied basing upon the security classification assigned to the information resource.

Examples of common access control mechanisms in use today include role-based access control available in many advanced database management systems—simple file permissions provided in the UNIX and Windows operating systems, Group Policy Objects provided in Windows network systems, Kerberos, RADIUS, TACACS, and the simple access lists used in many firewalls and routers.

To be effective, policies and other security controls must be enforceable and upheld. Effective policies ensure that people are held accountable for their actions. All failed and successful authentication attempts must be logged, and all access to information must leave some type of audit trail.

Also, need-to-know principle needs to be in effect when talking about access control. Need-to-know principle gives access rights to a person to perform their job functions. This principle is used in the government, when dealing with difference clearances. Even though two employees in different departments have a top-secret clearance, they must have a need-to-know in order for information to be exchanged. Within the need-to-know principle, network administrators grant the employee least amount privileges to prevent employees access and doing more than what they are supposed to. Need-to-know helps to enforce the confidentiality-integrity-availability (CIA) triad. Need-to-know directly impacts the confidential area of the triad.

Cryptography

Information security uses cryptography to transform usable information into a form that renders it unusable by anyone other than an authorized user; this process is called encryption. Information that has been encrypted (rendered unusable) can be transformed back into its original usable form by an authorized user, who possesses the cryptographic key, through the process of decryption. Cryptography is used in information security to protect information from unauthorized or accidental disclosure while the information is in transit (either electronically or physically) and while information is in storage.

Cryptography provides information security with other useful applications as well including improved authentication methods, message digests, digital signatures, non-repudiation, and encrypted network communications. Older less secure applications such as telnet and ftp are slowly being replaced with more secure applications such as ssh that use encrypted network communications. Wireless communications can be encrypted using protocols such as WPA/WPA2 or the older (and less secure) WEP. Wired communications (such as ITUT G.hn) are secured using AES for encryption and X.1035 for authentication and key exchange. Software applications such as GnuPG or PGP can be used to encrypt data files and Email.

Cryptography can introduce security problems when it is not implemented correctly. Cryptographic solutions need to be implemented using industry accepted solutions that have undergone rigorous peer review by independent experts in cryptography. The length and strength of the encryption key is also an important consideration. A key that is weak or too short will produce weak encryption. The keys used for encryption and decryption must be protected with the same degree of rigor as any other confidential information. They must be protected from unauthorized disclosure and destruction and they must be available when needed. Public key infrastructure (PKI) solutions address many of the problems that surround key management.

Process

The terms reasonable and prudent person, due care and due diligence have been used in the fields of Finance, Securities, and Law for many years. In recent years these terms have found their way into the fields of computing and information security. U.S.A. Federal Sentencing Guidelines now make it possible to hold corporate officers liable for failing to exercise due care and due diligence in the management of their information systems.

In the business world, stockholders, customers, business partners and governments have the expectation that corporate officers will run the business in accordance with accepted business practices and in compliance with laws and other regulatory requirements. This is often described as the "reasonable and prudent person" rule. A prudent person takes due care to ensure that everything necessary is done to operate the business by sound business principles and in a legal ethical manner. A prudent person is also diligent (mindful, attentive, and ongoing) in their due care of the business.

In the field of Information Security, Harris offers the following definitions of due care and due diligence:

"Due care are steps that are taken to show that a company has taken responsibility for the activities that take place within the corporation and has taken the necessary steps to help protect the company, its resources, and employees." And, [Due diligence are the] *"continual activities that make sure the protection mechanisms are continually maintained and operational."*

Attention should be made to two important points in these definitions. First, in due care, steps are taken to *show* - this means that the steps can be verified, measured, or even produce tangible artifacts. Second, in due diligence, there are continual activities - this means that people are actually doing things to monitor and maintain the protection mechanisms, and these activities are ongoing.

Security Governance

The Software Engineering Institute at Carnegie Mellon University, in a publication titled "Governing for Enterprise Security (GES)", defines characteristics of effective security governance. These include:

- An enterprise-wide issue
- Leaders are accountable
- Viewed as a business requirement
- Risk-based
- Roles, responsibilities, and segregation of duties defined
- Addressed and enforced in policy
- Adequate resources committed
- Staff aware and trained
- A development life cycle requirement
- Planned, managed, measurable, and measured
- Reviewed and audited

Incident Response Plans

1 to 3 paragraphs (non technical) that discuss:

- Selecting team members
- Define roles, responsibilities and lines of authority
- Define a security incident
- Define a reportable incident
- Training
- Detection
- Classification
- Escalation

- Containment

- Eradication

- Documentation

Change Management

Change management is a formal process for directing and controlling alterations to the information processing environment. This includes alterations to desktop computers, the network, servers and software. The objectives of change management are to reduce the risks posed by changes to the information processing environment and improve the stability and reliability of the processing environment as changes are made. It is not the objective of change management to prevent or hinder necessary changes from being implemented.

Any change to the information processing environment introduces an element of risk. Even apparently simple changes can have unexpected effects. One of Management's many responsibilities is the management of risk. Change management is a tool for managing the risks introduced by changes to the information processing environment. Part of the change management process ensures that changes are not implemented at inopportune times when they may disrupt critical business processes or interfere with other changes being implemented.

Not every change needs to be managed. Some kinds of changes are a part of the everyday routine of information processing and adhere to a predefined procedure, which reduces the overall level of risk to the processing environment. Creating a new user account or deploying a new desktop computer are examples of changes that do not generally require change management. However, relocating user file shares, or upgrading the Email server pose a much higher level of risk to the processing environment and are not a normal everyday activity. The critical first steps in change management are (a) defining change (and communicating that definition) and (b) defining the scope of the change system.

Change management is usually overseen by a Change Review Board composed of representatives from key business areas, security, networking, systems administrators, Database administration, applications development, desktop support and the help desk. The tasks of the Change Review Board can be facilitated with the use of automated work flow application. The responsibility of the Change Review Board is to ensure the organizations documented change management procedures are followed. The change management process is as follows:

- Requested: Anyone can request a change. The person making the change request may or may not be the same person that performs the analysis or implements the change. When a request for change is received, it may undergo a preliminary review to determine if the requested change is compatible with the organizations business model and practices, and to determine the amount of resources needed to implement the change.

- Approved: Management runs the business and controls the allocation of resources therefore, Management must approve requests for changes and assign a priority for every change. Management might choose to reject a change request if the change is not compatible with the business model, industry standards or best practices. Management might also choose to reject a change request if the change requires more resources than can be allocated for the change.

- Planned: Planning a change involves discovering the scope and impact of the proposed change; analyzing the complexity of the change; allocation of resources and, developing, testing and documenting both implementation and backout plans. Need to define the criteria on which a decision to back out will be made.

- Tested: Every change must be tested in a safe test environment, which closely reflects the actual production environment, before the change is applied to the production environment. The backout plan must also be tested.

- Scheduled: Part of the change review board's responsibility is to assist in the scheduling of changes by reviewing the proposed implementation date for potential conflicts with other scheduled changes or critical business activities.

- Communicated: Once a change has been scheduled it must be communicated. The communication is to give others the opportunity to remind the change review board about other changes or critical business activities that might have been overlooked when scheduling the change. The communication also serves to make the Help Desk and users aware that a change is about to occur. Another responsibility of the change review board is to ensure that scheduled changes have been properly communicated to those who will be affected by the change or otherwise have an interest in the change.

- Implemented: At the appointed date and time, the changes must be implemented. Part of the planning process was to develop an implementation plan, testing plan and, a back out plan. If the implementation of the change should fail or, the post implementation testing fails or, other "drop dead" criteria have been met, the back out plan should be implemented.

- Documented: All changes must be documented. The documentation includes the initial request for change, its approval, the priority assigned to it, the implementation, testing and back out plans, the results of the change review board critique, the date/time the change was implemented, who implemented it, and whether the change was implemented successfully, failed or postponed.

- Post change review: The change review board should hold a post implementation review of changes. It is particularly important to review failed and backed out changes. The review board should try to understand the problems that were encountered, and look for areas for improvement.

Change management procedures that are simple to follow and easy to use can greatly reduce the overall risks created when changes are made to the information processing environment. Good change management procedures improve the overall quality and success of changes as they are implemented. This is accomplished through planning, peer review, documentation and communication.

ISO/IEC 20000, The Visible OPS Handbook: Implementing ITIL in 4 Practical and Auditable

Steps (Full book summary), and Information Technology Infrastructure Library all provide valuable guidance on implementing an efficient and effective change management program information security.

Business Continuity

Business continuity is the mechanism by which an organization continues to operate its critical business units, during planned or unplanned disruptions that affect normal business operations, by invoking planned and managed procedures.

Not only is business continuity simply about the business, but it is also an IT system and process. Today disasters or disruptions to business are a reality. Whether the disaster is natural or man-made, it affects normal life and so business. Therefore, planning is important.

The planning is merely getting better prepared to face it, knowing fully well that the best plans may fail. Planning helps to reduce cost of recovery, operational overheads and most importantly sail through some smaller ones effortlessly.

For businesses to create effective plans they need to focus upon the following key questions. Most of these are common knowledge, and anyone can do a BCP.

1. Should a disaster strike, what are the first few things that I should do? Should I call people to find if they are OK or call up the bank to figure out my money is safe? This is Emergency Response. Emergency Response services help take the first hit when the disaster strikes and if the disaster is serious enough the Emergency Response teams need to quickly get a Crisis Management team in place.

2. What parts of my business should I recover first? The one that brings me most money or the one where I spend the most, or the one that will ensure I shall be able to get sustained future growth? The identified sections are the critical business units. There is no magic bullet here, no one answer satisfies all. Businesses need to find answers that meet business requirements.

3. How soon should I target to recover my critical business units? In BCP technical jargon, this is called Recovery Time Objective, or RTO. This objective will define what costs the business will need to spend to recover from a disruption. For example, it is cheaper to recover a business in 1 day than in 1 hour.

4. What do I need to recover the business? IT, machinery, records...food, water, people...So many aspects to dwell upon. The cost factor becomes clearer now...Business leaders need to drive business continuity. Hold on. My IT manager spent $200000 last month and created a DRP (Disaster Recovery Plan), whatever happened to that? A DRP is about continuing an IT system, and is one of the sections of a comprehensive Business Continuity Plan. Look below for more on this.

5. And where do I recover my business from... Will the business center give me space to work, or would it be flooded by many people queuing up for the same reasons that I am.

6. But once I do recover from the disaster and work in reduced production capacity since my

main operational sites are unavailable, how long can this go on. How long can I do without my original sites, systems, people? this defines the amount of business resilience a business may have.

7. Now that I know how to recover my business. How do I make sure my plan works? Most BCP pundits would recommend testing the plan at least once a year, reviewing it for adequacy and rewriting or updating the plans either annually or when businesses change.

Disaster Recovery Planning

While a business continuity plan (BCP) takes a broad approach to dealing with organizational-wide effects of a disaster, a disaster recovery plan (DRP), which is a subset of the business continuity plan, is instead focused on taking the necessary steps to resume normal business operations as quickly as possible. A disaster recovery plan is executed immediately after the disaster occurs and details what steps are to be taken in order to recover critical information technology infrastructure. Disaster recovery planning includes establishing a planning group, performing risk assessment, establishing priorities, developing recovery strategies, preparing inventories and documentation of the plan, developing verification criteria and procedure, and lastly implementing the plan.

Laws and Regulations

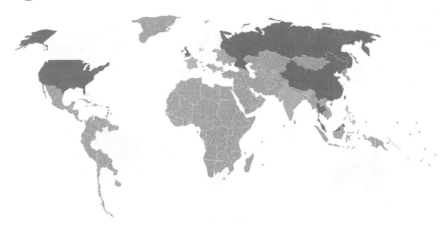

Privacy International 2007 privacy ranking
green: Protections and safeguards
red: Endemic surveillance societies

*Below is a **partial** listing of European, United Kingdom, Canadian and US governmental laws and regulations that have, or will have, a significant effect on data processing and information security. Important industry sector regulations have also been included when they have a significant impact on information security.*

- UK Data Protection Act 1998 makes new provisions for the regulation of the processing of information relating to individuals, including the obtaining, holding, use or disclosure of such information. The European Union Data Protection Directive (EUDPD) requires that all EU member must adopt national regulations to standardize the protection of data privacy for citizens throughout the EU.

- The Computer Misuse Act 1990 is an Act of the UK Parliament making computer crime (e.g. hacking) a criminal offence. The Act has become a model upon which several other countries including Canada and the Republic of Ireland have drawn inspiration when subsequently drafting their own information security laws.

- EU Data Retention laws requires Internet service providers and phone companies to keep data on every electronic message sent and phone call made for between six months and two years.

- The Family Educational Rights and Privacy Act (FERPA) (20 U.S.C. § 1232 g; 34 CFR Part 99) is a US Federal law that protects the privacy of student education records. The law applies to all schools that receive funds under an applicable program of the U.S. Department of Education. Generally, schools must have written permission from the parent or eligible student in order to release any information from a student's education record.

- Federal Financial Institutions Examination Council's (FFIEC) security guidelines for auditors specifies requirements for online banking security.

- Health Insurance Portability and Accountability Act (HIPAA) of 1996 requires the adoption of national standards for electronic health care transactions and national identifiers for providers, health insurance plans, and employers. And, it requires health care providers, insurance providers and employers to safeguard the security and privacy of health data.

- Gramm–Leach–Bliley Act of 1999 (GLBA), also known as the Financial Services Modernization Act of 1999, protects the privacy and security of private financial information that financial institutions collect, hold, and process.

- Sarbanes–Oxley Act of 2002 (SOX). Section 404 of the act requires publicly traded companies to assess the effectiveness of their internal controls for financial reporting in annual reports they submit at the end of each fiscal year. Chief information officers are responsible for the security, accuracy and the reliability of the systems that manage and report the financial data. The act also requires publicly traded companies to engage independent auditors who must attest to, and report on, the validity of their assessments.

- Payment Card Industry Data Security Standard (PCI DSS) establishes comprehensive requirements for enhancing payment account data security. It was developed by the founding payment brands of the PCI Security Standards Council, including American Express, Discover Financial Services, JCB, MasterCard Worldwide and Visa International, to help facilitate the broad adoption of consistent data security measures on a global basis. The PCI DSS is a multifaceted security standard that includes requirements for security management, policies, procedures, network architecture, software design and other critical protective measures.

- State security breach notification laws (California and many others) require businesses, nonprofits, and state institutions to notify consumers when unencrypted "personal information" may have been compromised, lost, or stolen.

- Personal Information Protection and Electronics Document Act (PIPEDA) – An Act to support and promote electronic commerce by protecting personal information that is collected, used or disclosed in certain circumstances, by providing for the use of electronic means to communicate or record information or transactions and by amending the Canada Evidence Act, the Statutory Instruments Act and the Statute Revision Act.

- Hellenic Authority for Communication Security and Privacy (ADAE) (Law 165/2011) - The Greek Law establishes and describes the minimum Information Security controls that should be deployed by every company which provides electronic communication networks and/or services in Greece in order to protect customers' Confidentiality. These include both managerial and technical controls (i.e. log records should be stored for two years).

- Hellenic Authority for Communication Security and Privacy (ADAE) (Law 205/2013)- The latest Greek Law published by ADAE concentrates around the protection of the Integrity and Availability of the services and data offered by the Greek Telecommunication Companies.The new Law forces Telcos and associated companies to build, deploy and test appropriate Business Continuity Plans and redundant infrastructures.

Information Security Culture

Employee's behavior has a big impact to information security in organizations. Cultural concept can help different segments of the organization to concern about the information security within the organization."Exploring the Relationship between Organizational Culture and Information Security Culture" provides the following definition of information security culture: "ISC is the totality of patterns of behavior in an organization that contribute to the protection of information of all kinds."

Information security culture needs to be improved continuously. In "Information Security Culture from Analysis to Change", authors commented, "It's a never ending process, a cycle of evaluation and change or maintenance." To manage the information security culture, five steps should be taken: Pre-evaluation, strategic planning, operative planning, implementation, and post-evaluation.

- Pre-Evaluation : to identify the awareness of information security within employees and to analysis current security policy.

- Strategic Planning: to come up a better awareness-program, we need to set clear targets. Clustering people is helpful to achieve it.

- Operative Planning: we can set a good security culture based on internal communication, management-buy-in, and security awareness and training program.

- Implementation: four stages should be used to implement the information security culture. They are commitment of the management, communication with organizational members, courses for all organizational members, and commitment of the employees.

Sources of Standards

International Organization for Standardization (ISO) is a consortium of national standards institutes from 157 countries, coordinated through a secretariat in Geneva, Switzerland. ISO is the world's largest developer of standards. ISO 15443: "Information technology - Security techniques

- A framework for IT security assurance", ISO/IEC 27002: "Information technology - Security techniques - Code of practice for information security management", ISO-20000: "Information technology - Service management", and ISO/IEC 27001: "Information technology - Security techniques - Information security management systems - Requirements" are of particular interest to information security professionals.

The US National Institute of Standards and Technology (NIST) is a non-regulatory federal agency within the U.S. Department of Commerce. The NIST Computer Security Division develops standards, metrics, tests and validation programs as well as publishes standards and guidelines to increase secure IT planning, implementation, management and operation. NIST is also the custodian of the US Federal Information Processing Standard publications (FIPS).

The Internet Society is a professional membership society with more than 100 organizations and over 20,000 individual members in over 180 countries. It provides leadership in addressing issues that confront the future of the Internet, and is the organization home for the groups responsible for Internet infrastructure standards, including the Internet Engineering Task Force (IETF) and the Internet Architecture Board (IAB). The ISOC hosts the Requests for Comments (RFCs) which includes the Official Internet Protocol Standards and the RFC-2196 Site Security Handbook.

The Information Security Forum is a global nonprofit organization of several hundred leading organizations in financial services, manufacturing, telecommunications, consumer goods, government, and other areas. It undertakes research into information security practices and offers advice in its biannual Standard of Good Practice and more detailed advisories for members.

The Institute of Information Security Professionals (IISP) is an independent, non-profit body governed by its members, with the principal objective of advancing the professionalism of information security practitioners and thereby the professionalism of the industry as a whole. The Institute developed the IISP Skills Framework©. This framework describes the range of competencies expected of Information Security and Information Assurance Professionals in the effective performance of their roles. It was developed through collaboration between both private and public sector organisations and world-renowned academics and security leaders.

The German Federal Office for Information Security (in German *Bundesamt für Sicherheit in der Informationstechnik (BSI)*) BSI-Standards 100-1 to 100-4 are a set of recommendations including "methods, processes, procedures, approaches and measures relating to information security". The BSI-Standard 100-2 *IT-Grundschutz Methodology* describes how an information security management can be implemented and operated. The Standard includes a very specific guide, the IT Baseline Protection Catalogs (also known as IT-Grundschutz Catalogs). Before 2005 the catalogs were formerly known as "IT Baseline Protection Manual". The Catalogs are a collection of documents useful for detecting and combating security-relevant weak points in the IT environment (IT cluster). The collection encompasses as of September 2013 over 4.400 pages with the introduction and catalogs. The IT-Grundschutz approach is aligned with to the ISO/IEC 2700x family.

At the European Telecommunications Standards Institute a catalog of Information security indicators have been standardized by the Industrial Specification Group (ISG) ISI.

Scholars Working in the Field

- Adam Back
- Annie Anton
- Brian LaMacchia
- Bruce Schneier
- Cynthia Dwork
- Dawn Song
- Deborah Estrin
- Gene Spafford
- Ian Goldberg
- Lawrence A. Gordon
- Martin P. Loeb
- Monica S. Lam
- Joan Feigenbaum
- L Jean Camp
- Lance Cottrell
- Lorrie Cranor
- Khalil Sehnaoui
- Paul C. van Oorschot
- Peter Gutmann
- Peter Landrock
- Ross J. Anderson
- Stefan Brands

References

- ISACA (2006). CISA Review Manual 2006. Information Systems Audit and Control Association. p. 85. ISBN 1-933284-15-3.
- Kiountouzis, E.A.; Kokolakis, S.A. Information systems security: facing the information society of the 21st century. London: Chapman & Hall, Ltd. ISBN 0-412-78120-4.
- Shon Harris (2003). All-in-one CISSP Certification Exam Guide (2nd ed.). Emeryville, California: McGraw-Hill/Osborne. ISBN 0-07-222966-7.
- Harris, Shon (2008). All-in-one CISSP Certification Exam Guide (4th ed.). New York, NY: McGraw-Hill. ISBN 978-0-07-149786-2.

- "book summary of The Visible Ops Handbook: Implementing ITIL in 4 Practical and Auditable Steps". wikisummaries.org. Retrieved 2016-06-22.

- Y. Cherdantseva and J. Hilton, "A Reference Model of Information Assurance & Security," Availability, Reliability and Security (ARES), 2013 Eighth International Conference on , vol., no., pp.546-555, IEEE, doi: 10.1109/ARES.2013.72, 2–6 September 2013.

- Boritz, J. Efrim. "IS Practitioners' Views on Core Concepts of Information Integrity". International Journal of Accounting Information Systems. Elsevier. Retrieved 12 August 2011.

2

Approaches Towards Information Security

This chapter elucidates the various approaches to information security like data-centric security, bottom-up, top-down etc. The chapter also talks about the various techniques that help in the implementation of these approaches like data masking, cyber security standards, global surveillance etc.

Data-centric Security

Data-centric security is an approach to security that emphasizes the security of the data itself rather than the security of networks, servers, or applications. Data-centric security is evolving rapidly as enterprises increasingly rely on digital information to run their business and big data projects become mainstream. Data-centric security also allows organizations to overcome the disconnect between IT security technology and the objectives of business strategy by relating security services directly to the data they implicitly protect; a relationship that is often obscured by the presentation of security as an end in itself.

Key Concepts

Common processes in a data-centric security model include:
- Discover: the ability to inspect data storage areas at rest to detect sensitive information.
- Manage: the ability to define access policies that will determine if certain data is accessible, editable, or blocked from specific users, or locations.
- Protect: the ability to defend against data loss or unauthorized use of data and prevent sensitive data from being sent to unauthorized users or locations.
- Track: the constant monitoring of data usage to identify meaningful deviations from normal behavior that would point to possible malicious intent.

From a technical point of view, information(data)-centric security relies on the implementation of the following:
- Information (data) that is self-describing and defending.
- Policies and controls that account for business context.
- Information that remains protected as it moves in and out of applications and storage systems, and changing business context.
- Policies that work consistently through the different defensive layers and technologies implemented.

Technology

Data Access Controls and Policies: Data access control is the selective restriction of access to data.

Accessing may mean viewing, editing, or using. Defining proper access controls requires to map out the information, where it resides, how important it is, who it is important to, how sensitive it is and then designing appropriate controls. Controls need to be able to match the most granular level of access a subject (the user) should have to a data element. Applied to relational databases, data access controls that support a data-centric security model should be able to define and control access at the table, field/column, cell and partial cell levels. In the case of complex enterprise data environments, the organization might need to enforce standards, and manage centrally the use of data protection techniques and security policies

Encryption

Encryption is a proven data-centric technique to address the risk of data theft in smartphones, laptops, desktops and even servers, including the cloud. One limitation is that encryption becomes useless once a network intrusion has occurred and cybercriminals operate with stolen valid user credentials.

Data Masking

Data Masking is the process of hiding specific data within a database table or cell to ensure that data security is maintained and that sensitive information is not exposed to unauthorized personnel. This may include masking the data from users, developers, third-party and outsourcing vendors, etc. Data masking can be achieved multiple ways: by duplicating data to eliminate the subset of the data that needs to be hidden or by obscuring the data dynamically as users perform requests.

Data-centric Security and Cloud Computing

Cloud computing is an evolving paradigm with tremendous momentum, but its unique aspects exacerbate security and privacy challenges. Heterogeneity and diversity of cloud services and environments demand fine-grained access control policies and services that should be flexible enough to capture dynamic, context, or attribute- or credential-based access requirements and data protection.

Data Masking

Data masking or data obfuscation is the process of hiding original data with random characters or data.

The main reason for applying masking to a data field is to protect data that is classified as personal identifiable data, personal sensitive data or commercially sensitive data, however the data must remain usable for the purposes of undertaking valid test cycles. It must also look real and appear consistent. It is more common to have masking applied to data that is represented outside of a corporate production system. In other words, where data is needed for the purpose of application development, building program extensions and conducting various test cycles. It is common practice in enterprise computing to take data from the production systems to fill the data component, required for these non-production environments. However the practice is not always restricted to non-production environments. In some organizations, data that appears on terminal screens to call centre operators may have masking dynamically applied based on user security permissions. (e.g.: Preventing call centre operators from viewing Credit Card Numbers in billing systems)

The primary concern from a corporate governance perspective is that personnel conducting work in these non-production environments are not always security cleared to operate with the information contained in the production data. This practice represents a security hole where data can be copied by unauthorised personnel and security measures associated with standard production level controls can be easily bypassed. This represents an access point for a data security breach.

The overall practice of Data Masking at an organisational level should be tightly coupled with the Test Management Practice and underlying Methodology and should incorporate processes for the distribution of masked test data subsets.

Background

Data involved in any data-masking or obfuscation must remain meaningful at several levels:

1. The data must remain meaningful for the application logic. For example, if elements of addresses are to be obfuscated and city and suburbs are replaced with substitute cities or suburbs, then, if within the application there is a feature that validates postcode or post code lookup, that function must still be allowed to operate without error and operate as expected. The same is also true for credit-card algorithm validation checks and Social Security Number validations.

2. The data must undergo enough changes so that it is not obvious that the masked data is from a source of production data. For example, it may be common knowledge in an organisation that there are 10 senior managers all earning in excess of $300K. If a test environment of the organisation's HR System also includes 10 identities in the same earning-bracket, then other information could be pieced together to reverse-engineer a real-life identity. Theoretically, if the data is obviously masked or obfuscated, then it would be reasonable for someone intending a data breach to assume that they could reverse engineer identity-data if they had some degree of knowledge of the identities in the production data-set. Accordingly, data obfuscation or masking of a data-set applies in such a manner as to ensure that identity and sensitive data records are protected - not just the individual data elements in discrete fields and tables.

Data Masking Techniques

Substitution

Substitution is one of the most effective methods of applying data masking and being able to preserve the authentic look and feel of the data records.

It allows the masking to be performed in such a manner that another authentic looking value can be substituted for the existing value. There are several data field types where this approach provides optimal benefit in disguising the overall data sub set as to whether or not it is a masked data set. For example, if dealing with source data which contains customer records, real life surname or first name can be randomly substituted from a supplied or customised look up file. If the first pass of the substitution allows for applying a male first name to all first names, then the second pass would need to allow for applying a female first name to all first names where gender equals "F". Using this approach we could easily maintain the gender mix within the data structure, apply anonymity to the data records but also maintain a realistic looking database which could not easily be identified as a database consisting of masked data.

This substitution method needs to be applied for many of the fields that are in DB structures across the world, such as telephone numbers, zip codes and postcodes, as well as credit card numbers and other card type numbers like Social Security numbers and Medicare numbers where these numbers actually need to conform to a checksum test of the Luhn algorithm.

In most cases the substitution files will need to be fairly extensive so having large substitution datasets as well the ability to apply customised data substitution sets should be a key element of the evaluation criteria for any data masking solution.

Shuffling

The shuffling method is a very common form of data obfuscation. It is similar to the substitution method but it derives the substitution set from the same column of data that is being masked. In very simple terms, the data is randomly shuffled within the column. However, if used in isolation, anyone with any knowledge of the original data can then apply a "What If" scenario to the data set and then piece back together a real identity. The shuffling method is also open be reversed if the shuffling algorithm can be deciphered.

Shuffling however has some real strengths in certain areas. If for instance, the end of year figures for financial information in a test data base, one can mask the names of the suppliers and then shuffle the value of the accounts throughout the masked database. It is highly unlikely that anyone, even someone with intimate knowledge of the original data could derive a true data record back to its original values.

Number and Date Variance

The numeric variance method is very useful for applying to financial and date driven information fields. Effectively, a method utilising this manner of masking can still leave a meaningful range in a financial data set such as payroll. If the variance applied is around +/- 10% then it is still a very meaningful data set in terms of the ranges of salaries that are paid to the recipients.

The same also applies to the date information. If the overall data set needs to retain demographic and actuarial data integrity then applying a random numeric variance of +/- 120 days to date fields would preserve the date distribution but still prevent traceability back to a known entity based on their known actual date or birth or a known date value of whatever record is being masked.

Encryption

Encryption is often the most complex approach to solving the data masking problem. The encryption algorithm often requires that a "key" be applied to view the data based on user rights. This often sounds like the best solution but in practice the key may then be given out to personnel without the proper rights to view the data and this then defeats the purpose of the masking exercise. Old databases may then be copied with the original credentials of the supplied key and the same uncontrolled problem lives on.

Recently, the problem of encrypting data while preserving the properties of the entities got a recognition and newly acquired interest among the vendors and academia. New challenge gave birth to algorithms called FPE (format preserving encryption). They are based on the accepted AES algorithmic mode that makes them being recognized by NIST.

Nulling Out or Deletion

Sometimes a very simplistic approach to masking is adopted through applying a null value to a particular field. The null value approach is really only useful to prevent visibility of the data element.

In almost all cases it lessens the degree of data integrity that is maintained in the masked data set. It is not a realistic value and will then fail any application logic validation that may have been applied in the front end software that is in the system under test. It also highlights to anyone that wishes to reverse engineer any of the identity data that data masking has been applied to some degree on the data set.

Masking Out

Character scrambling or masking out of certain fields is also another simplistic yet very effective method of preventing sensitive information to be viewed. It is really an extension of the previous method of nulling out but there is greater emphasis on keeping the data real and not fully masked all together.

This is commonly applied to credit card data in production systems. For instance, you may have spoken with an operator in a Call Centre and they have suggested they could bill an item to your credit card. They then quote you a billing reference to your card with the last 4 digits of XXXX XXXX xxxx 6789. As an operator they can only see the last 4 digits of your card number but once the billing system passes your details for charging the full number is revealed to the payment gateway systems.

This system is not very effective for test systems but is very useful for the billing scenario detailed above. It is also commonly known as a dynamic data masking method.

Additional Complex Rules

Additional rules can also be factored into any masking solution regardless of how the masking methods are constructed. Product agnostic White Papers are a good source of information for exploring some of the more common complex requirements for enterprise masking solutions which include Row Internal Synchronisation Rules, Table Internal Synchronisation Rules and Table to Table Synchronisation Rules.

Different Types of Data Masking

Data masking is tightly coupled with building test data. Two major types of data masking are static and on-the-fly data masking.

Static Data Masking

Static Data Masking is done on the golden copy of the database. Production DBAs load the backup in a separate environment, reduce the data set to a subset that holds the data necessary for a particular round of testing (a technique called "subsetting"), apply data masking rules while data is in stasis, apply necessary code changes from source control and push data to desired environment.

On-the-fly Data Masking

On-the-Fly Data Masking happens in the process of transferring data from environment to environment without data touching the disk on its way. The same technique is applied to "Dynamic Data Masking" but one record at a time. This type of data masking is most useful for environments that do continuous deployments as well as for heavily integrated applications. Organizations that employ continuous deployment or continuous delivery practices do not have the time necessary to create a backup and load it to the golden copy of the database. Thus, continuously sending smaller subsets (deltas) of masked testing data from production is important. In heavily integrated applications, developers get feeds from other production systems at the very onset of development and masking of these feeds is either overlooked and not budgeted until later, making organizations non-compliant. Having on-the-fly data masking in place becomes essential.

Dynamic Data Masking

Dynamic Data Masking is similar to On-the-Fly Data Masking but it differs in the sense that On-the-Fly Data Masking is about copying data from one source to another source so that the latter can be shared. Dynamic data masking happens at runtime, dynamically, and on-demand so that there need not be a second data source where to store the masked data dynamically.

Dynamic data masking enables several scenarios, many of which revolve around strict privacy regulations e.g. the Singapore Monetary Authority or the Privacy regulations in Europe.

Dynamic data masking is attribute-based and policy-driven. Policies include:

- Doctors can view the medical records of patients they are assigned to (data filtering)
- Doctors cannot view the SSN field inside a medical record (data masking).

Dynamic data masking can also be used to encrypt or decrypt values on the fly especially when using format-preserving encryption.

Data Masking and the Cloud

In latest years, organizations develop their new applications in the cloud more and more often, regardless of whether final applications will be hosted in the cloud or on- premises. The cloud solutions as of now allow organizations to use Infrastructure as a Service or IaaS, Platform as a Service or PaaS, and Software as a Service or SaaS. There are various modes of creating test data and moving it from on-premises databases to the cloud, or between different environments within the cloud. Data masking invariably becomes the part of these processes in SDLC as the development environments' SLAs are usually not as stringent as the production environments' SLAs regardless of whether application is hosted in the cloud or on-premises.

Cyber Security Standards

Cybersecurity Standards (also styled cyber security standards) are techniques generally set forth in published materials that attempt to protect the cyber environment of a user or organization. This environment includes users themselves, networks, devices, all software, processes, information in storage or transit, applications, services, and systems that can be connected directly or indirectly to networks. The principal objective is to reduce the risks, including prevention or mitigation of cyber-attacks. These published materials consist of collections of tools, policies, security concepts, security safeguards, guidelines, risk management approaches, actions, training, best practices, assurance and technologies.

(Writing cybersecurity as two words (*cyber security*) or one (*cybersecurity*) depends on the institution. The spelling in Europe tends to consist of two words.)

History

Cybersecurity standards have existed over several decades as users and providers have collaborated in many domestic and international forums to effect the necessary capabilities, policies, and practices - generally emerging from work at the Stanford Consortium for Research on Information Security and Policy in the 1990s. Also many tasks that were once carried out by hand are now carried out by computer; therefore there is a need for information assurance (IA) and security.

ETSI Cyber Security Technical Committee (TC CYBER)

TC CYBER is responsible for the standardisation of Cyber Security internationally and for providing a centre of relevant expertise for other ETSI committees. Growing dependence on networked digital systems has brought with it an increase in both the variety and quantity of cyber-threats. The different methods governing secure transactions in the various Member States of the European Union sometimes make it difficult to assess the respective risks and to ensure adequate security. Building on ETSI's world-leading expertise in the security of Information and Communications Technologies (ICT), it set up a new Cyber Security committee (TC CYBER) in 2014 to meet the growing demand for standards to protect the Internet and the communications and business it carries.

TC CYBER is working closely with relevant stakeholders to develop appropriate standards to increase privacy and security for organisations and citizens across Europe. The committee is looking in particular at the security of infrastructures, devices, services and protocols, as well as security tools and techniques to ensure security. It offers security advice and guidance to users, manufacturers and network and infrastructure operators. Its standards are freely available on-line. A principal work item effort is the production of a global cyber security ecosystem of standardization and other activities.

ISO 27001 and 27002

ISO/IEC 27001:2013, part of the growing ISO/IEC 27000 family of standards, is an information security management system (ISMS) standard published in October 2013 by the International Organization for Standardization (ISO) and the International Electrotechnical Commission (IEC). Its full name is *ISO/IEC 27001:2013 – Information technology – Security techniques – Information security management systems – Requirements.*

ISO/IEC 27001:2013 formally specifies a management system that is intended to bring information security under explicit management control.

ISO/IEC 27002 incorporates mainly part 1 of the BS 7799 good security management practice standard. The latest versions of BS7799 is BS7799-3. Sometimes ISO/IEC 27002 is therefore referred to as ISO 17799 or BS 7799 part 1 and sometimes it refers to part 1 and part 7. BS 7799 part 1 provides an outline or good practice guide for cybersecurity management; whereas BS 7799 part 2 and ISO 27001 are normative and therefore provide a framework for certification. ISO/IEC 27002 is a high level guide to cybersecurity. It is most beneficial as explanatory guidance for the management of an organisation to obtain certification to the ISO 27001 standard. The certification once obtained lasts three years. Depending on the auditing organisation, no or some intermediate audits may be carried out during the three years.

ISO 27001 (ISMS) replaces BS 7799 part 2, but since it is backward compatible any organization working toward BS 7799 part 2 can easily transition to the ISO 27001 certification process. There is also a transitional audit available to make it easier once an organization is BS 7799 part 2-certified for the organization to become ISO 27001-certified. ISO/IEC 27002 provides best practice recommendations on information security management for use by those responsible for initiating, implementing or maintaining information security management systems (ISMS). It states the information security systems required to implement ISO 27002 control objectives. Without ISO 27001, ISO 27002 control objectives are ineffective. ISO 27002 controls objectives are incorporated into ISO 27001 in Annex A.

ISO/IEC 21827 (SSE-CMM – ISO/IEC 21827) is an International Standard based on the Systems Security Engineering Capability Maturity Model (SSE-CMM) that can measure the maturity of ISO controls objectives.

Standard of Good Practice

In the 1990s, the Information Security Forum (ISF) published a comprehensive list of best practices for information security, published as the *Standard of Good Practice* (SoGP). The ISF continues to update the SoGP every two years (with the exception of 2013-2014); the latest version was published in 2016.

Originally the *Standard of Good Practice* was a private document available only to ISF members, but the ISF has since made the full document available for sale to the general public.

Among other programs, the ISF offers its member organizations a comprehensive benchmarking program based on the SoGP. Furthermore, it is important for those in charge of security management to understand and adhere to NERC CIP compliance requirements.

NERC

The North American Electric Reliability Corporation (NERC) has created many standards. The most widely recognized is NERC 1300 which is a modification/update of NERC 1200. The newest version of NERC 1300 is called CIP-002-3 through CIP-009-3 (CIP=Critical Infrastructure Protection). These standards are used to secure bulk electric systems although NERC has created standards within other areas. The bulk electric system standards also provide network security administration while still supporting best-practice industry processes.

NIST

1. Special publication 800-12 provides a broad overview of computer security and control areas. It also emphasizes the importance of the security controls and ways to implement them. Initially this document was aimed at the federal government although most practices in this document can be applied to the private sector as well. Specifically it was written for those people in the federal government responsible for handling sensitive systems.

2. Special publication 800-14 describes common security principles that are used. It provides a high level description of what should be incorporated within a computer security policy. It describes what can be done to improve existing security as well as how to develop a new security practice. Eight principles and fourteen practices are described within this document.

3. Special publication 800-26 provides advice on how to manage IT security. Superseded by NIST SP 800-53 rev3. This document emphasizes the importance of self assessments as well as risk assessments.

4. Special publication 800-37, updated in 2010 provides a new risk approach: "Guide for Applying the Risk Management Framework to Federal Information Systems"

5. Special publication 800-53 rev4, "Security and Privacy Controls for Federal Information Systems and Organizations", Published April 2013 updated to include updates as of January 15, 2014, specifically addresses the 194 security controls that are applied to a system to make it "more secure".

6. Special Publication 800-82, Revision 2, "Guide to Industrial Control System (ICS) Security", revised May 2015, describes how to secure multiple types of Industrial Control Systems against cyber attacks while considering the performance, reliability and safety requirements specific to ICS.

ISO 15408

This standard develops what is called the "Common Criteria". It allows many different software applications to be integrated and tested in a secure way.

RFC 2196

RFC (Request For Comments) 2196 is memorandum published by Internet Engineering Task Force for developing security policies and procedures for information systems connected on the Internet. The RFC 2196 provides a general and broad overview of information security including network security, incident response, or security policies. The document is very practical and focusing on day-to-day operations.

ISA/IEC-62443 (Formerly ISA-99)

ISA/IEC-62443 is a series of standards, technical reports, and related information that define procedures for implementing electronically secure Industrial Automation and Control Systems (IACS). This guidance applies to end-users (i.e. asset owner), system integrators, security practitioners, and control systems manufacturers responsible for manufacturing, designing, implementing, or managing industrial automation and control systems.

These documents were originally referred to as ANSI/ISA-99 or ISA99 standards, as they were created by the International Society for Automation (ISA) and publicly released as American National Standards Institute (ANSI) documents. In 2010, they were renumbered to be the ANSI/ISA-62443 series. This change was intended to align the ISA and ANSI document numbering with the corresponding International Electrotechnical Commission (IEC) standards.

All ISA work products are now numbered using the convention "ISA-62443-x-y" and previous ISA99 nomenclature is maintained for continuity purposes only. Corresponding IEC documents are referenced as "IEC 62443-x-y". The approved IEC and ISA versions are generally identical for all functional purposes.

ISA99 remains the name of the Industrial Automation and Control System Security Committee of the ISA. Since 2002, the committee has been developing a multi-part series of standards and technical reports on the subject. These work products are then submitted to the ISA approval and publishing under ANSI. They are also submitted to IEC for review and approval as standards and specifications in the IEC 62443 series.

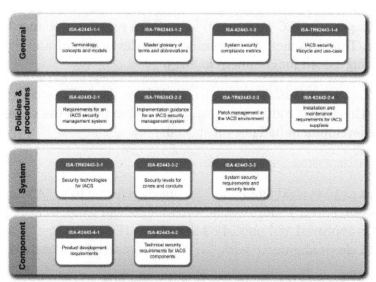

Planned and published ISA-62443 work products for IACS Security.

All ISA-62443 standards and technical reports are organized into four general categories called General, Policies and Procedures, System, and Component.

1. The first (top) category includes common or foundational information such as concepts, models and terminology. Also included are work products that describe security metrics and security life cycles for IACS.

2. The second category of work products targets the Asset Owner. These address various aspects of creating and maintaining an effective IACS security program.

3. The third category includes work products that describe system design guidance and requirements for the secure integration of control systems. Core in this is the zone and conduit design model.

4. The fourth category includes work products that describe the specific product development and technical requirements of control system products. This is primarily intended for control product vendors, but can be used by integrator and asset owners for to assist in the procurement of secure products.

The planned and published ISA-62443 documents are as follows:

- **Group 1: General**

   o ISA-62443-1-1 (IEC/TS 62443-1-1) (formerly referred to as "ISA-99 Part 1") was originally published as ISA standard ANSI/ISA-99.00.01-2007, as well as an IEC technical specification IEC/TS 62443-1-1. The ISA99 committee is currently revising it to make it align with other documents in the series, and to clarify normative content.

   o ISA-TR62443-1-2 (IEC 62443-1-2) is a master glossary of terms used by the ISA99 committee. This document is a working draft, but the content is available on the ISA99 committee Wiki.

   o ISA-62443-1-3 (IEC 62443-1-3) identifies a set of compliance metrics for IACS security. This document is currently under development and the committee will be releasing a draft for comment in 2013.

   o ISA-62443-1-4 (IEC/TS 62443-1-4) defines the IACS security life cycle and use case. This work product has been proposed as part of the series, but as of January 2013 development had not yet started.

- **Group 2: Policy and Procedure**

   o ISA-62443-2-1 (IEC 62443-2-1) (formerly referred to as "ANSI/ISA 99.02.01-2009 or ISA-99 Part 2") addresses how to establish an IACS security program. This standard is approved and published the IEC as IEC 62443-2-1. It now being revised to permit closer alignment with the ISO 27000 series of standards.

   o ISA-62443-2-2 (IEC 62443-2-2) addresses how to operate an IACS security program. This standard is currently under development.

   o ISA-TR62443-2-3 (IEC/TR 62443-2-3) is a technical report on the subject of patch management in IACS environments. This report is currently under development.

   o ISA-62443-2-4 (IEC 62443-2-4) focuses on the certification of IACS supplier security policies and practices. This document was adopted from the WIB organization and is now a working product of the IEC TC65/WG10 committee. The proposed ISA version will be a U.S. national publication of the IEC standard.

- **Group 3: System Integrator**

  o ISA-TR62443-3-1 (IEC/TR 62443-3-1) is a technical report on the subject of suitable technologies for IACS security. This report is approved and published as ANSI/ISA-TR99.00.01-2007 and is now being revised.

  o ISA-62443-3-2 (IEC 62443-3-2) addresses how to define security assurance levels using the zones and conduits concept. This standard is currently under development.

  o ISA-62443-3-3 (IEC 62443-3-3) defines detailed technical requirements for IACS security. This standard has been published as ANSI/ISA-62443-3-3 (99.03.03)-2013. It was previously numbered as ISA-99.03.03.

- **Group 4: Component Provider**

  o ISA-62443-4-1 (IEC 62443-4-1) addresses the requirements for the development of secure IACS products and solutions. This standard is currently under development.

  o ISA-62443-4-2 (IEC 62443-4-2) series address detailed technical requirements for IACS components level. This standard is currently under development.

IEC 62443 Conformity Assessment Program

The ISA Security Compliance Institute (ISCI) www.isasecure.org operates the first conformity assessment scheme for IEC 62443 IACS cybersecurity standards. This program certifies Commercial Off-the-shelf (COTS) IACS products and systems, addressing securing the IACS supply chain.

Certification Offerings Two COTS product certifications are available under the ISASecure® brand: ISASecure-EDSA (Embedded Device Security Assurance) certifying IACS products to the IEC 62443-4-2 IACS cybersecurity standard and ISASecure-SSA (System Security Assurance), certifying IACS systems to the IEC 62443-3-3 IACS cybersecurity standard.

A third certification, SDLA (Secure Development Lifecycle Assurance) is available which certifies IACS development organizations to the IEC 62443-4-1 cybersecurity standard, providing assurances that a supplier organization has institutionalized cybersecurity into their product development practices.

ISO 17065 and Global Accreditation The ISASecure 62443 conformity assessment scheme is an ISO 17065 program whose labs (certification bodies or CB) are independently accredited by ANSI/ANAB, JAB and other global ISO 17011 accreditation bodies (AB). The certification labs must also meet ISO 17025 lab accreditation requirements to ensure consistent application of certification requirements and recognized tools.

Through Mutual Recognition Arrangements (MRA) with IAF, ILAC and others, the accreditation of the ISASecure labs by the ISA 17011 accreditation bodies ensures that certificates issued by any of the ISASecure labs are globally recognized.

Test Tool Recognition The ISASecure scheme includes a process for recognizing test tools to ensure the tools meet functional requirements necessary and sufficient to execute all required product tests and that test results will be consistent among the recognized tools.

Chemicals, Oil and Gas Industries ISCI development processes include maintenance policies to ensure that the ISASecure certifications remain in alignment with the IEC 62443 standards as they evolve. While the IEC 62443 standards are designed to horizontally address technical cybersecurity requirements of a cross-section of process industries, the ISASecure scheme's certification requirements have been vetted by representatives from the chemical and oil and gas industries and are reflective of their cybersecurity needs.

IASME

IASME is a UK-based standard for information assurance at small-to-medium enterprises (SMEs). It provides criteria and certification for small-to-medium business cybersecurity readiness. It also allows small to medium business to provide potential and existing customers and clients with an accredited measurement of the cybersecurity posture of the enterprise and its protection of personal/business data.

IASME was established to enable businesses with capitalization of 1.2 billion pounds or less (1.5 billion Euros; 2 billion US dollars) to achieve an accreditation similar to ISO 27001 but with reduced complexity, cost, and administrative overhead (specifically focused on SME in recognition that it is difficult for small cap businesses to achieve and maintain ISO 27001).

The cost of the certification is progressively graduated based upon the employee population of the SME (e.g., 10 & fewer, 11 to 25, 26 - 100, 101 - 250 employees); the certification can be based upon a self-assessment with an IASME questionnaire or by a third-party professional assessor. Some insurance companies reduce premiums for cybersecurity related coverage based upon the IASME certification.

Global Surveillance

Global surveillance refers to the mass surveillance of entire populations across national borders. Its roots can be traced back to the middle of the 20th century, when the UKUSA Agreement was jointly enacted by the United Kingdom and the United States, which later expanded to Canada, Australia, and New Zealand to create the Five Eyes alliance. The alliance developed cooperation arrangements with several "third-party" nations. Eventually, this resulted in the establishment of a global surveillance network, code-named "ECHELON", in 1971.

Its existence, however, was not widely acknowledged by governments and the mainstream media until the global surveillance disclosures by Edward Snowden triggered a debate about the right to privacy in the digital age.

Historical Background

According to Snowden's documents, the United Nations Headquarters and the United Nations General Assembly were targeted by NSA employees disguised as diplomats.

Citing Snowden's documents, *The Guardian* reported that British officials had set up fake internet cafes at the 2009 G-20 London summit to spy on the delegates' use of computers, and to install key-logging software on the delegates' phones. This allowed British representatives to gain a "negotiating advantage" at the summit

According to Snowden's interview with the *South China Morning Post*, the U.S. government has been hacking numerous non-military targets in China for years. Other high-priority targets include academic institutions such as the prestigious Tsinghua University in Beijing

The Council of the European Union, with its headquarters at the Justus Lipsius building in Brussels, was targeted by NSA employees working near the headquarters of NATO. An NSA document dated September 2010 explicitly names the Europeans as a "location target".

The reservations system of Russia's Aeroflot airline was hacked by the NSA

Petrobras, currently the world's leader in offshore deepwater drilling, is a "prominent" target of the U.S. government

From 2002 to 2013, the German Chancellor Angela Merkel was targeted by the U.S. Special Collection Service

Israeli Prime Minister Ehud Olmert (pictured) and Defense Minister Ehud Barak were included
in a list of surveillance targets used by the GCHQ and the NSA

Joaquín Almunia, who served as the European Commissioner for Competition and the Vice-President
of the European Commission, was targeted by Britain's GCHQ agency

Indonesia's President Susilo Bambang Yudhoyono and his wife were placed under surveillance by the Australian Signals Directorate (ASD). During the 2007 United Nations Climate Change Conference in Bali, the ASD cooperated with the NSA to conduct mass surveillance on the Indonesian hosts

The video gaming network Xbox Live was placed under surveillance to unravel possible terrorist plots

The origins of global surveillance can be traced back to the late 1940s, after the UKUSA Agreement was jointly enacted by the United Kingdom and the United States, which eventually culminated in the creation of the global surveillance network code-named "ECHELON" in 1971.

In the aftermath of the 1970s Watergate affair and a subsequent congressional inquiry led by Sen. Frank Church, it was revealed that the NSA, in collaboration with Britain's GCHQ, had routinely intercepted the international communications of prominent anti-Vietnam War leaders such as Jane Fonda and Dr. Benjamin Spock. Decades later, a multi-year investigation by the European Parliament highlighted the NSA's role in economic espionage in a report entitled 'Development of Surveillance Technology and Risk of Abuse of Economic Information', in 1999.

However, for the general public, it was a series of detailed disclosures of internal NSA documents in June 2013 that first revealed the massive extent of the NSA's spying, both foreign and domestic. Most of these were leaked by an ex-contractor, Edward Snowden. Even so, a number of these older global surveillance programs such as PRISM, XKeyscore, and Tempora were referenced in the 2013 release of thousands of documents. Many countries around the world, including Western

Allies and member states of NATO, have been targeted by the "Five Eyes" strategic alliance of Australia, Canada, New Zealand, the UK and the USA—five English-speaking Western democracies aiming to achieve Total Information Awareness by mastering the Internet with analytical tools such as the Boundless Informant. As confirmed by the NSA's director Keith B. Alexander on September 26, 2013, the NSA collects and stores all phone records of all American citizens. Much of the data is kept in large storage facilities such as the Utah Data Center, a US$1.5 billion megaproject referred to by *The Wall Street Journal* as a "symbol of the spy agency's surveillance prowess."

"Today, this global surveillance system continues to grow. It now collects so much digital detritus — e-mails, calls, text messages, cellphone location data and a catalog of computer viruses - that the N.S.A. is building a 1-million-square-foot facility in the Utah desert to store and process it."

— *The New York Times (August 2012)*

On June 6, 2013, Britain's *The Guardian* newspaper began publishing a series of revelations by an as yet unknown American whistleblower, revealed several days later to be ex-CIA and ex-NSA-contracted systems analyst Edward Snowden. Snowden gave a cache of documents to two journalists: Glenn Greenwald and Laura Poitras, Greenwald later estimated that the cache contains 15,000 – 20,000 documents, some very large and very detailed, and some very small. In over two subsequent months of publications, it became clear that the NSA had operated a complex web of spying programs which allowed it to intercept internet and telephone conversations from over a billion users from dozens of countries around the world. Specific revelations were made about China, the European Union, Latin America, Iran and Pakistan, and Australia and New Zealand, however the published documentation reveals that many of the programs indiscriminately collected bulk information directly from central servers and internet backbones, which almost invariably carry and reroute information from distant countries.

Due to this central server and backbone monitoring, many of the programs overlapped and interrelated among one another. These programs were often carried out with the assistance of US entities such as the United States Department of Justice and the FBI, were sanctioned by US laws such as the FISA Amendments Act, and the necessary court orders for them were signed by the secret Foreign Intelligence Surveillance Court. Some of the NSA's programs were directly aided by national and foreign intelligence agencies, Britain's GCHQ and Australia's DSD, as well as by large private telecommunications and internet corporations, such as Verizon, Telstra, Google and Facebook.

Purposes

According to the April 2013 summary of documents leaked by Snowden, other than to combat terrorism, these surveillance programs were employed to assess the foreign policy and economic stability of other countries, and to gather "commercial secrets".

In a statement addressed to the National Congress of Brazil in early August 2013, journalist Glenn Greenwald maintained that the U.S. government had used counter-terrorism as a pretext for clandestine surveillance in order to compete with other countries in the "business, industrial and economic fields". In a December 2013 letter to the Brazilian government, Snowden wrote that "These programs were never about terrorism: they're about economic spying, social control, and diplomatic manipulation. They're about power." According to White House panel member NSA didn't stop any terrorist attack. However NSA chief said, that surveillance programs stopped 54 terrorist plots.

In an interview with *Der Spiegel* published on August 12, 2013, former NSA Director Michael Hayden admitted that "We (the NSA) steal secrets. We're number one in it". Hayden also added: "We steal stuff to make you safe, not to make you rich".

According to documents seen by the news agency Reuters, these "secrets" were subsequently funnelled to authorities across the nation to help them launch criminal investigations of Americans. Federal agents are then instructed to "recreate" the investigative trail in order to "cover up" where the information originated.

According to the congressional testimony of Keith B. Alexander, Director of the National Security Agency, one of the purposes of its data collection is to store all the phone records inside a place that can be searched and assessed at all times. When asked by Senator Mark Udall if the goal of the NSA is to collect the phone records of all Americans, Alexander replied:

"Yes, I believe it is in the nation's best interest to put all the phone records into a lockbox that we could search when the nation needs to do it."

— *Gen. Keith B. Alexander*

Targets and Methods

Socioeconomical

Collection of Metadata and Other Content

In the United States, the NSA is collecting the phone records of more than 300 million Americans. The international surveillance tool XKeyscore allows government analysts to search through vast databases containing emails, online chats and the browsing histories of millions of individuals. Britain's global surveillance program Tempora intercepts the fibre-optic cables that form the backbone of the Internet. Under the NSA's PRISM surveillance program, data that has already reached its final destination would be directly harvested from the servers of the following U.S. service providers: Microsoft, Yahoo!, Google, Facebook, Paltalk, AOL, Skype, YouTube, and Apple Inc.

Contact Chaining

The NSA uses the analysis of phone call and e-mail logs of American citizens to create sophisticated graphs of their social connections that can identify their associates, their locations at certain times, their traveling companions and other personal information.

According to top secret NSA documents leaked by Edward Snowden, during a single day in 2012, the NSA collected e-mail address books from:

- 22,881 Gmail accounts
- 82,857 Facebook accounts
- 105,068 Hotmail accounts

- 444,743 Yahoo! accounts

Each day, the NSA collects contacts from an estimated 500,000 buddy lists on live-chat services as well as from the inbox displays of Web-based e-mail accounts. Taken together, the data enables the NSA to draw detailed maps of a person's life based on their personal, professional, religious and political connections.

Data Transfer

Federal Agencies in the United States

Data gathered by these surveillance programs is routinely shared with the U.S. Federal Bureau of Investigation (FBI) and the U.S. Central Intelligence Agency (CIA). In addition, the NSA supplies domestic intercepts to the Drug Enforcement Administration (DEA), Internal Revenue Service (IRS), and other law enforcement agencies.

Foreign Countries

As a result of the NSA's secret treaties with foreign countries, data gathered by its surveillance programs is routinely shared with countries who are signatories to the UKUSA Agreement. These foreign countries also help to operate several NSA programs such as XKEYSCORE·

Financial Payments Monitoring

A special branch of the NSA called "Follow the Money" (FTM) monitors international payments, banking and credit card transactions and later stores the collected data in the NSA's financial databank, "Tracfin".

Mobile Phone Location Tracking

Mobile phone tracking refers to the act of attaining the position and coordinates of a mobile phone. According to *The Washington Post*, the NSA has been tracking the locations of mobile phones from all over the world by tapping into the cables that connect mobile networks globally and that serve U.S. cellphones as well as foreign ones. In the process of doing so, the NSA collects more than 5 billion records of phone locations on a daily basis. This enables NSA analysts to map cellphone owners' relationships by correlating their patterns of movement over time with thousands or millions of other phone users who cross their paths.

In order to decode private conversations, the NSA has cracked the most commonly used cellphone encryption technology, A5/1. According to a classified document leaked by Snowden, the agency can "process encrypted A5/1" even when it has not acquired an encryption key. In addition, the NSA uses various types of cellphone infrastructure, such as the links between carrier networks, to determine the location of a cellphone user tracked by Visitor Location Registers.

Infiltration of Smartphones

As worldwide sales of smartphones grew rapidly, the NSA decided to take advantage of the smartphone boom. This is particularly advantageous because the smartphone contains a variety of data sets that would interest an intelligence agency, such as social contacts, user behavior, interests, location, photos and credit card numbers and passwords.

According to documents leaked by Edward Snowden, the NSA has set up task forces assigned to several smartphone manufacturers and operating systems, including Apple Inc.'s iPhone and iOS operating system, as well as Google's Android mobile operating system. Similarly, Britain's GCHQ assigned a team to study and crack the BlackBerry. In addition, there are smaller NSA programs, known as "scripts", that can perform surveillance on 38 different features of the iOS 3 and iOS 4 operating systems. These include the mapping feature, voicemail and photos, as well as Google Earth, Facebook and Yahoo! Messenger.

Infiltration of Commercial Data Centers

In contrast to the PRISM surveillance program, which is a front-door method of access that is nominally approved by the FISA court, the MUSCULAR surveillance program is noted to be "unusually aggressive" in its usage of unorthodox hacking methods to infiltrate Yahoo! and Google data centers around the world. As the program is operated overseas (United Kingdom), the NSA presumes that anyone using a foreign data link is a foreigner, and is therefore able to collect content and metadata on a previously unknown scale from U.S. citizens and residents. According to documents leaked by Edward Snowden, the MUSCULAR surveillance program is jointly operated by the NSA and Britain's GCHQ agency.

Infiltration of Anonymous Networks

The Five Eyes have made repeated attempts to spy on Internet users communicating in secret via the anonymity network Tor. Several of their clandestine operations involve the implantation of malicious code into the computers of anonymous Tor users who visit infested websites. In some cases, the NSA and GCHQ have succeeded in blocking access to the anonymous network, diverting Tor users to insecure channels. In other cases, the NSA and the GCHQ were able to uncover the identity of these anonymous users.

Monitoring of Hotel Reservation Systems

Under the Royal Concierge surveillance program, Britain's GCHQ agency uses an automated monitoring system to infiltrate the reservation systems of at least 350 luxury hotels in many different parts of the world. Other related surveillance programs involve the wiretapping of room telephones and fax machines used in targeted hotels as well as the monitoring of computers hooked up to the hotel network.

Virtual Reality Surveillance

The U.S. National Security Agency (NSA), the U.S. Central Intelligence Agency (CIA), and Britain's Government Communications Headquarters (GCHQ) have been conducting surveillance on the networks of many online games, including massively multiplayer online role-playing games (MMORPGs) such as World of Warcraft, as well as virtual worlds such as Second Life, and the Xbox gaming console.

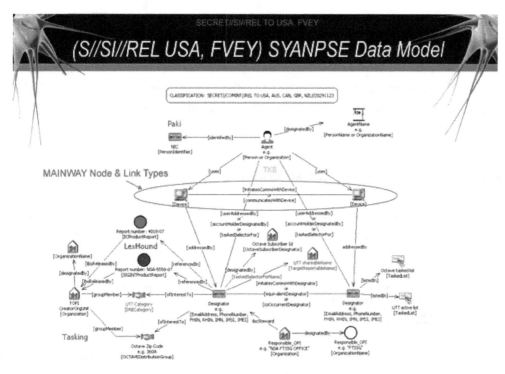

The New York Times, citing documents leaked by Edward Snowden, reported in September 2013 on the NSA's "push to exploit phone and e-mail data of Americans after it lifted restrictions in 2010", which enables "large-scale graph analysis on very large sets of communications metadata". This slide from an NSA presentation shows one of the methods in which the agency uses e-mail and phone data to analyze the relationship network of a target. According to The *Times*, the NSA can "augment the communications data with material from public, commercial and other sources, including bank codes, insurance information, Facebook profiles, passenger manifests, voter registration rolls and GPS location information, as well as property records and unspecified tax data". Such types of data were collected from U.S. citizens as well as foreign nationals.

Political Espionage

According to the April 2013 summary of disclosures, the NSA defined its "intelligence priorities" on a scale of "1" (highest interest) to "5" (lowest interest). It classified about 30 countries as "3rd parties", with whom it cooperates but also spies on:

- Main targets: China, Russia, Iran, Pakistan and Afghanistan were ranked highly on the NSA's list of spying priorities, followed by France, Germany, Japan, and Brazil. The European Union's "international trade" and "economic stability" are also of interest. Other high priority targets include Cuba, Israel, and North Korea.

- Irrelevant : From a US intelligence perspective, countries such as Cambodia, Laos and Nepal were largely irrelevant, as were governments of smaller European Union countries such as Finland, Denmark, Croatia and the Czech Republic.

Other prominent targets included members and adherents of the internet group known as "Anonymous", as well as potential whistleblowers. According to Edward Snowden, the NSA targeted reporters who wrote critically about the government after 9/11.

As part of a joint operation with the Central Intelligence Agency (CIA), the NSA deployed secret eavesdropping posts in eighty U.S. embassies and consulates worldwide. The headquarters of NATO were also used by NSA experts to spy on the European Union.

In 2013, documents provided by Edward Snowden revealed that the following intergovernmental organizations, diplomatic missions, and government ministries have been subjected to surveillance by the "Five Eyes":

Country/ Organization	Target	Method(s)
Brazil	Ministry of Energy	Collection of metadata records by the Communications Security Establishment of Canada (CSEC)
France	Ministry of Foreign and European Affairs	Infiltration of virtual private networks (VPN)
France	Embassy of France in Washington, D.C	Infiltration of virtual private networks (VPN)
Germany	Embassy of Germany in Rwanda	
Italy	Embassy of Italy in Washington, D.C	• Installation of physical implants • Copying of entire hard disk drives
India	Embassy of India in Washington, D.C	• Copying entire hard disk drives
India	Permanent Representative of India to the United Nations	• Picking data from screenshots
Mexico	Secretariat of Public Security	• Hacking of e-mail accounts as part of an operation code-named "*Whitetamale*"
European Union	Council of the European Union in Brussels	• Installation of covert listening devices
European Union	Delegation to the United Nations in New York	• Hacking and infiltration of virtual private networks
European Union	Delegation to the United States in Washington, D.C	• Disk cloning
United Nations	United Nations Headquarters	
United Nations	International Atomic Energy Agency (IAEA)	• Hacking of encrypted communications
United Nations	United Nations Development Programme (UNDP)	• Infiltration of internal video conferences
United Nations	United Nations Children's Fund (UNICEF)	

International Cooperation

During World War II, the BRUSA Agreement was signed by the governments of the United States and the United Kingdom for the purpose of intelligence sharing. This was later formalized in the

UKUSA Agreement of 1946 as a secret treaty. The full text of the agreement was released to the public on June 25, 2010.

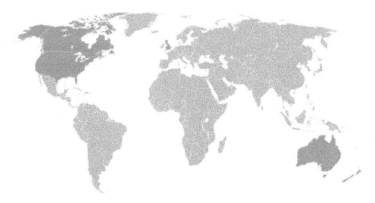

The "Five Eyes" of Australia, Canada, New Zealand, the United Kingdom and the United States

Although the treaty was later revised to include other countries such as Denmark, Germany, Ireland, Norway, Turkey, and the Philippines, most of the information sharing has been performed by the so-called "Five Eyes", a term referring to the following English-speaking western democracies and their respective intelligence agencies:

- ▰▰ – The Defence Signals Directorate of Australia

- ▰◆▰ – The Communications Security Establishment of Canada

- ▰▰ – The Government Communications Security Bureau of New Zealand

- ▰▰ – The Government Communications Headquarters of the United Kingdom, which is widely considered to be a leader in traditional spying due to its influence on countries that were once part of the British Empire.

- ▰▰ – The National Security Agency of the United States, which has the biggest budget and the most advanced technical abilities among the *"five eyes"*.

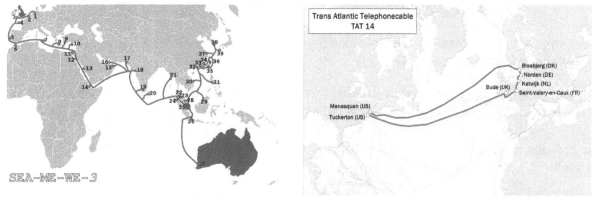

Top secret documents leaked by Edward Snowden revealed that the "Five Eyes" have gained access to the majority of internet and telephone communications flowing throughout Europe, the United States, and other parts of the world.

Left: SEA-ME-WE 3, which runs across the Afro-Eurasian supercontinent from Japan to Northern

Germany, is one of the most important submarine cables accessed by the "Five Eyes". Singapore, a former British colony in the Asia-Pacific region (blue dot), plays a vital role in intercepting internet and telecommunications traffic heading from Australia/Japan to Europe, and vice versa. An intelligence sharing agreement between Singapore and Australia allows the rest of the "Five Eyes" to gain access to SEA-ME-WE 3. Right: TAT-14, a telecommunications cable linking Europe with the United States, was identified as one of few assets of "Critical Infrastructure and Key Resources" of the USA on foreign territory. In 2013, it was revealed that British officials "pressured a handful of telecommunications and internet companies" to allow the British government to gain access to TAT-14.

According to the leaked documents, aside from the Five Eyes, most other Western countries have also participatied in the NSA surveillance system and are sharing information with each other. However, being a partner of the NSA does not automatically exempt a country from being targeted by the NSA. According to an internal NSA document leaked by Snowden, "We (the NSA) can, and often do, target the signals of most 3rd party foreign partners."

Australia

Pine Gap, near the Australian town of Alice Springs, is run by the CIA and it is part of the global surveillance program ECHELON.

The Australian Signals Directorate (ASD), formerly known as the Defence Signals Directorate (DSD), shares information on Australian citizens with the other members of the UKUSA Agreement. According to a 2008 Five Eyes document leaked by Edward Snowden, data of Australian citizens shared with foreign countries include "bulk, unselected, unminimised metadata" as well as "medical, legal or religious information".

In close cooperation with other members of the Five Eyes community, the ASD runs secret surveillance facilities in many parts of Southeast Asia without the knowledge of Australian diplomats. In addition, the ASD cooperates with the Security and Intelligence Division (SID) of the Republic of Singapore in an international operation to intercept underwater telecommunications cables across the Eastern Hemisphere and the Pacific Ocean.

Canada

The Communications Security Establishment Canada (CSEC) offers the NSA resources for advanced collection, processing, and analysis. It has set up covert sites at the request of NSA. The US-Canada SIGNT relationship dates back to a secret alliance formed during World War II, and was formalized in 1949 under the CANUSA Agreement.

On behalf of the NSA, the CSEC opened secret surveillance facilities in 20 countries around the world.

NSA's relationship with Canada's CSEC

As well, the Communications Security Establishment Canada has been revealed, following the global surveillance disclosures to be engaging in surveillance on Wifi Hotspots of major Canadian Airports, collecting meta-data to use for engaging in surveillance on travelers, even days after their departure from said airports.

NSA document on a mass surveillance operation with Canada's CSEC agency during
the G8 and G20 summits in Toronto in 2010

Denmark

The Politiets Efterretningstjeneste (PET) of Denmark, a domestic intelligence agency, exchanges data with the NSA on a regular basis, as part of a secret agreement with the United States. Being one of the "9-Eyes" of the UKUSA Agreement, Denmark's relationship with the NSA is closer than the NSA's relationship with Germany, Sweden, Spain, Belgium or Italy.

France

The Directorate-General for External Security (DGSE) of France maintains a close relationship with both the NSA and the GCHQ after discussions for increased cooperation began in November 2006. By the early 2010s, the extent of cooperation in the joint interception of digital data by the DGSE and the NSA was noted to have increased dramatically.

In 2011, a formal memorandum for data exchange was signed by the DGSE and the NSA, which facilitated the transfer of millions of metadata records from the DGSE to the NSA. From December 2012 to 8 January 2013, over 70 million metadata records were handed over to the NSA by French intelligence agencies.

Germany

The Bundesnachrichtendienst (BND) of Germany systematically transfers metadata from German intelligence sources to the NSA. In December 2012 alone, the BND provided the NSA with 500 million metadata records. The NSA granted the Bundesnachrichtendienst access to X-Keyscore, in exchange for the German surveillance programs Mira4 and Veras.

In early 2013, Hans-Georg Maaßen, President of the German domestic security agency Bundesamt für Verfassungsschutz (BfV), made several visits to the headquarters of the NSA. According to classified documents of the German government, Maaßen agreed to transfer all data records of persons monitored in Germany by the BfV via XKeyscore to the NSA. In addition, the BfV works very closely with eight other U.S. government agencies, including the CIA. Under Project 6, which is jointly operated by the CIA, BfV, and BND, a massive database containing personal information such as photos, license plate numbers, Internet search histories and telephone metadata was developed to gain a better understanding of the social relationships of presumed jihadists.

In 2012, the BfV handed over 864 data sets of personal information to the CIA, NSA and seven other U.S. intelligence agencies. In exchange, the BND received data from U.S. intelligence agencies on 1,830 occasions. The newly acquired data was handed over to the BfV and stored in a domestically accessible system known as NADIS WN.

The Dagger Complex in Darmstadt, Germany, is operated by the United States Army on behalf of the NSA. Similar to the NSA's Utah Data Center, the Dagger Complex is able to process, store, and decrypt millions of data pieces

The Bad Aibling Station in Bavaria, Germany, was operated by the NSA until the early 2000s. It is currently run by the BND. As part of the global surveillance network ECHELON, it is the largest listening post outside Britain and the USA.

> The BND XKEYSCORE system successfully processed DSL wiretap collection belonging to a German domestic CT target. As a result of this demonstration, the BfV Vice President formally requested the XKEYSCORE software from DIRNSA to further enable the BfV to achieve its mission goal of countering terrorist activities in Germany. By enhancing BfV's Internet analytic capabilities through the provision of XKEYSCORE, NSA will enable Germany to provide unique contributions in the form of collection, data summaries, and/or finished intelligence to the high-priority NSA CT mission.

In 2013, the German news magazine *Der Spiegel* published an excerpt of an NSA document leaked by Edward Snowden, showing that the BND used the NSA's XKEYSCORE to wiretap a German domestic target

Israel

On 11 September 2013, *The Guardian* released a secret NSA document leaked by Edward Snowden, which reveals how Israel's Unit 8200 (ISNU) was given raw, unfiltered data of U.S. citizens, as part of a secret agreement with the U.S. National Security Agency

The Israeli SIGINT National Unit (ISNU) routinely receives raw, unfiltered data of U.S. citizens from the NSA. However, a secret NSA document leaked by Snowden revealed that U.S. government officials are explicitly exempted from such forms of data sharing with the ISNU. As stated in a memorandum detailing the rules of data sharing on U.S. citizens, the ISNU is obligated to:

"Destroy upon recognition any communication contained in raw SIGINT provided by NSA that is either to or from an official of the U.S. government. "U.S. government officials" include officials of the Executive Branch (including White House, Cabinet Departments, and independent agencies); the U.S. House of Representatives and Senate (members and staff); and the U.S. Federal Court system (including, but not limited to, the Supreme Court)."

—*Memorandum of understanding between the NSA and Israel (circa 2009)*

According to the undated memorandum, the ground rules for intelligence sharing between the NSA and the ISNU were laid out in March 2009. Under the data sharing agreement, the ISNU is allowed to retain the identities of U.S. citizens (excluding U.S. government officials) for up to a year.

Japan

In 2011, the NSA asked the Japanese government to intercept underwater fiber-optic cables carrying phone and Internet data in the Asia-Pacific region. However, the Japanese government refused to comply.

Netherlands

The Algemene Inlichtingen en Veiligheidsdienst (AIVD) of the Netherlands has been receiving and storing data of Internet users gathered by U.S. intelligence sources such as the NSA's PRISM surveillance program. During a meeting in February 2013, the AIVD and the MIVD briefed the NSA on their attempts to hack Internet forums and to collect the data of all users using a technology known as Computer Network Exploitation (CNE).

Summary of a meeting held in February 2013 between the NSA and the Dutch intelligence services AIVD and MIVD

Norway

The Norwegian Intelligence Service (NIS) has confirmed that data collected by the agency is "shared with the Americans". Kjell Grandhagen, head of Norwegian military intelligence told reporters at a news conference that "We share this information with partners, and partners share with us...We are talking about huge amounts of traffic data".

In cooperation with the NSA, the NIS has gained access to Russian targets in the Kola Peninsula and other civilian targets. In general, the NIS provides information to the NSA about "Politicians", "Energy" and "Armament". A top secret memo of the NSA lists the following years as milestones of the Norway-United States of America SIGNT agreement, or NORUS Agreement:

- 1952 - Informal starting year of cooperation between the NIS and the NSA

- 1954 - Formalization of the NORUS Agreement

- 1963 - Extension of the agreement for coverage of foreign instrumentation signals intelligence (FISINT)

- 1970 - Extension of the agreement for coverage of electronic intelligence (ELINT)

- 1994 - Extension of the agreement for coverage of communications intelligence (COMINT)

The NSA perceives the NIS as one of its most reliable partners. Both agencies also cooperate to crack the encryption systems of mutual targets. According to the NSA, Norway has made no objections to its requests.

Singapore

The Defence Ministry of Singapore and its Security and Intelligence Division (SID) have been secretly intercepting much of the fibre optic cable traffic passing through the Asian continent. In close cooperation with the Australian Signals Directorate (ASD/DSD), Singapore's SID has been able to intercept SEA-ME-WE 3 (Southeast Asia-Middle East-Western Europe 3) as well as SEA-ME-WE 4 telecommunications cables. Access to these international telecommunications channels is facilitated by Singapore's government-owned operator, SingTel. Temasek Holdings, a multibillion-dollar sovereign wealth fund with a majority stake in SingTel, has maintained close relations with the country's intelligence agencies.

Information gathered by the Government of Singapore is transferred to the Government of Australia as part of an intelligence sharing agreement. This allows the "Five Eyes" to maintain a "stranglehold on communications across the Eastern Hemisphere".

Spain

In close cooperation with Spanish intelligence agencies, the NSA intercepted 60.5 million phone calls in Spain in a single month.

Sweden

The Försvarets radioanstalt (FRA) of Sweden (codenamed Sardines) has allowed the "Five Eyes" to access underwater cables in the Baltic Sea. On 5 December 2013, Sveriges Television (*Swedish Television*) revealed that the FRA has been conducting a clandestine surveillance operation targeting the internal politics of Russia. The operation was conducted on behalf of the NSA, which receives data handed over to it by the FRA.

According to documents leaked by Snowden, the FRA of Sweden has been granted access to the NSA's international surveillance program XKeyscore.

NSA's relationship with Sweden's FRA under the UKUSA Agreement

Switzerland

The Federal Intelligence Service (NDB) of Switzerland exchanges information with the NSA regularly, on the basis of a secret agreement to circumvent domestic surveillance restrictions. In addition, the NSA has been granted access to Swiss surveillance facilities in Leuk (canton of Valais) and Herrenschwanden (canton of Bern), which are part of the Swiss surveillance program Onyx.

According to the NDB, the agency maintains working relationships with about 100 international organizations. However, the NDB has denied any form of cooperation with the NSA. Although the NSA does not have direct access to Switzerland's Onyx surveillance program, the Director of the NDB acknowledged that it is possible for other U.S. intelligence agencies to gain access to Switzerland's surveillance system.

United Kingdom

The British government allowed the NSA to store personal data of British citizens.

Under Project MINARET, anti-Vietnam War dissidents in the United States were jointly targeted by the GCHQ and the NSA.

RAF Menwith Hill, near Harrogate, North Yorkshire, is the biggest listening post outside the United States. It was used by U.S. military personnel to spy on Britons on behalf of MI5 and MI6

United States

Central Intelligence Agency (CIA)

The CIA pays AT&T more than US$10 million a year to gain access to international phone records, including those of U.S. citizens.

National Security Agency (NSA)

The NSA's Foreign Affairs Directorate interacts with foreign intelligence services and members of the Five Eyes to implement global surveillance.

Federal Bureau of Investigation (FBI)

The FBI acts as the liaison between U.S. intelligence agencies and Silicon Valley giants such as Microsoft.

Department of Homeland Security (DHS)

In the early 2010s, the DHS conducted a joint surveillance operation with the FBI to crack down on dissidents of the Occupy Wall Street protest movement.

Other law Enforcement Agencies

The NSA supplies domestic intercepts to the Drug Enforcement Administration (DEA), Internal Revenue Service (IRS), and other law enforcement agencies, who use intercepted data to initiate criminal investigations against US citizens. Federal agents are instructed to "recreate" the investigative trail in order to "cover up" where the information originated.

White House

Weeks after the September 11 attacks, U.S. President George W. Bush signed the Patriot Act to ensure no disruption in the government's ability to conduct global surveillance:

This new law that I sign today will allow surveillance of all communications used by terrorists, including e-mails, the Internet and cell phones.

U.S. President Barack Obama emphasizing the importance of global surveillance to prevent terrorist attacks

*— U.S. President George W. Bush on the implementation of the **Patriot Act** after the September 11 attacks*

The Patriot Act was extended by U.S. President Barack Obama in May 2011 to further extend the federal government's legal authority to conduct additional forms of surveillance such as roving wiretaps.

Commercial Cooperation

Over 70 percent of the United States Intelligence Community's budget is earmarked for payment to private firms. According to *Forbes* magazine, the defense technology company Lockheed Martin is currently the USA's biggest defense contractor, and it is destined to be the NSA's most powerful commercial partner and biggest contractor in terms of dollar revenue.

AT&T

In a joint operation with the NSA, the American telecommunications corporation AT&T operates Room 641A in the SBC Communications building in San Francisco to spy on internet traffic. The CIA pays AT&T more than US$10 million a year to gain access to international phone records, including those of U.S. citizens.

Booz Allen Hamilton

Projects developed by Booz Allen Hamilton include the Strategic Innovation Group to identify terrorists through social media, on behalf of government agencies. During the fiscal year of 2013, Booz Allen Hamilton derived 99% of its income from the government, with the largest portion of its revenue coming from the U.S. Army. In 2013, Booz Allen Hamilton was hailed by Bloomberg Businessweek as "the World's Most Profitable Spy Organization".

British Telecommunications

British Telecommunications (code-named Remedy), a major supplier of telecommunications, granted Britain's intelligence agency GCHQ "unlimited access" to its network of undersea cables, according to documents leaked by Snowden.

Microsoft

The American multinational corporation Microsoft helped the NSA to circumvent software encryption safeguards. It also allowed the federal government to monitor web chats on the *Outlook.com* portal. In 2013, Microsoft worked with the FBI to allow the NSA to gain access to the company's cloud storage service SkyDrive.

Orange S.A.

French telecommunications corporation Orange S.A. shares customer call data with intelligence agencies

The French telecommunications corporation Orange S.A. shares customer call data with the French intelligence agency DGSE, and the intercepted data is handed over to GCHQ.

RSA Security

RSA Security was paid US$10 million by the NSA to introduce a cryptographic backdoor in its encryption products.

Stratfor

Strategic Forecasting, Inc., more commonly known as Stratfor, is a global intelligence company offering information to governments and private clients including Dow Chemical Company, Lockheed Martin, Northrop Grumman, Raytheon, the U.S. Department of Homeland Security, the U.S. Defense Intelligence Agency, and the U.S. Marine Corps.

Vodafone

The British telecommunications company Vodafone (code-named Gerontic) granted Britain's intelligence agency GCHQ "unlimited access" to its network of undersea cables, according to documents leaked by Snowden.

In-Q-Tel

In-Q-Tel, which receives more than US$56 million a year in government support, is a venture capital firm that enables the CIA to invest in Silicon Valley.

Palantir Technologies

Palantir Technologies is a data mining corporation with close ties to the FBI, NSA and CIA.

Based in Palo Alto, California, the company developed a data collection and analytical program known as Prism.

Surveillance Evasion

Several countries have evaded global surveillance by constructing secret bunker facilities deep below the Earth's surface.

North Korea

Despite North Korea being a priority target, the NSA's internal documents acknowledged that it did not know much about Kim Jong Un and his regime's intentions.

Iran

In October 2012, Iran's police chief Esmail Ahmadi Moghaddam alleged that Google is not a search engine but "a spying tool" for Western intelligence agencies. Six months later in April 2013, the country announced plans to introduce an "Islamic Google Earth" to evade global surveillance.

Libya

Libya evaded surveillance by building "hardened and buried" bunkers at least 40 feet below ground level.

Timeline of Disclosures

Edward Snowden's disclosures of the NSA's surveillance activities are a continuation of news leaks which have been ongoing since the early 2000s. One year after the September 11, 2001 attacks, former U.S. intelligence official William Binney, was publicly critical of the NSA for spying on U.S. citizens.

Further disclosures followed. On December 16, 2005, *The New York Times* published a report under the headline "Bush Lets U.S. Spy on Callers Without Courts." In 2006, further evidence of the NSA's domestic surveillance of U.S. citizens was provided by *USA Today*. The newspaper released a report on May 11, 2006 regarding the NSA's "massive database" of phone records collected from "tens of millions" of U.S. citizens. According to *USA Today*, these phone records were provided by several telecom companies such as AT&T, Verizon and BellSouth. In 2008, the security analyst Babak Pasdar revealed the existence of the so-called "Quantico circuit" that he and his team discovered in 2003 when brought on to update the carrier's security system. The circuit provided the U.S. federal government with a backdoor into the network of an unnamed wireless provider, which was later independently identified as Verizon.

Snowden made his first contact with journalist Glenn Greenwald of *The Guardian* in late 2012. The timeline of mass surveillance disclosures by Snowden continued throughout the entire year of 2013.

By Category

Documents leaked by Edward Snowden in 2013 include court orders, memos, and policy documents related to a wide range of surveillance activities.

Impact

The global surveillance disclosure has caused tension in the bilateral relations of the United States with several of its allies and economic partners as well as in its relationship with the European Union. On August 12, 2013, President Obama announced the creation of an "independent" panel of "outside experts" to review the NSA's surveillance programs. The panel is due to be established by the Director of National Intelligence, James R. Clapper, who will consult and provide assistance to them.

According to a survey undertaken by the human rights group PEN International, these disclosures have had a chilling effect on American writers. Fearing the risk of being targeted by government surveillance, 28% of PEN's American members have curbed their usage of social media, and 16% have self-censored themselves by avoiding controversial topics in their writings.

References

- Webb, Maureen (2007). Illusions of Security: Global Surveillance and Democracy in the Post-9/11 World (1st ed.). San Francisco: City Lights Books. ISBN 0872864766.

- Robert Dover; Michael S. Goodman; Claudia Hillebrand, eds. (2013). Routledge Companion to Intelligence Studies. Routledge. p. 164. ISBN 9781134480296.

- Shafir, Reinhard Wobst ; translated by Angelika (2007). Cryptology unlocked. Chichester: John Wiley & Sons. p. 5. ISBN 0470516194.

- Ranger, Steve (24 March 2015). "The undercover war on your internet secrets: How online surveillance cracked our trust in the web". TechRepublic. Archived from the original on 2016-06-12. Retrieved 2016-06-12.

- "CSEC used airport Wi-Fi to track Canadian travellers: Edward Snowden documents". cbc.ca. 31 January 2014. Retrieved 8 March 2015.

- Michael Hastings (28 February 2012). "Exclusive: Homeland Security Kept Tabs on Occupy Wall Street". Rolling Stone. Retrieved 5 January 2014.

- Naomi Wolf (29 December 2012). "Revealed: how the FBI coordinated the crackdown on Occupy". The Guardian. Retrieved 5 January 2014.

- Follorou, Jacques (20 March 2014). "Espionnage : comment Orange et les services secrets coopèrent" (in French). Le Monde. Retrieved 22 March 2014.

- Andy Greenberg (2013-08-14). "How A 'Deviant' Philosopher Built Palantir, A CIA-Funded Data-Mining Juggernaut". Forbes. Retrieved 5 January 2014.

- Ryan W. Neal (June 7, 2013). "NSA Scandal: Is Palantir's Prism Powering PRISM?". International Business Times. Retrieved 5 January 2014.

- "Edward Snowden: US government has been hacking Hong Kong and China for years". South China Morning Post. Retrieved September 9, 2013.

- Laura Poitras; Marcel Rosenbach; Fidelius Schmid; Holger Stark. "Attacks from America: NSA Spied on European Union Offices". Der Spiegel. Retrieved September 9, 2013.

- ROMERO, SIMON (9 September 2013). "N.S.A. Spied on Brazilian Oil Company, Report Says". The New York Times. Retrieved September 9, 2013.

• Ofer Aderet. "Snowden documents reveal U.S., British intelligence spied on former Prime Minister Olmert, Defense Minister Barak". Haaretz. Retrieved 20 December 2013.

• James Ball; Nick Hopkins. "GCHQ and NSA targeted charities, Germans, Israeli PM and EU chief". The Guardian. Retrieved 20 December 2013.

• Michael Brissenden (18 Nov 2013). "Australia spied on Indonesian president Susilo Bambang Yudhoyono, leaked Edward Snowden documents reveal". Australian Broadcasting Corporation. Retrieved 13 December 2013.

• Ewen MacAskill nd Lenore Taylor. "NSA: Australia and US used climate change conference to spy on Indonesia". The Guardian. Retrieved 21 December 2013.

• Duran-Sanchez, Mabel (August 10, 2013). "Greenwald Testifies to Brazilian Senate about NSA Espionage Targeting Brazil and Latin America". Retrieved August 13, 2013.

• "Glenn Greenwald afirma que documentos dizem respeito à interesses comerciais do governo americano". August 6, 2013. Retrieved August 13, 2013.

• "Greenwald diz que espionagem dá vantagens comerciais e industriais aos Estados Unidos" (in Portuguese). Federal Senate of Brazil. Retrieved August 13, 2013.

• "NSA's activity in Latin America is 'collection of data on oil and military purchases from Venezuela, energy and narcotics from Mexico' – Greenwald". Voice of Russia. Retrieved August 13, 2013.

3

Protection Method of Information Systems

Sometimes referred to as IT security, computer security indicates the security involved in the protection of technology. Information systems are prone to attacks by hackers who steal sensitive data or try and disrupt the functioning of businesses. IT security ensures that the systems are protected on a real-time basis. This chapter describes the various methods of protection of information systems.

Computer security

Computer security, also known as cybersecurity or IT security, is the protection of information systems from theft or damage to the hardware, the software, and to the information on them, as well as from disruption or misdirection of the services they provide.

It includes controlling physical access to the hardware, as well as protecting against harm that may come via network access, data and code injection, and due to malpractice by operators, whether intentional, accidental, or due to them being tricked into deviating from secure procedures.

The field is of growing importance due to the increasing reliance on computer systems in most societies and the growth of "smart" devices, including smartphones, televisions and tiny devices as part of the Internet of Things – and of the Internet and wireless network such as Bluetooth and Wi-Fi.

Some organizations are turning to big data platforms, such as Apache Hadoop, to extend data accessibility and machine learning to detect advanced persistent threats.

Vulnerabilities and Attacks

A vulnerability is a system susceptibility or flaw, and many vulnerabilities are documented in the Common Vulnerabilities and Exposures (CVE) database and vulnerability management is the cyclical practice of identifying, classifying, remediating, and mitigating vulnerabilities as they are discovered. An *exploitable* vulnerability is one for which at least one working attack or "exploit" exists.

To secure a computer system, it is important to understand the attacks that can be made against it, and these threats can typically be classified into one of the categories below:

Backdoors

A backdoor in a computer system, a cryptosystem or an algorithm, is any secret method of bypassing normal authentication or security controls. They may exist for a number of reasons, including by original design or from poor configuration. They may also have been added later by an authorized party to allow some legitimate access, or by an attacker for malicious reasons; but regardless of the motives for their existence, they create a vulnerability.

Denial-of-service Attack

Denial of service attacks are designed to make a machine or network resource unavailable to its intended users. Attackers can deny service to individual victims, such as by deliberately entering a wrong password enough consecutive times to cause the victim account to be locked, or they may overload the capabilities of a machine or network and block all users at once. While a network attack from a single IP address can be blocked by adding a new firewall rule, many forms of Distributed denial of service (DDoS) attacks are possible, where the attack comes from a large number of points – and defending is much more difficult. Such attacks can originate from the zombie computers of a botnet, but a range of other techniques are possible including reflection and amplification attacks, where innocent systems are fooled into sending traffic to the victim.

Direct-access Attacks

An unauthorized user gaining physical access to a computer is most likely able to directly copy data from it. They may also compromise security by making operating system modifications, installing software worms, keyloggers, covert listening devices or using wireless mice. Even when the system is protected by standard security measures, these may be able to be by passed by booting another operating system or tool from a CD-ROM or other bootable media. Disk encryption and Trusted Platform Module are designed to prevent these attacks.

Eavesdropping

Eavesdropping is the act of surreptitiously listening to a private conversation, typically between hosts on a network. For instance, programs such as Carnivore and NarusInsight have been used by the FBI and NSA to eavesdrop on the systems of internet service providers. Even machines that operate as a closed system (i.e., with no contact to the outside world) can be eavesdropped upon via monitoring the faint electro-magnetic transmissions generated by the hardware; TEMPEST is a specification by the NSA referring to these attacks.

Spoofing

Spoofing, in general, is a fraudulent or malicious practice in which communication is sent from an unknown source disguised as a source known to the receiver. Spoofing is most prevalent in communication mechanisms that lack a high level of security.

Tampering

Tampering describes a malicious modification of products. So-called "Evil Maid" attacks and security services planting of surveillance capability into routers are examples.

Privilege Escalation

Privilege escalation describes a situation where an attacker with some level of restricted access is able to, without authorization, elevate their privileges or access level. So for example a standard computer user may be able to fool the system into giving them access to restricted data; or even to "become root" and have full unrestricted access to a system.

Phishing

Phishing is the attempt to acquire sensitive information such as usernames, passwords, and credit card details directly from users. Phishing is typically carried out by email spoofing or instant messaging, and it often directs users to enter details at a fake website whose look and feel are almost identical to the legitimate one. Preying on a victim's trusting, phishing can be classified as a form of social engineering.

Clickjacking

Clickjacking, also known as "UI redress attack or User Interface redress attack", is a malicious technique in which an attacker tricks a user into clicking on a button or link on another webpage while the user intended to click on the top level page. This is done using multiple transparent or opaque layers. The attacker is basically "hijacking" the clicks meant for the top level page and routing them to some other irrelevant page, most likely owned by someone else. A similar technique can be used to hijack keystrokes. Carefully drafting a combination of stylesheets, iframes, buttons and text boxes, a user can be led into believing that they are typing the password or other information on some authentic webpage while it is being channeled into an invisible frame controlled by the attacker.

Social Engineering

Social engineering aims to convince a user to disclose secrets such as passwords, card numbers, etc. by, for example, impersonating a bank, a contractor, or a customer.

A popular and profitable cyber scam involves fake CEO emails sent to accounting and finance departments. In early 2016, the FBI reported that the scam has cost US businesses more than $2bn in about two years.

In May 2016, the Milwaukee Bucks NBA team was the victim of this type of cyber scam with a perpetrator impersonating the team's president Peter Feigin, resulting in the handover of all the team's employees' 2015 W-2 tax forms.

Systems at Risk

Computer security is critical in almost any industry which uses computers. Currently, most electronic devices such as computers, laptops and cellphones come with built in firewall security software, but despite this, computers are not 100 percent accurate and dependable to protect our data (Smith, Grabosky & Urbas, 2004.) There are many different ways of hacking into computers. It can be done through a network system, clicking into unknown links, connecting to unfamiliar Wi-Fi, downloading software and files from unsafe sites, power consumption, electromagnetic radiation waves, and many more. However, computers can be protected through well built software and hardware. By having strong internal interactions of properties, software complexity can prevent software crash and security failure.

Financial Systems

Web sites and apps that accept or store credit card numbers, brokerage accounts, and bank account information are prominent hacking targets, because of the potential for immediate financial gain from transferring money, making purchases, or selling the information on the black market. In-store payment systems and ATMs have also been tampered with in order to gather customer account data and PINs.

Utilities and Industrial Equipment

Computers control functions at many utilities, including coordination of telecommunications, the power grid, nuclear power plants, and valve opening and closing in water and gas networks. The Internet is a potential attack vector for such machines if connected, but the Stuxnet worm demonstrated that even equipment controlled by computers not connected to the Internet can be vulnerable to physical damage caused by malicious commands sent to industrial equipment (in that case uranium enrichment centrifuges) which are infected via removable media. In 2014, the Computer Emergency Readiness Team, a division of the Department of Homeland Security, investigated 79 hacking incidents at energy companies. Vulnerabilities in smart meters (many of which use local radio or cellular communications) can cause problems with billing fraud.

Aviation

The aviation industry is very reliant on a series of complex system which could be attacked. A simple power outage at one airport can cause repercussions worldwide, much of the system relies on radio transmissions which could be disrupted, and controlling aircraft over oceans is especially dangerous because radar surveillance only extends 175 to 225 miles offshore. There is also potential for attack from within an aircraft.

The consequences of a successful attack range from loss of confidentiality to loss of system integrity, which may lead to more serious concerns such as exfiltration of data, network and air traffic control outages, which in turn can lead to airport closures, loss of aircraft, loss of passenger life, damages on the ground and to transportation infrastructure. A successful attack on a military aviation system that controls munitions could have even more serious consequences.

Consumer Devices

Desktop computers and laptops are commonly infected with malware either to gather passwords or financial account information, or to construct a botnet to attack another target. Smart phones, tablet computers, smart watches, and other mobile devices such as Quantified Self devices like activity trackers have also become targets and many of these have sensors such as cameras, microphones, GPS receivers, compasses, and accelerometers which could be exploited, and may collect personal information, including sensitive health information. Wifi, Bluetooth, and cell phone networks on any of these devices could be used as attack vectors, and sensors might be remotely activated after a successful breach.

Home automation devices such as the Nest thermostat are also potential targets.

Large Corporations

Large corporations are common targets. In many cases this is aimed at financial gain through identity theft and involves data breaches such as the loss of millions of clients' credit card details by Home Depot, Staples, and Target Corporation. Medical records have been targeted for use in general identify theft, health insurance fraud, and impersonating patients to obtain prescription drugs for recreational purposes or resale.

Not all attacks are financially motivated however; for example security firm HBGary Federal suffered a serious series of attacks in 2011 from hacktivist group Anonymous in retaliation for the firm's CEO claiming to have infiltrated their group, and Sony Pictures was attacked in 2014 where the motive appears to have been to embarrass with data leaks, and cripple the company by wiping workstations and servers.

Automobiles

If access is gained to a car's internal controller area network, it is possible to disable the brakes and turn the steering wheel. Computerized engine timing, cruise control, anti-lock brakes, seat belt tensioners, door locks, airbags and advanced driver assistance systems make these disruptions possible, and self-driving cars go even further. Connected cars may use wifi and bluetooth to communicate with onboard consumer devices, and the cell phone network to contact concierge and emergency assistance services or get navigational or entertainment information; each of these networks is a potential entry point for malware or an attacker. Researchers in 2011 were even able to use a malicious compact disc in a car's stereo system as a successful attack vector, and cars with built-in voice recognition or remote assistance features have onboard microphones which could be used for eavesdropping.

A 2015 report by U.S. Senator Edward Markey criticized manufacturers' security measures as inadequate, and also highlighted privacy concerns about driving, location, and diagnostic data being collected, which is vulnerable to abuse by both manufacturers and hackers.

Government

Government and military computer systems are commonly attacked by activists and foreign powers. Local and regional government infrastructure such as traffic light controls, police and intelligence agency communications, personnel records, student records, and financial systems are also potential targets as they are now all largely computerized. Passports and government ID cards that control access to facilities which use RFID can be vulnerable to cloning.

Internet of Things and Physical Vulnerabilities

The Internet of Things (IoT) is the network of physical objects such as devices, vehicles, buildings and that are embedded with electronics, software, sensors, and network connectivity that enables them to collect and exchange data - and concerns have been raised that this is being developed without appropriate consideration of the security challenges involved.

While the IoT creates opportunities for more direct integration of the physical world into computer-based systems, it also provides opportunities for misuse. In particular, as the Internet of Things spreads widely, cyber attacks are likely to become an increasingly physical (rather than simply virtual) threat. If a front door's lock is connected to the Internet, and can be locked/unlocked from a phone, then a criminal could enter the home at the press of a button from a stolen or hacked phone. People could stand to lose much more than their credit card numbers in a world controlled by IoT-enabled devices. Thieves have also used electronic means to circumvent non-Internet-connected hotel door locks.

Medical devices have either been successfully attacked or had potentially deadly vulnerabilities demonstrated, including both in-hospital diagnostic equipment and implanted devices including pacemakers and insulin pumps.

Impact of Security Breaches

Serious financial damage has been caused by security breaches, but because there is no standard model for estimating the cost of an incident, the only data available is that which is made public by the organizations involved. "Several computer security consulting firms produce estimates of total worldwide losses attributable to virus and worm attacks and to hostile digital acts in general. The 2003 loss estimates by these firms range from $13 billion (worms and viruses only) to $226 billion (for all forms of covert attacks). The reliability of these estimates is often challenged; the underlying methodology is basically anecdotal."

However, reasonable estimates of the financial cost of security breaches can actually help organizations make rational investment decisions. According to the classic Gordon-Loeb Model analyzing the optimal investment level in information security, one can conclude that the amount a firm spends to protect information should generally be only a small fraction of the expected loss (i.e., the expected value of the loss resulting from a cyber/information security breach).

Attacker Motivation

As with physical security, the motivations for breaches of computer security vary between attackers. Some are thrill-seekers or vandals, others are activists or criminals looking for financial gain. State-sponsored attackers are now common and well resourced, but started with amateurs such as Markus Hess who hacked for the KGB, as recounted by Clifford Stoll, in *The Cuckoo's Egg*.

A standard part of threat modelling for any particular system is to identify what might motivate an attack on that system, and who might be motivated to breach it. The level and detail of precautions will vary depending on the system to be secured. A home personal computer, bank, and classified military network face very different threats, even when the underlying technologies in use are similar.

Computer Protection (Countermeasures)

In computer security a countermeasure is an action, device, procedure, or technique that reduces a threat, a vulnerability, or an attack by eliminating or preventing it, by minimizing the harm it can cause, or by discovering and reporting it so that corrective action can be taken.

Some common countermeasures are listed in the following sections:

Security Measures

A state of computer "security" is the conceptual ideal, attained by the use of the three processes: threat prevention, detection, and response. These processes are based on various policies and system components, which include the following:

- User account access controls and cryptography can protect systems files and data, respectively.

- Firewalls are by far the most common prevention systems from a network security perspective as they can (if properly configured) shield access to internal network services, and block certain kinds of attacks through packet filtering. Firewalls can be both hardware- or software-based.

- Intrusion Detection System (IDS) products are designed to detect network attacks in-progress and assist in post-attack forensics, while audit trails and logs serve a similar function for individual systems.

- "Response" is necessarily defined by the assessed security requirements of an individual system and may cover the range from simple upgrade of protections to notification of legal authorities, counter-attacks, and the like. In some special cases, a complete destruction of the compromised system is favored, as it may happen that not all the compromised resources are detected.

Today, computer security comprises mainly "preventive" measures, like firewalls or an exit procedure. A firewall can be defined as a way of filtering network data between a host or a network and another network, such as the Internet, and can be implemented as software running on the machine, hooking into the network stack (or, in the case of most UNIX-based operating systems such as Linux, built into the operating system kernel) to provide real time filtering and blocking. Another implementation is a so-called physical firewall which consists of a separate machine filtering network traffic. Firewalls are common amongst machines that are permanently connected to the Internet.

However, relatively few organisations maintain computer systems with effective detection systems, and fewer still have organised response mechanisms in place. As result, as Reuters points out: "Companies for the first time report they are losing more through electronic theft of data than physical stealing of assets". The primary obstacle to effective eradication of cyber crime could be traced to excessive reliance on firewalls and other automated "detection" systems. Yet it is basic evidence gathering by using packet capture appliances that puts criminals behind bars.

Reducing Vulnerabilities

While formal verification of the correctness of computer systems is possible, it is not yet common. Operating systems formally verified include seL4, and SYSGO's PikeOS – but these make up a very small percentage of the market.

Cryptography properly implemented is now virtually impossible to directly break. Breaking them requires some non-cryptographic input, such as a stolen key, stolen plaintext (at either end of the transmission), or some other extra cryptanalytic information.

Two factor authentication is a method for mitigating unauthorized access to a system or sensitive information. It requires "something you know"; a password or PIN, and "something you have"; a card, dongle, cellphone, or other piece of hardware. This increases security as an unauthorized person needs both of these to gain access.

Social engineering and direct computer access (physical) attacks can only be prevented by non-computer means, which can be difficult to enforce, relative to the sensitivity of the information. Training is often involved to help mitigate this risk, but even in a highly disciplined environments (e.g. military organizations), social engineering attacks can still be difficult to foresee and prevent.

It is possible to reduce an attacker's chances by keeping systems up to date with security patches and updates, using a security scanner or/and hiring competent people responsible for security. The effects of data loss/damage can be reduced by careful backing up and insurance.

Security by Design

Security by design, or alternately secure by design, means that the software has been designed from the ground up to be secure. In this case, security is considered as a main feature.

Some of the techniques in this approach include:

- The principle of least privilege, where each part of the system has only the privileges that are needed for its function. That way even if an attacker gains access to that part, they have only limited access to the whole system.

- Automated theorem proving to prove the correctness of crucial software subsystems.

- Code reviews and unit testing, approaches to make modules more secure where formal correctness proofs are not possible.

- Defense in depth, where the design is such that more than one subsystem needs to be violated to compromise the integrity of the system and the information it holds.

- Default secure settings, and design to "fail secure" rather than "fail insecure". Ideally, a secure system should require a deliberate, conscious, knowledgeable and free decision on the part of legitimate authorities in order to make it insecure.

- Audit trails tracking system activity, so that when a security breach occurs, the mechanism and extent of the breach can be determined. Storing audit trails remotely, where they can only be appended to, can keep intruders from covering their tracks.

- Full disclosure of all vulnerabilities, to ensure that the "window of vulnerability" is kept as short as possible when bugs are discovered.

Security Architecture

The Open Security Architecture organization defines IT security architecture as "the design artifacts that describe how the security controls (security countermeasures) are positioned, and how they relate to the overall information technology architecture. These controls serve the purpose to maintain the system's quality attributes: confidentiality, integrity, availability, accountability and assurance services".

Techopedia defines security architecture as "a unified security design that addresses the necessities and potential risks involved in a certain scenario or environment. It also specifies when and where to apply security controls. The design process is generally reproducible." The key attributes of security architecture are:

- the relationship of different components and how they depend on each other.

- the determination of controls based on risk assessment, good practice, finances, and legal matters.

- the standardization of controls.

Hardware Protection Mechanisms

While hardware may be a source of insecurity, such as with microchip vulnerabilities maliciously introduced during the manufacturing process, hardware-based or assisted computer security also offers an alternative to software-only computer security. Using devices and methods such as dongles, trusted platform modules, intrusion-aware cases, drive locks, disabling USB ports, and mobile-enabled access may be considered more secure due to the physical access (or sophisticated backdoor access) required in order to be compromised. Each of these is covered in more detail below.

- USB dongles are typically used in software licensing schemes to unlock software capabilities, but they can also be seen as a way to prevent unauthorized access to a computer or other device's software. The dongle, or key, essentially creates a secure encrypted tunnel between the software application and the key. The principle is that an encryption scheme on the dongle, such as Advanced Encryption Standard (AES) provides a stronger measure of security, since it is harder to hack and replicate the dongle than to simply copy the native software to another machine and use it. Another security application for dongles is to use them for accessing web-based content such as cloud software or Virtual Private Networks (VPNs). In addition, a USB dongle can be configured to lock or unlock a computer.

- Trusted platform modules (TPMs) secure devices by integrating cryptographic capabilities onto access devices, through the use of microprocessors, or so-called computers-on-a-chip. TPMs used in conjunction with server-side software offer a way to detect and authenticate hardware devices, preventing unauthorized network and data access.

- Computer case intrusion detection refers to a push-button switch which is triggered when a computer case is opened. The firmware or BIOS is programmed to show an alert to the operator when the computer is booted up the next time.

- Drive locks are essentially software tools to encrypt hard drives, making them inaccessible to thieves. Tools exist specifically for encrypting external drives as well.

- Disabling USB ports is a security option for preventing unauthorized and malicious access to an otherwise secure computer. Infected USB dongles connected to a network from a computer inside the firewall are considered by the magazine Network World as the most common hardware threat facing computer networks.

- Mobile-enabled access devices are growing in popularity due to the ubiquitous nature of cell phones. Built-in capabilities such as Bluetooth, the newer Bluetooth low energy (LE), Near field communication (NFC) on non-iOS devices and biometric validation such as thumb print readers, as well as QR code reader software designed for mobile devices, offer new, secure ways for mobile phones to connect to access control systems. These control systems provide computer security and can also be used for controlling access to secure buildings.

Secure Operating Systems

One use of the term "computer security" refers to technology that is used to implement secure operating systems. In the 1980s the United States Department of Defense (DoD) used the "Orange Book" standards, but the current international standard ISO/IEC 15408, "Common Criteria" defines a number of progressively more stringent Evaluation Assurance Levels. Many common operating systems meet the EAL4 standard of being "Methodically Designed, Tested and Reviewed", but the formal verification required for the highest levels means that they are uncommon. An example of an EAL6 ("Semiformally Verified Design and Tested") system is Integrity-178B, which is used in the Airbus A380 and several military jets.

Secure Coding

In software engineering, secure coding aims to guard against the accidental introduction of security vulnerabilities. It is also possible to create software designed from the ground up to be secure. Such systems are "secure by design". Beyond this, formal verification aims to prove the correctness of the algorithms underlying a system; important for cryptographic protocols for example.

Capabilities and Access Control Lists

Within computer systems, two of many security models capable of enforcing privilege separation are access control lists (ACLs) and capability-based security. Using ACLs to confine programs has been proven to be insecure in many situations, such as if the host computer can be tricked into indirectly allowing restricted file access, an issue known as the confused deputy problem. It has also been shown that the promise of ACLs of giving access to an object to only one person can never be guaranteed in practice. Both of these problems are resolved by capabilities. This does not mean practical flaws exist in all ACL-based systems, but only that the designers of certain utilities must take responsibility to ensure that they do not introduce flaws.

Capabilities have been mostly restricted to research operating systems, while commercial OSs still use ACLs. Capabilities can, however, also be implemented at the language level, leading to a style of programming that is essentially a refinement of standard object-oriented design. An open source project in the area is the E language.

The most secure computers are those not connected to the Internet and shielded from any interference. In the real world, the most secure systems are operating systems where security is not an add-on.

Response to Breaches

Responding forcefully to attempted security breaches (in the manner that one would for attempted physical security breaches) is often very difficult for a variety of reasons:

- Identifying attackers is difficult, as they are often in a different jurisdiction to the systems they attempt to breach, and operate through proxies, temporary anonymous dial-up accounts, wireless connections, and other anonymising procedures which make backtracing difficult and are often located in yet another jurisdiction. If they successfully breach security, they are often able to delete logs to cover their tracks.

- The sheer number of attempted attacks is so large that organisations cannot spend time pursuing each attacker (a typical home user with a permanent (e.g., cable modem) connection will be attacked at least several times per day, so more attractive targets could be presumed to see many more). Note however, that most of the sheer bulk of these attacks are made by automated vulnerability scanners and computer worms.

- Law enforcement officers are often unfamiliar with information technology, and so lack the skills and interest in pursuing attackers. There are also budgetary constraints. It has been argued that the high cost of technology, such as DNA testing, and improved forensics mean less money for other kinds of law enforcement, so the overall rate of criminals not getting dealt with goes up as the cost of the technology increases. In addition, the identification of attackers across a network may require logs from various points in the network and in many countries, the release of these records to law enforcement (with the exception of being voluntarily surrendered by a network administrator or a system administrator) requires a search warrant and, depending on the circumstances, the legal proceedings required can be drawn out to the point where the records are either regularly destroyed, or the information is no longer relevant.

Notable Attacks and Breaches

Some illustrative examples of different types of computer security breaches are given below.

Robert Morris and the First Computer Worm

In 1988, only 60,000 computers were connected to the Internet, and most were mainframes, minicomputers and professional workstations. On November 2, 1988, many started to slow down, because they were running a malicious code that demanded processor time and that spread itself to other computers – the first internet "computer worm". The software was traced back to 23-year-old Cornell University graduate student Robert Tappan Morris, Jr. who said 'he wanted to count how many machines were connected to the Internet'.

Rome Laboratory

In 1994, over a hundred intrusions were made by unidentified crackers into the Rome Laboratory, the US Air Force's main command and research facility. Using trojan horses, hackers were able to obtain unrestricted access to Rome's networking systems and remove traces of their activities. The intruders were able to obtain classified files, such as air tasking order systems data and furthermore able to penetrate connected networks of National Aeronautics and Space Administration's Goddard Space Flight Center, Wright-Patterson Air Force Base, some Defense contractors, and other private sector organizations, by posing as a trusted Rome center user.

TJX Loses 45.7m Customer Credit Card Details

In early 2007, American apparel and home goods company TJX announced that it was the victim of an unauthorized computer systems intrusion and that the hackers had accessed a system that stored data on credit card, debit card, check, and merchandise return transactions.

Stuxnet Attack

The computer worm known as Stuxnet reportedly ruined almost one-fifth of Iran's nuclear centrifuges by disrupting industrial programmable logic controllers (PLCs) in a targeted attack generally believed to have been launched by Israel and the United States although neither has publicly acknowledged this.

Global Surveillance Disclosures

In early 2013, massive breaches of computer security by the NSA were revealed, including deliberately inserting a backdoor in a NIST standard for encryption and tapping the links between Google's data centres. These were disclosed by NSA contractor Edward Snowden.

Target and Home Depot Breaches

In 2013 and 2014, a Russian/Ukrainian hacking ring known as "Rescator" broke into Target Corporation computers in 2013, stealing roughly 40 million credit cards, and then Home Depot computers in 2014, stealing between 53 and 56 million credit card numbers. Warnings were delivered at both corporations, but ignored; physical security breaches using self checkout machines are believed to have played a large role. "The malware utilized is absolutely unsophisticated and uninteresting," says Jim Walter, director of threat intelligence operations at security technology company McAfee – meaning that the heists could have easily been stopped by existing antivirus software had administrators responded to the warnings. The size of the thefts has resulted in major attention from state and Federal United States authorities and the investigation is ongoing.

Ashley Madison Breach

In July 2015, a hacker group known as "The Impact Team" successfully breached the extramarital relationship website Ashley Madison. The group claimed that they had taken not only company data but user data as well. After the breach, The Impact Team dumped emails from the company's CEO, to prove their point, and threatened to dump customer data unless the website was taken down permanently. With this initial data release, the group stated "Avid Life Media has been instructed to take Ashley Madison and Established Men offline permanently in all forms, or we will release all customer records, including profiles with all the customers' secret sexual fantasies and matching credit card transactions, real names and addresses, and employee documents and emails. The other websites may stay online." When Avid Life Media, the parent company that created the Ashley Madison website, did not take the site offline, The Impact Group released two more compressed files, one 9.7GB and the second 20GB. After the second data dump, Avid Life Media CEO Noel Biderman resigned, but the website remained functional.

Legal Issues and Global Regulation

Conflict of laws in cyberspace has become a major cause of concern for computer security community. Some of the main challenges and complaints about the antivirus industry are the lack of global web regulations, a global base of common rules to judge, and eventually punish, cyber crimes and cyber criminals. There is no global cyber law and cybersecurity treaty that can be invoked for enforcing global cybersecurity issues.

International legal issues of cyber attacks are complicated in nature. Even if an antivirus firm locates the cyber criminal behind the creation of a particular virus or piece of malware or form of cyber attack, often the local authorities cannot take action due to lack of laws under which to prosecute. Authorship attribution for cyber crimes and cyber attacks is a major problem for all law enforcement agencies.

"[Computer viruses] switch from one country to another, from one jurisdiction to another — moving around the world, using the fact that we don't have the capability to globally police operations like this. So the Internet is as if someone [had] given free plane tickets to all the online criminals of the world." Use of dynamic DNS, fast flux and bullet proof servers have added own complexities to this situation.

Government

The role of the government is to make regulations to force companies and organizations to protect their systems, infrastructure and information from any cyber-attacks, but also to protect its own national infrastructure such as the national power-grid.

The question of whether the government should intervene or not in the regulation of the cyberspace is a very polemical one. Indeed, for as long as it has existed and by definition, the cyberspace is a virtual space free of any government intervention. Where everyone agree that an improvement on cybersecurity is more than vital, is the government the best actor to solve this issue? Many government officials and experts think that the government should step in and that there is a crucial need for regulation, mainly due to the failure of the private sector to solve efficiently the cybersecurity problem. R. Clarke said during a panel discussion at the RSA Security Conference in San Francisco, he believes that the "industry only responds when you threaten regulation. If industry doesn't respond (to the threat), you have to follow through." On the other hand, executives from the private sector agree that improvements are necessary, but think that the government intervention would affect their ability to innovate efficiently.

Actions and Teams in the US

Legislation

The 1986 18 U.S.C. § 1030, more commonly known as the Computer Fraud and Abuse Act is the key legislation. It prohibits unauthorized access or damage of "protected computers" as defined in 18 U.S.C. § 1030(e)(2).

Although various other measures have been proposed, such as the "Cybersecurity Act of 2010 – S. 773" in 2009, the "International Cybercrime Reporting and Cooperation Act – H.R.4962" and "Protecting Cyberspace as a National Asset Act of 2010 – S.3480" in 2010 – none of these has succeeded.

Executive order 13636 *Improving Critical Infrastructure Cybersecurity* was signed February 12, 2013.

Agencies

The Department of Homeland Security has a dedicated division responsible for the response system, risk management program and requirements for cybersecurity in the United States called the National Cyber Security Division. The division is home to US-CERT operations and the National Cyber Alert System. The National Cybersecurity and Communications Integration Center brings together government organizations responsible for protecting computer networks and networked infrastructure.

The third priority of the Federal Bureau of Investigation (FBI) is to: *"Protect the United States against cyber-based attacks and high-technology crimes"*, and they, along with the National White Collar Crime Center (NW3C), and the Bureau of Justice Assistance (BJA) are part of the multi-agency task force, The Internet Crime Complaint Center, also known as IC3.

In addition to its own specific duties, the FBI participates alongside non-profit organizations such as InfraGard.

In the criminal division of the United States Department of Justice operates a section called the Computer Crime and Intellectual Property Section. The CCIPS is in charge of investigating computer crime and intellectual property crime and is specialized in the search and seizure of digital evidence in computers and networks.

The United States Cyber Command, also known as USCYBERCOM, is tasked with the defense of specified Department of Defense information networks and *"ensure US/Allied freedom of action in cyberspace and deny the same to our adversaries."* It has no role in the protection of civilian networks.

The U.S. Federal Communications Commission's role in cybersecurity is to strengthen the protection of critical communications infrastructure, to assist in maintaining the reliability of networks during disasters, to aid in swift recovery after, and to ensure that first responders have access to effective communications services.

The Food and Drug Administration has issued guidance for medical devices, and the National Highway Traffic Safety Administration is concerned with automotive cybersecurity. After being criticized by the Government Accountability Office, and following successful attacks on airports and claimed attacks on airplanes, the Federal Aviation Administration has devoted funding to securing systems on board the planes of private manufacturers, and the Aircraft Communications Addressing and Reporting System. Concerns have also been raised about the future Next Generation Air Transportation System.

Computer Emergency Readiness Team

"Computer emergency response team" is a name given to expert groups that handle computer security incidents. In the US, two distinct organization exist, although they do work closely together.

- US-CERT: part of the National Cyber Security Division of the United States Department of Homeland Security.

- CERT/CC: created by the Defense Advanced Research Projects Agency (DARPA) and run by the Software Engineering Institute (SEI).

International Actions

Many different teams and organisations exist, including:

- The Forum of Incident Response and Security Teams (FIRST) is the global association of CSIRTs. The US-CERT, AT&T, Apple, Cisco, McAfee, Microsoft are all members of this international team.

- The Council of Europe helps protect societies worldwide from the threat of cybercrime through the Convention on Cybercrime.

- The purpose of the Messaging Anti-Abuse Working Group (MAAWG) is to bring the messaging industry together to work collaboratively and to successfully address the various forms of messaging abuse, such as spam, viruses, denial-of-service attacks and other messaging exploitations. France Telecom, Facebook, AT&T, Apple, Cisco, Sprint are some of the members of the MAAWG.

- ENISA : The European Network and Information Security Agency (ENISA) is an agency of the European Union with the objective to improve network and information security in the European Union.

Europe

CSIRTs in Europe collaborate in the TERENA task force TF-CSIRT. TERENA's Trusted Introducer service provides an accreditation and certification scheme for CSIRTs in Europe. A full list of known CSIRTs in Europe is available from the Trusted Introducer website.

National Teams

Here are the main computer emergency response teams around the world. Most countries have their own team to protect network security.

Canada

On October 3, 2010, Public Safety Canada unveiled Canada's Cyber Security Strategy, following a Speech from the Throne commitment to boost the security of Canadian cyberspace. The aim of the strategy is to strengthen Canada's "cyber systems and critical infrastructure sectors, support economic growth and protect Canadians as they connect to each other and to the world." Three main pillars define the strategy: securing government systems, partnering to secure vital cyber systems outside the federal government, and helping Canadians to be secure online. The strategy involves multiple departments and agencies across the Government of Canada. The Cyber Incident Management Framework for Canada outlines these responsibilities, and provides a plan for coordinated response between government and other partners in the event of a cyber incident. The Action Plan 2010–2015 for Canada's Cyber Security Strategy outlines the ongoing implementation of the strategy.

Public Safety Canada's Canadian Cyber Incident Response Centre (CCIRC) is responsible for mitigating and responding to threats to Canada's critical infrastructure and cyber systems. The CCIRC provides support to mitigate cyber threats, technical support to respond and recover from targeted cyber attacks, and provides online tools for members of Canada's critical infrastructure sectors. The CCIRC posts regular cyber security bulletins on the Public Safety Canada website. The CCIRC also operates an online reporting tool where individuals and organizations can report a cyber incident. Canada's Cyber Security Strategy is part of a larger, integrated approach to critical infrastructure protection, and functions as a counterpart document to the National Strategy and Action Plan for Critical Infrastructure.

On September 27, 2010, Public Safety Canada partnered with STOP.THINK.CONNECT, a coalition of non-profit, private sector, and government organizations dedicated to informing the general public on how to protect themselves online. On February 4, 2014, the Government of Canada launched the Cyber Security Cooperation Program. The program is a $1.5 million five-year initiative aimed at improving Canada's cyber systems through grants and contributions to projects in support of this objective. Public Safety Canada aims to begin an evaluation of Canada's Cyber Security Strategy in early 2015. Public Safety Canada administers and routinely updates the Get-CyberSafe portal for Canadian citizens, and carries out Cyber Security Awareness Month during October.

China

China's network security and information technology leadership team was established February 27, 2014. The leadership team is tasked with national security and long-term development and co-ordination of major issues related to network security and information technology. Economic, political, cultural, social and military fields as related to network security and information technology strategy, planning and major macroeconomic policy are being researched. The promotion of national network security and information technology law are constantly under study for enhanced national security capabilities.

Germany

Berlin starts National Cyber Defense Initiative: On June 16, 2011, the German Minister for Home Affairs, officially opened the new German NCAZ (National Center for Cyber Defense) Nationales Cyber-Abwehrzentrum located in Bonn. The NCAZ closely cooperates with BSI (Federal Office for Information Security) Bundesamt für Sicherheit in der Informationstechnik, BKA (Federal Police Organisation) Bundeskriminalamt (Deutschland), BND (Federal Intelligence Service) Bundesnachrichtendienst, MAD (Military Intelligence Service) Amt für den Militärischen Abschirmdienst and other national organisations in Germany taking care of national security aspects. According to the Minister the primary task of the new organisation founded on February 23, 2011, is to detect and prevent attacks against the national infrastructure and mentioned incidents like Stuxnet.

India

Some provisions for cybersecurity have been incorporated into rules framed under the Information Technology Act 2000.

The National Cyber Security Policy 2013 is a policy framework by Department of Electronics and Information Technology (DeitY) which aims to protect the public and private infrastructure from cyber attacks, and safeguard "information, such as personal information (of web users), financial and banking information and sovereign data".

The Indian Companies Act 2013 has also introduced cyber law and cyber security obligations on the part of Indian directors.

Pakistan

Cyber-crime has risen rapidly in Pakistan. There are about 30 million Internet users with 15 million mobile subscribers in Pakistan. According to Cyber Crime Unit (CCU), a branch of Federal Investigation Agency, only 62 cases were reported to the unit in 2007, 287 cases in 2008, ratio dropped in 2009 but in 2010, more than 312 cases were registered. However, there are many unreported incidents of cyber-crime.

"Pakistan's Cyber Crime Bill 2007", the first pertinent law, focuses on electronic crimes, for example cyber-terrorism, criminal access, electronic system fraud, electronic forgery, and misuse of encryption.

National Response Centre for Cyber Crime (NR3C) – FIA is a law enforcement agency dedicated to fight cybercrime. Inception of this Hi-Tech crime fighting unit transpired in 2007 to identify and curb the phenomenon of technological abuse in society. However, certain private firms are also working in cohesion with the government to improve cyber security and curb cyberattacks.

South Korea

Following cyberattacks in the first half of 2013, when government, news-media, television station, and bank websites were compromised, the national government committed to the training of 5,000 new cybersecurity experts by 2017. The South Korean government blamed its northern counterpart for these attacks, as well as incidents that occurred in 2009, 2011, and 2012, but Pyongyang denies the accusations.

Other Countries

- CERT Brazil, member of FIRST (Forum for Incident Response and Security Teams)
- CARNet CERT, Croatia, member of FIRST
- AE CERT, United Arab Emirates
- SingCERT, Singapore
- CERT-LEXSI, France, Canada, Singapore

Modern Warfare

Cybersecurity is becoming increasingly important as more information and technology is being made available on cyberspace. There is growing concern among governments that cyberspace will become the next theatre of warfare. As Mark Clayton from the *Christian Science Monitor* described in an article titled "The New Cyber Arms Race":

In the future, wars will not just be fought by soldiers with guns or with planes that drop bombs. They will also be fought with the click of a mouse a half a world away that unleashes carefully weaponized computer programs that disrupt or destroy critical industries like utilities, transportation, communications, and energy. Such attacks could also disable military networks that control the movement of troops, the path of jet fighters, the command and control of warships.

This has led to new terms such as *cyberwarfare* and *cyberterrorism*. More and more critical infrastructure is being controlled via computer programs that, while increasing efficiency, exposes new vulnerabilities. The test will be to see if governments and corporations that control critical systems such as energy, communications and other information will be able to prevent attacks before they occur. As Jay Cross, the chief scientist of the Internet Time Group, remarked, "Connectedness begets vulnerability."

Job Market

Cybersecurity is a fast-growing field of IT concerned with reducing organizations' risk of hack or data breach. According to research from the Enterprise Strategy Group, 46% of organizations say that they have a "problematic shortage" of cybersecurity skills in 2016, up from 28% in 2015. Commercial, government and non-governmental organizations all employ cybersecurity professionals. The fastest increases in demand for cybersecurity workers are in industries managing increasing volumes of consumer data such as finance, health care, and retail. However, the use of the term "cybersecurity" is more prevalent in government job descriptions.

Typical cybersecurity job titles and descriptions include:

Security Analyst

Analyzes and assesses vulnerabilities in the infrastructure (software, hardware, networks), investigates available tools and countermeasures to remedy the detected vulnerabilities, and recommends solutions and best practices. Analyzes and assesses damage to the data/infrastructure as a result of security incidents, examines available recovery tools and processes, and recommends solutions. Tests for compliance with security policies and procedures. May assist in the creation, implementation, and/or management of security solutions.

Security Engineer

Performs security monitoring, security and data/logs analysis, and forensic analysis, to detect security incidents, and mounts incident response. Investigates and utilizes new technologies and processes to enhance security capabilities and implement improvements. May also review code or perform other security engineering methodologies.

Security Architect

Designs a security system or major components of a security system, and may head a security design team building a new security system.

Security Administrator

Installs and manages organization-wide security systems. May also take on some of the tasks of a security analyst in smaller organizations.

Chief Information Security Officer (CISO)

A high-level management position responsible for the entire information security division/ staff. The position may include hands-on technical work.

Chief Security Officer (CSO)

A high-level management position responsible for the entire security division/staff. A newer position now deemed needed as security risks grow.

Security Consultant/Specialist/Intelligence

Broad titles that encompass any one or all of the other roles/titles, tasked with protecting computers, networks, software, data, and/or information systems against viruses, worms, spyware, malware, intrusion detection, unauthorized access, denial-of-service attacks, and an ever increasing list of attacks by hackers acting as individuals or as part of organized crime or foreign governments.

Student programs are also available to people interested in beginning a career in cybersecurity. Meanwhile, a flexible and effective option for information security professionals of all experience levels to keep studying is online security training, including webcasts.

Terminology

The following terms used with regards to engineering secure systems are explained below.

- Access authorization restricts access to a computer to group of users through the use of authentication systems. These systems can protect either the whole computer – such as through an interactive login screen – or individual services, such as an FTP server. There are many methods for identifying and authenticating users, such as passwords, identification cards, and, more recently, smart cards and biometric systems.

- Anti-virus software consists of computer programs that attempt to identify, thwart and eliminate computer viruses and other malicious software (malware).

- Applications with known security flaws should not be run. Either leave it turned off until it can be patched or otherwise fixed, or delete it and replace it with some other application. Publicly known flaws are the main entry used by worms to automatically break into a system and then spread to other systems connected to it. The security website Secunia provides a search tool for unpatched known flaws in popular products.

- Authentication techniques can be used to ensure that communication end-points are who they say they are.

- Automated theorem proving and other verification tools can enable critical algorithms and code used in secure systems to be mathematically proven to meet their specifications.

- Backups are a way of securing information; they are another copy of all the important computer files kept in another location. These files are kept on hard disks, CD-Rs, CD-RWs, tapes and more recently on the cloud. Suggested locations for backups are a fireproof, waterproof, and heat proof safe, or in a separate, offsite location than that in which the original files are contained. Some individuals and companies also keep their backups in safe deposit boxes inside bank vaults. There is also a fourth option, which involves using one of the file hosting services that backs up files over the Internet for both business and individuals, known as the cloud.

  o Backups are also important for reasons other than security. Natural disasters, such as earthquakes, hurricanes, or tornadoes, may strike the building where the computer is located. The building can be on fire, or an explosion may occur. There needs to be a recent backup at an alternate secure location, in case of such kind of disaster. Further, it is recommended that the alternate location be placed where the same disaster would not affect both locations. Examples of alternate disaster recovery sites being compromised by the same disaster that affected the primary site include having had a primary site in World Trade Center I and the recovery site in 7 World Trade Center, both of which were destroyed in the 9/11 attack, and having one's primary site and recovery site in the same coastal region, which leads to both being vulnerable to hurricane damage (for example, primary site in New Orleans and recovery site in Jefferson Parish, both of which were hit by Hurricane Katrina in 2005). The backup media should be moved between the geographic sites in a secure manner, in order to prevent them from being stolen.

- Capability and access control list techniques can be used to ensure privilege separation and mandatory access control. This section discusses their use.

- Chain of trust techniques can be used to attempt to ensure that all software loaded has been certified as authentic by the system's designers.

- Confidentiality is the nondisclosure of information except to another authorized person.

- Cryptographic techniques can be used to defend data in transit between systems, reducing the probability that data exchanged between systems can be intercepted or modified.

- Cyberwarfare is an internet-based conflict that involves politically motivated attacks on information and information systems. Such attacks can, for example, disable official websites and networks, disrupt or disable essential services, steal or alter classified data, and criple financial systems.

- Data integrity is the accuracy and consistency of stored data, indicated by an absence of any alteration in data between two updates of a data record.

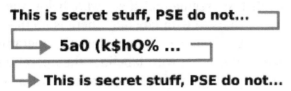

Cryptographic techniques involve transforming information, scrambling it so it becomes unreadable during transmission. The intended recipient can unscramble the message; ideally, eavesdroppers cannot.

- Encryption is used to protect the message from the eyes of others. Cryptographically secure ciphers are designed to make any practical attempt of breaking infeasible. Symmetric-key ciphers are suitable for bulk encryption using shared keys, and public-key encryption using digital certificates can provide a practical solution for the problem of securely communicating when no key is shared in advance.

- Endpoint security software helps networks to prevent exfiltration (data theft) and virus infection at network entry points made vulnerable by the prevalence of potentially infected portable computing devices, such as laptops and mobile devices, and external storage devices, such as USB drives.

- Firewalls are an important method for control and security on the Internet and other networks. A network firewall can be a communications processor, typically a router, or a dedicated server, along with firewall software. A firewall serves as a gatekeeper system that protects a company's intranets and other computer networks from intrusion by providing a filter and safe transfer point for access to and from the Internet and other networks. It screens all network traffic for proper passwords or other security codes and only allows authorized transmission in and out of the network. Firewalls can deter, but not completely prevent, unauthorized access (hacking) into computer networks; they can also provide some protection from online intrusion.

- Honey pots are computers that are either intentionally or unintentionally left vulnerable to attack by crackers. They can be used to catch crackers or fix vulnerabilities.

- Intrusion-detection systems can scan a network for people that are on the network but who should not be there or are doing things that they should not be doing, for example trying a lot of passwords to gain access to the network.

- A microkernel is the near-minimum amount of software that can provide the mechanisms to implement an operating system. It is used solely to provide very low-level, very precisely defined machine code upon which an operating system can be developed. A simple example is the early '90s GEMSOS (Gemini Computers), which provided extremely low-level machine code, such as "segment" management, atop which an operating system could be built. The theory (in the case of "segments") was that—rather than have the operating system itself worry about mandatory access separation by means of military-style labeling—it is safer if a low-level, independently scrutinized module can be charged solely with the management of individually labeled segments, be they memory "segments" or file system "segments" or executable text "segments." If software below the visibility of the operating system is (as in this case) charged with labeling, there is no theoretically viable means for a clever hacker to subvert the labeling scheme, since the operating system *per se* does not provide mechanisms for interfering with labeling: the operating system is, essentially, a client (an "application," arguably) atop the microkernel and, as such, subject to its restrictions.

- Pinging The ping application can be used by potential crackers to find if an IP address is reachable. If a cracker finds a computer, they can try a port scan to detect and attack services on that computer.

- Social engineering awareness keeps employees aware of the dangers of social engineering and/or having a policy in place to prevent social engineering can reduce successful breaches of the network and servers.

Scholars

- Ross J. Anderson
- Annie Anton
- Adam Back
- Daniel J. Bernstein
- Matt Blaze
- Stefan Brands
- L. Jean Camp
- Lance Cottrell
- Lorrie Cranor
- Dorothy E. Denning
- Peter J. Denning
- Cynthia Dwork
- Deborah Estrin
- Joan Feigenbaum
- Ian Goldberg
- Shafi Goldwasser
- Lawrence A. Gordon

- Peter Gutmann

- Paul Kocher

- Monica S. Lam

- Butler Lampson

- Brian LaMacchia

- Carl Landwehr

- Kevin Mitnick

- Peter G. Neumann

- Susan Nycum

- Roger R. Schell

- Bruce Schneier

- Dawn Song

- Gene Spafford

- Joseph Steinberg

- Salvatore J. Stolfo

- Willis Ware

- Moti Yung

References

- Gasser, Morrie (1988). Building a Secure Computer System (PDF). Van Nostrand Reinhold. p. 3. ISBN 0-442-23022-2. Retrieved 6 September 2015.

- Umrigar, Zerksis D.; Pitchumani, Vijay (1983). "Formal verification of a real-time hardware design". Proceeding DAC '83 Proceedings of the 20th Design Automation Conference. IEEE Press. pp. 221–7. ISBN 0-8186-0026-8.

- Arachchilage, Nalin; Love, Steve; Scott, Michael (June 1, 2012). "Designing a Mobile Game to Teach Conceptual Knowledge of Avoiding 'Phishing Attacks'". International Journal for e-Learning Security (Infonomics Society) 2 (1): 127–132. Retrieved April 1, 2016.

- Scott, Michael; Ghinea, Gheorghita; Arachchilage, Nalin (7 July 2014). Assessing the Role of Conceptual Knowledge in an Anti-Phishing Educational Game (pdf). Proceedings of the 14th IEEE International Conference on Advanced Learning Technologies. IEEE. p. 218. doi:10.1109/ICALT.2014.70. Retrieved April 1, 2016.

- "U.S. GAO - Air Traffic Control: FAA Needs a More Comprehensive Approach to Address Cybersecurity As Agency Transitions to NextGen". Retrieved 23 May 2016.

- Aliya Sternstein (4 March 2016). "FAA Working on New Guidelines for Hack-Proof Planes". Nextgov. Retrieved 23 May 2016.

- "Ensuring the Security of Federal Information Systems and Cyber Critical Infrastructure and Protecting the

Privacy of Personally Identifiable Information". Government Accountability Office. Retrieved November 3, 2015.

- "Action Plan 2010–2015 for Canada's Cyber Security Strategy". Public Safety Canada. Government of Canada. Retrieved 1 November 2014.

- "Cyber Security Awareness Free Training and Webcasts". MS-ISAC (Multi-State Information Sharing & Analysis Center. Retrieved 9 January 2015.

- Pagliery, Jose. "Hackers attacked the U.S. energy grid 79 times this year". CNN Money. Cable News Network. Retrieved 16 April 2015.

- James Cook (December 16, 2014). "Sony Hackers Have Over 100 Terabytes Of Documents. Only Released 200 Gigabytes So Far". Business Insider. Retrieved December 18, 2014.

- de Silva, Richard (11 Oct 2011). "Government vs. Commerce: The Cyber Security Industry and You (Part One)". Defence IQ. Retrieved 24 Apr 2014.

4

Challenges and Threats to Information Technology

Organizations are becoming largely dependent on information and its processing hence there is always a potential to risk and this can unfold in the manner of a security incident or event. To mitigate this, there are several IT risk laws and regulations in place. This chapter provides an insight into these areas and provides valuable information about the various challenges and threats to computer technology.

IT risk

Information technology risk, or IT risk, IT-related risk, is any risk related to information technology. While information has long been appreciated as a valuable and important asset, the rise of the knowledge economy has led to organizations becoming increasingly dependent on information, information processing and especially IT. Various events or incidents that compromise IT in some way can therefore cause adverse impacts on the organization's business processes or mission, ranging from inconsequential to catastrophic in scale.

Assessing the probability of likelihood of various types of event/incident with their predicted impacts or consequences should they occur is a common way to assess and measure IT risks. Alternative methods of measuring IT risk typically involve assessing other contributory factors such as the threats, vulnerabilities, exposures, and asset values.

Definitions of IT Risk

ISO

IT risk: *the potential that a given threat will exploit vulnerabilities of an asset or group of assets and thereby cause harm to the organization. It is measured in terms of a combination of the probability of occurrence of an event and its consequence.*

Committee on National Security Systems

The Committee on National Security Systems of United States of America defined risk in different documents:

- From CNSS Instruction No. 4009 dated 26 April 2010 the basic and more technical focused definition:

  Risk - Possibility that a particular threat will adversely impact an IS by exploiting a par-

ticular vulnerability.

• National Security Telecommunications and Information Systems Security Instruction (NS-TISSI) No. 1000, introduces a probability aspect, quite similar to NIST SP 800-30 one:

Risk - A combination of the likelihood that a threat will occur, the likelihood that a threat occurrence will result in an adverse impact, and the severity of the resulting impact

National Information Assurance Training and Education Center defines risk in the IT field as:

1. The loss potential that exists as the result of threat-vulnerability pairs. Reducing either the threat or the vulnerability reduces the risk.

2. The uncertainty of loss expressed in terms of probability of such loss.

3. The probability that a hostile entity will successfully exploit a particular telecommunications or COMSEC system for intelligence purposes; its factors are threat and vulnerability.

4. A combination of the likelihood that a threat shall occur, the likelihood that a threat occurrence shall result in an adverse impact, and the severity of the resulting adverse impact.

5. the probability that a particular threat will exploit a particular vulnerability of the system.

NIST

Many NIST publications define risk in IT context in different publications: FISMApedia term provide a list. Between them:

• According to NIST SP 800-30:

Risk is a function of the likelihood of a given threat-source's exercising a particular potential vulnerability, and the resulting impact of that adverse event on the organization.

• From NIST FIPS 200

Risk - The level of impact on organizational operations (including mission, functions, image, or reputation), organizational assets, or individuals resulting from the operation of an information system given the potential impact of a threat and the likelihood of that threat occurring.

NIST SP 800-30 defines:

IT-related Risk

The net mission impact considering:

1. *the probability that a particular threat-source will exercise (accidentally trigger or intentionally exploit) a particular information system vulnerability and*

2. *the resulting impact if this should occur. IT-related risks arise from legal liability or mission loss due to:*

    1. *Unauthorized (malicious or accidental) disclosure, modification, or de-*

struction of information

2. *Unintentional errors and omissions*

3. *IT disruptions due to natural or man-made disasters*

4. *Failure to exercise due care and diligence in the implementation and operation of the IT system.*

Risk Management Insight

IT risk is the probable frequency and probable magnitude of future loss.

ISACA

ISACA published the Risk IT Framework in order to provides an end-to-end, comprehensive view of all risks related to the use of IT. There, IT risk is defined as:

The business risk associated with the use, ownership, operation, involvement, influence and adoption of IT within an enterprise

According to Risk IT, IT risk has a broader meaning: it encompasses not just only the negative impact of operations and service delivery which can bring destruction or reduction of the value of the organization, but also the benefit\value enabling risk associated to missing opportunities to use technology to enable or enhance business or the IT project management for aspects like overspending or late delivery with adverse business impact

Measuring IT Risk

It is useful to introduce related terms, to properly measure IT risk.

Information Security Event

An identified occurrence of a system, service or network state indicating a possible breach of information security policy or failure of safeguards, or a previously unknown situation that may be security relevant.

Occurrence of a particular set of circumstances

- *The event can be certain or uncertain.*

- *The event can be a single occurrence or a series of occurrences. :(ISO/IEC Guide 73)*

Information security incident is indicated by a single or a series of unwanted information security events that have a significant probability of compromising business operations and threatening informa-tion security.

An event [G.11] that has been assessed as having an actual or potentially adverse effect on the security or performance of a system.

Impact

> The result of an unwanted incident [G.17].(ISO/IEC PDTR 13335-1)

Consequence

> *Outcome of an event [G.11]*
>
> - *There can be more than one consequence from one event.*
>
> - *Consequences can range from positive to negative.*
>
> - *Consequences can be expressed qualitatively or quantitatively (ISO/IEC Guide 73)*

The risk R is the product of the likelihood L of a security incident occurring times the impact I that will be incurred to the organization due to the incident, that is:

$$R = L \times I$$

The likelihood of a security incident occurrence is a function of the likelihood that a threat appears and the likelihood that the threat can successfully exploit the relevant system vulnerabilities.

The consequence of the occurrence of a security incident are a function of likely impact that the incident will have on the organization as a result of the harm the organization assets will sustain. Harm is related to the value of the assets to the organization; the same asset can have different values to different organizations.

So R can be function of four factors:

- A = Value of the assets

- T = the likelihood of the threat

- V = the nature of vulnerability i.e. the likelihood that can be exploited (proportional to the potential benefit for the attacker and inversely proportional to the cost of exploitation)

- I = the likely impact, the extent of the harm

If numerical values (money for impact and probabilities for the other factors), the risk can be expressed in monetary terms and compared to the cost of countermeasures and the residual risk after applying the security control. It is not always practical to express this values, so in the first step of risk evaluation, risk are graded dimensionless in three or five steps scales.

OWASP proposes a practical risk measurement guideline based on:

- Estimation of Likelihood as a mean between different factors in a 0 to 9 scale:

    o   Threat agent factors

☐ Skill level: How technically skilled is this group of threat agents? No technical skills (1), some technical skills (3), advanced computer user (4), network and programming skills (6), security penetration skills (9)

☐ Motive: How motivated is this group of threat agents to find and exploit this vulnerability? Low or no reward (1), possible reward (4), high reward (9)

☐ Opportunity: What resources and opportunity are required for this group of threat agents to find and exploit this vulnerability? full access or expensive resources required (0), special access or resources required (4), some access or resources required (7), no access or resources required (9)

☐ Size: How large is this group of threat agents? Developers (2), system administrators (2), intranet users (4), partners (5), authenticated users (6), anonymous Internet users (9)

o Vulnerability Factors: the next set of factors are related to the vulnerability involved. The goal here is to estimate the likelihood of the particular vulnerability involved being discovered and exploited. Assume the threat agent selected above.

☐ Ease of discovery: How easy is it for this group of threat agents to discover this vulnerability? Practically impossible (1), difficult (3), easy (7), automated tools available (9)

☐ Ease of exploit: How easy is it for this group of threat agents to actually exploit this vulnerability? Theoretical (1), difficult (3), easy (5), automated tools available (9)

☐ Awareness: How well known is this vulnerability to this group of threat agents? Unknown (1), hidden (4), obvious (6), public knowledge (9)

☐ Intrusion detection: How likely is an exploit to be detected? Active detection in application (1), logged and reviewed (3), logged without review (8), not logged (9)

• Estimation of Impact as a mean between different factors in a 0 to 9 scale

o Technical Impact Factors; technical impact can be broken down into factors aligned with the traditional security areas of concern: confidentiality, integrity, availability, and accountability. The goal is to estimate the magnitude of the impact on the system if the vulnerability were to be exploited.

☐ Loss of confidentiality: How much data could be disclosed and how sensitive is it? Minimal non-sensitive data disclosed (2), minimal critical data disclosed (6), extensive non-sensitive data disclosed (6), extensive critical data disclosed (7), all data disclosed (9)

☐ Loss of integrity: How much data could be corrupted and how damaged is it? Minimal slightly corrupt data (1), minimal seriously corrupt data (3), extensive slightly corrupt data (5), extensive seriously corrupt data (7), all data totally corrupt (9)

☐ Loss of availability How much service could be lost and how vital is it? Minimal secondary services interrupted (1), minimal primary services interrupted (5), extensive secondary services interrupted (5), extensive primary services interrupted (7), all services completely lost (9)

☐ Loss of accountability: Are the threat agents' actions traceable to an individual? Fully traceable (1), possibly traceable (7), completely anonymous (9)

o Business Impact Factors: The business impact stems from the technical impact, but requires a deep understanding of what is important to the company running the application. In general, you should be aiming to support your risks with business impact, particularly if your audience is executive level. The business risk is what justifies investment in fixing security problems.

☐ Financial damage: How much financial damage will result from an exploit? Less than the cost to fix the vulnerability (1), minor effect on annual profit (3), significant effect on annual profit (7), bankruptcy (9)

☐ Reputation damage: Would an exploit result in reputation damage that would harm the business? Minimal damage (1), Loss of major accounts (4), loss of goodwill (5), brand damage (9)

☐ Non-compliance: How much exposure does non-compliance introduce? Minor violation (2), clear violation (5), high-profile violation (7)

☐ Privacy violation: How much personally identifiable information could be disclosed? One individual (3), hundreds of people (5), thousands of people (7), millions of people (9)

o If the business impact is calculated accurately use it in the following otherwise use the Technical impact

• Rate likelihood and impact in a LOW, MEDIUM, HIGH scale assuming that less than 3 is LOW, 3 to less than 6 is MEDIUM, and 6 to 9 is HIGH.

• Calculate the risk using the following table

Overall Risk Severity			
Impact	HIGH	Medium	High	Critical
	MEDIUM	Low	Medium	High
	LOW	None	Low	Medium
		LOW	MEDIUM	HIGH
		Likelihood		

IT Risk Management

IT risk management can be considered a component of a wider enterprise risk management system.

The establishment, maintenance and continuous update of an ISMS provide a strong indication that a company is using a systematic approach for the identification, assessment and management of information security risks.

A Continuous Interlocked Process—Not an Event

Risk Management Elements

Different methodologies have been proposed to manage IT risks, each of them divided in processes and steps.

The Certified Information Systems Auditor Review Manual 2006 produced by ISACA is an international professional association focused on IT Governance, provides the following definition of risk management: *"Risk management is the process of identifying vulnerabilities and threats to the information resources used by an organization in achieving business objectives, and deciding what countermeasures, if any, to take in reducing risk to an acceptable level, based on the value of the information resource to the organization."*

IT Risk Laws and Regulations

In the following a brief description of applicable rules organized by source.

United Nations

United Nations issued the following:

- UN Guidelines concerning computerized personal data files of 14 December 1990 Generic data processing activities using digital processing methods. Nonbinding guideline to UN nations calling for national regulation in this field

OECD

OECD issued the following:

- Organisation for Economic Co-operation and Development (OECD) Recommendation of the Council concerning guidelines governing the protection of privacy and trans-border flows of personal data (23 September 1980)

- OECD Guidelines for the Security of Information Systems and Networks: Towards a Culture of Security (25 July 2002). Topic: General information security. Scope: Non binding guidelines to any OECD entities (governments, businesses, other organisations and individual users who develop, own, provide, manage, service, and use information systems and networks). The OECD Guidelines state the basic principles underpinning risk management and information security practices. While no part of the text is binding as such, non-compliance with any of the principles is indicative of a serious breach of RM/RA good practices that can potentially incur liability.

European Union

The European Union issued the following, divided by topic:

- Privacy

  - Regulation (EC) No 45/2001 on the protection of individuals with regard to the processing of personal data by the Community institutions and bodies and on the free movement of such data provide an internal regulation which is a practical application of the principles of the Privacy Directive described below. Furthermore, article 35 of the Regulation requires the Community institutions and bodies to take similar precautions with regard to their telecommunications infrastructure, and to properly inform the users of any specific risks of security breaches.

  - Directive 95/46/EC on the protection of individuals with regard to the processing of personal data and on the free movement of such data require that any personal data processing activity undergoes a prior risk analysis in order to determine the privacy implications of the activity, and to determine the appropriate legal, technical and organisation measures to protect such activities;is effectively protected by such measures, which must be state of the art keeping into account the sensitivity and privacy implications of the activity (including when a third party is charged with the processing task) is notified to a national data protection authority, including the measures taken to ensure the security of the activity. Furthermore, article 25 and following of the Directive requires Member States to ban the transfer of personal data to non-Member States, unless such countries have provided adequate legal protection for such personal data, or barring certain other exceptions.

  - Commission Decision 2001/497/EC of 15 June 2001 on standard contractual clauses for the transfer of personal data to third countries, under Directive 95/46/EC; and Commission Decision 2004/915/EC of 27 December 2004 amending Decision 2001/497/EC as regards the introduction of an alternative set of standard contractual clauses for the transfer of personal data to third countries. Topic: Export of personal data to third countries, specifically non-E.U. countries which have not been recognised as having a data protection level that is adequate (i.e. equivalent to that of the E.U.). Both Commission Decisions provide a set of voluntary model clauses which can be used to export personal data from a data controller (who is subject to E.U. data protection rules) to a data processor outside the E.U. who is not subject to these rules or to a similar set of adequate rules.

o International Safe Harbor Privacy Principles

o Directive 2002/58/EC of 12 July 2002 concerning the processing of personal data and the protection of privacy in the electronic communications sector

- National Security

o Directive 2006/24/EC of 15 March 2006 on the retention of data generated or processed in connection with the provision of publicly available electronic communications services or of public communications networks and amending Directive 2002/58/EC ('Data Retention Directive'). Topic: Requirement for the providers of public electronic telecommunications service providers to retain certain information for the purposes of the investigation, detection and prosecution of serious crime

o Council Directive 2008/114/EC of 8 December 2008 on the identification and designation of European critical infrastructures and the assessment of the need to improve their protection. Topic: Identification and protection of European Critical Infrastructures. Scope: Applicable to Member States and to the operators of European Critical Infrastructure (defined by the draft directive as 'critical infrastructures the disruption or destruction of which would significantly affect two or more Member States, or a single Member State if the critical infrastructure is located in another Member State. This includes effects resulting from cross-sector dependencies on other types of infrastructure'). Requires Member States to identify critical infrastructures on their territories, and to designate them as ECIs. Following this designation, the owners/operators of ECIs are required to create Operator Security Plans (OSPs), which should establish relevant security solutions for their protection

- Civil and Penal law

o Council Framework Decision 2005/222/JHA of 24 February 2005 on attacks against information systems. Topic: General decision aiming to harmonise national provisions in the field of cyber crime, encompassing material criminal law (i.e. definitions of specific crimes), procedural criminal law (including investigative measures and international cooperation) and liability issues. Scope: Requires Member States to implement the provisions of the Framework Decision in their national legal frameworks. Framework decision is relevant to RM/RA because it contains the conditions under which legal liability can be imposed on legal entities for conduct of certain natural persons of authority within the legal entity. Thus, the Framework decision requires that the conduct of such figures within an organisation is adequately monitored, also because the Decision states that a legal entity can be held liable for acts of omission in this regard.

Council of Europe

- Council of Europe Convention on Cybercrime, Budapest, 23.XI.2001, European Treaty Series-No. 185. Topic: General treaty aiming to harmonise national provisions in the field of cyber crime, encompassing material criminal law (i.e. definitions of specific crimes), procedural criminal law (including investigative measures and international cooperation), liability issues and data retention. Apart from the definitions of a series of criminal offences in articles 2 to 10, the Convention is relevant to RM/RA because it states the conditions under which legal liability can be imposed on legal entities for conduct of certain natural persons of authority within the legal entity. Thus, the Convention requires that the conduct of such figures within an organisation is adequately monitored, also because the Convention states that a legal entity can be held liable for acts of omission in this regard.

USA

United States issued the following, divided by topic:

- Civil and Penal law

  - o Amendments to the Federal Rules of Civil Procedure with regard to electronic discovery. Topic: U.S. Federal rules with regard to the production of electronic documents in civil proceedings. The discovery rules allow a party in civil proceedings to demand that the opposing party produce all relevant documentation (to be defined by the requesting party) in its possession, so as to allow the parties and the court to correctly assess the matter. Through the e-discovery amendment, which entered into force on 1 December 2006, such information may now include electronic information. This implies that any party being brought before a U.S. court in civil proceedings can be asked to produce such documents, which includes finalised reports, working documents, internal memos and e-mails with regard to a specific subject, which may or may not be specifically delineated. Any party whose activities imply a risk of being involved in such proceedings must therefore take adequate precautions for the management of such information, including the secure storage. Specifically: The party must be capable of initiating a 'litigation hold', a technical/organisational measure which must ensure that no relevant information can be modified any longer in any way. Storage policies must be responsible: while deletion of specific information of course remains allowed when this is a part of general information management policies ('routine, good-faith operation of the information system', Rule 37 (f)), the wilful destruction of potentially relevant information can be punished by extremely high fines (in one specific case of 1.6 billion US$). Thus, in practice, any businesses who risk civil litigation before U.S. courts must implement adequate information management policies, and must implement the necessary measures to initiate a litigation hold.

- Privacy

  - o Gramm–Leach–Bliley Act (GLBA)

  - o USA PATRIOT Act, Title III

o   Health Insurance Portability and Accountability Act (HIPAA) From an RM/RA
     perspective, the Act is particularly known for its provisions with regard to Adminis-
     trative Simplification (Title II of HIPAA). This title required the U.S. Department of
     Health and Human Services (HHS) to draft specific rule sets, each of which would
     provide specific standards which would improve the efficiency of the health care
     system and prevent abuse. As a result, the HHS has adopted five principal rules:
     the Privacy Rule, the Transactions and Code Sets Rule, the Unique Identifiers Rule,
     the Enforcement Rule, and the Security Rule. The latter, published in the Federal
     Register on 20 February 2003, is specifically relevant, as it specifies a series of
     administrative, technical, and physical security procedures to assure the confiden-
     tiality of electronic protected health information. These aspects have been further
     outlined in a set of Security Standards on Administrative, Physical, Organisational
     and Technical Safeguards, all of which have been published, along with a guidance
     document on the basics of HIPAA risk management and risk assessment <http://
     www.cms.hhs.gov/EducationMaterials/04_SecurityMaterials.asp>. European or
     other countries health care service providers will generally not be affected by HI-
     PAA obligations if they are not active on the U.S. market. However, since their data
     processing activities are subject to similar obligations under general European law
     (including the Privacy Directive), and since the underlying trends of
     modernisation and evolution towards electronic health files are the same, the HHS
     safeguards can be useful as an initial yardstick for measuring RM/RA strategies
     put in place by European health care service providers, specifically with regard to
     the processing of electronic health information. HIPAA security standards include
     the following:

     ☐ Administrative safeguards:

          ☐ Security Management Process

          ☐ Assigned Security Responsibility

          ☐ Workforce Security

          ☐ Information Access Management

          ☐ Security Awareness and Training

          ☐ Security Incident Procedures

          ☐ Contingency Plan

          ☐ Evaluation

          ☐ Business Associate Contracts and Other Arrangements

     ☐ Physical safeguards

          ☐ Facility Access Controls

          ☐ Workstation Use

        ☐ Workstation Security

        ☐ Device and Media Controls

    ☐ Technical safeguards

        ☐ Access Control

        ☐ Audit Controls

        ☐ Integrity

        ☐ Person or Entity Authentication

        ☐ Transmission Security

    ☐ Organisational requirements

        ☐ Business Associate Contracts & Other Arrangements

        ☐ Requirements for Group Health Plans

- o International Safe Harbor Privacy Principles issued by the US Department of Commerce on July 21, 2000 Export of personal data from a data controller who is subject to E.U. privacy regulations to a U.S. based destination; before personal data may be exported from an entity subject to E.U. privacy regulations to a destination subject to U.S. law, the European entity must ensure that the receiving entity provides adequate safeguards to protect such data against a number of mishaps. One way of complying with this obligation is to require the receiving entity to join the Safe Harbor, by requiring that the entity self-certifies its compliance with the so-called Safe Harbor Principles. If this road is chosen, the data controller exporting the data must verify that the U.S. destination is indeed on the Safe Harbor list

- Sarbanes–Oxley Act

- FISMA

Standards Organizations and Standards

- International standard bodies:

  - o International Organization for Standardization - ISO

  - o Payment Card Industry Security Standards Council

  - o Information Security Forum

  - o The Open Group

- United States standard bodies:

- o   National Institute of Standards and Technology - NIST

  - o   Federal Information Processing Standards - FIPS by NIST devoted to Federal Government and Agencies

- UK standard bodies

  - o   British Standard Institute

Short Description of Standards

The list is chiefly based on:

ISO

- ISO/IEC 13335-1:2004 - Information technology—Security techniques—Management of information and communications technology security—Part 1: Concepts and models for information and communications technology security management http://www.iso.org/iso/en/CatalogueDetailPage.CatalogueDetail?CSNUMBER=39066. Standard containing generally accepted descriptions of concepts and models for information and communications technology security management. The standard is a commonly used code of practice, and serves as a resource for the implementation of security management practices and as a yardstick for auditing such practices.

- ISO/IEC TR 15443-1:2005 – Information technology—Security techniques—A framework for IT security assurance reference:http://www.iso.org/iso/en/CatalogueDetailPage.CatalogueDetail?CSNUMBER=39733 (Note: this is a reference to the ISO page where the standard can be acquired. However, the standard is not free of charge, and its provisions are not publicly available. For this reason, specific provisions cannot be quoted). Topic: Security assurance – the Technical Report (TR) contains generally accepted guidelines which can be used to determine an appropriate assurance method for assessing a security service, product or environmental factor

- ISO/IEC 15816:2002 - Information technology—Security techniques—Security information objects for access control reference:http://www.iso.org/iso/en/CatalogueDetailPage.CatalogueDetail?CSNUMBER=29139 (Note: this is a reference to the ISO page where the standard can be acquired. However, the standard is not free of charge, and its provisions are not publicly available. For this reason, specific provisions cannot be quoted). Topic: Security management – Access control. The standard allows security professionals to rely on a specific set of syntactic definitions and explanations with regard to SIOs, thus avoiding duplication or divergence in other standardisation efforts.

- ISO/IEC TR 15947:2002 - Information technology—Security techniques—IT intrusion detection framework reference:http://www.iso.org/iso/en/CatalogueDetailPage.CatalogueDetail?CSNUMBER=29580 (Note: this is a reference to the ISO page where the standard can be acquired. However, the standard is not free of charge, and its provisions are not publicly available. For this reason, specific provisions cannot be quoted). Topic: Security management – Intrusion detection in IT systems. The standard allows security professionals to rely on a specific set of concepts and methodologies for describing and assessing security risks with regard to potential intrusions in IT systems. It does not contain any RM/RA obligations as such, but it is rather a tool for facilitating RM/RA activities in the affected field.

- ISO/IEC 15408-1/2/3:2005 - Information technology — Security techniques — Evaluation criteria for IT security — Part 1: Introduction and general model (15408-1) Part 2: Security functional requirements (15408-2) Part 3: Security assurance requirements (15408-3) reference: http://isotc.iso.org/livelink/livelink/fetch/2000/2489/Ittf_Home/PubliclyAvailableStandards.htm Topic: Standard containing a common set of requirements for the security functions of IT products and systems and for assurance measures applied to them during a security evaluation. Scope: Publicly available ISO standard, which can be voluntarily implemented. The text is a resource for the evaluation of the security of IT products and systems, and can thus be used as a tool for RM/RA. The standard is commonly used as a resource for the evaluation of the security of IT products and systems; including (if not specifically) for procurement decisions with regard to such products. The standard can thus be used as an RM/RA tool to determine the security of an IT product or system during its design, manufacturing or marketing, or before procuring it.

- ISO/IEC 17799:2005 - Information technology—Security techniques—Code of practice for information security management. reference: http://www.iso.org/iso/en/CatalogueDetailPage.CatalogueDetail?CSNUMBER=39612&ICS1=35&ICS2=40&ICS3= (Note: this is a reference to the ISO page where the standard can be acquired. However, the standard is not free of charge, and its provisions are not publicly available. For this reason, specific provisions cannot be quoted). Topic: Standard containing generally accepted guidelines and general principles for initiating, implementing, maintaining, and improving information security management in an organization, including business continuity management. The standard is a commonly used code of practice, and serves as a resource for the implementation of information security management practices and as a yardstick for auditing such practices.

- ISO/IEC TR 15446:2004 – Information technology—Security techniques—Guide for the production of Protection Profiles and Security Targets. reference: http://isotc.iso.org/livelink/livelink/fetch/2000/2489/Ittf_Home/PubliclyAvailableStandards.htm Topic: Technical Report (TR) containing guidelines for the construction of Protection Profiles (PPs) and Security Targets (STs) that are intended to be compliant with ISO/IEC 15408 (the "Common Criteria"). The standard is predominantly used as a tool for security professionals to develop PPs and STs, but can also be used to assess the validity of the same (by using the TR as a yardstick to determine if its standards have been obeyed). Thus, it is a (nonbinding) normative tool for the creation and assessment of RM/RA practices.

- ISO/IEC 18028:2006 - Information technology—Security techniques—IT network security reference: http://www.iso.org/iso/en/CatalogueDetailPage.CatalogueDetail?CSNUMBER=40008 (Note: this is a reference to the ISO page where the standard can be acquired. However, the standard is not free of charge, and its provisions are not publicly available. For this reason, specific provisions cannot be quoted). Topic: Five part standard (ISO/IEC

18028-1 to 18028-5) containing generally accepted guidelines on the security aspects of the management, operation and use of information technology networks. The standard is considered an extension of the guidelines provided in ISO/IEC 13335 and ISO/IEC 17799 focusing specifically on network security risks. The standard is a commonly used code of practice, and serves as a resource for the implementation of security management practices and as a yardstick for auditing such practices.

- ISO/IEC 27001:2005 - Information technology—Security techniques—Information security management systems—Requirements reference: http://www.iso.org/iso/en/CatalogueDetailPage.CatalogueDetail?CSNUMBER=42103 (Note: this is a reference to the ISO page where the standard can be acquired. However, the standard is not free of charge, and its provisions are not publicly available. For this reason, specific provisions cannot be quoted). Topic: Standard containing generally accepted guidelines for the implementation of an Information Security Management System within any given organisation. Scope: Not publicly available ISO standard, which can be voluntarily implemented. While not legally binding, the text contains direct guidelines for the creation of sound information security practices The standard is a very commonly used code of practice, and serves as a resource for the implementation of information security management systems and as a yardstick for auditing such systems and/or the surrounding practices. Its application in practice is often combined with related standards, such as BS 7799-3:2006 which provides additional guidance to support the requirements given in ISO/IEC 27001:2005 <http://www.bsiglobal.com/en/Shop/Publication-Detail/?pid=000000000030125022&recid=2491>

- ISO/IEC 27001:2013, the updated standard for information security management systems.

- ISO/IEC TR 18044:2004 – Information technology—Security techniques—Information security incident management reference: http://www.iso.org/iso/en/CatalogueDetailPage.CatalogueDetail?CSNUMBER=35396 (Note: this is a reference to the ISO page where the standard can be acquired. However, the standard is not free of charge, and its provisions are not publicly available. For this reason, specific provisions cannot be quoted). Topic: Technical Report (TR) containing generally accepted guidelines and general principles for information security incident management in an organization.Scope: Not publicly available ISO TR, which can be voluntarily used.While not legally binding, the text contains direct guidelines for incident management. The standard is a high level resource introducing basic concepts and considerations in the field of incident response. As such, it is mostly useful as a catalyst to awareness raising initiatives in this regard.

- ISO/IEC 18045:2005 - Information technology—Security techniques—Methodology for IT security evaluation reference: http://isotc.iso.org/livelink/livelink/fetch/2000/2489/Ittf_Home/PubliclyAvailableStandards.htm Topic: Standard containing auditing guidelines for assessment of compliance with ISO/IEC 15408 (Information technology—Security techniques—Evaluation criteria for IT security) Scope Publicly available ISO standard, to be followed when evaluating compliance with ISO/IEC 15408 (Information technology—Security techniques—Evaluation criteria for IT security). The standard is a 'companion document', which is thus primarily of used for security professionals involved in evaluating compliance with ISO/IEC 15408 (Information technology—Security techniques—Evaluation criteria for IT security). Since it describes minimum actions to be performed by such auditors, compliance with ISO/IEC 15408 is impossible if ISO/IEC 18045 has been disregarded.

- ISO/TR 13569:2005 - Financial services—Information security guidelines reference: http://www.iso.org/iso/en/CatalogueDetailPage.CatalogueDetail?CSNUMBER=37245 (Note: this is a reference to the ISO page where the standard can be acquired. However, the standard is not free of charge, and its provisions are not publicly available. For this reason, specific provisions cannot be quoted). Topic: Standard containing guidelines for the implementation and assessment of information security policies in financial services institutions. The standard is a commonly referenced guideline, and serves as a resource for the implementation of information security management programmes in institutions of the financial sector, and as a yardstick for auditing such programmes.

- ISO/IEC 21827:2008 - Information technology—Security techniques—Systems Security Engineering—Capability Maturity Model (SSE-CMM): ISO/IEC 21827:2008 specifies the Systems Security Engineering - Capability Maturity Model (SSE-CMM), which describes the essential characteristics of an organization's security engineering process that must exist to ensure good security engineering. ISO/IEC 21827:2008 does not prescribe a particular process or sequence, but captures practices generally observed in industry. The model is a standard metric for security engineering practices.

BSI

- BS 25999-1:2006 - Business continuity management Part 1: Code of practice Note: this is only part one of BS 25999, which was published in November 2006. Part two (which should contain more specific criteria with a view of possible accreditation) is yet to appear. reference: http://www.bsi-global.com/en/Shop/Publication-Detail/?pid=000000000030157563. Topic: Standard containing a business continuity code of practice. The standard is intended as a code of practice for business continuity management, and will be extended by a second part that should permit accreditation for adherence with the standard. Given its relative newness, the potential impact of the standard is difficult to assess, although it could be very influential to RM/RA practices, given the general lack of universally applicable standards in this regard and the increasing attention to business continuity and contingency planning in regulatory initiatives. Application of this standard can be complemented by other norms, in particular PAS 77:2006 - IT Service Continuity Management Code of Practice <http://www.bsi-global.com/en/Shop/Publication-Detail/?pid=000000000030141858>.The TR allows security professionals to determine a suitable methodology for assessing a security service, product or environmental factor (a deliverable). Following this TR, it can be determined which level of security assurance a deliverable is intended to meet, and if this threshold is actually met by the deliverable.

- BS 7799-3:2006 - Information security management systems—Guidelines for information security risk management reference: http://www.bsi-global.com/en/Shop/Publication-Detail/?pid=000000000030125022&recid=2491 (Note: this is a reference to the BSI page where the standard can be acquired. However, the standard is not free of charge, and its provisions are not publicly available. For this reason, specific provisions cannot be quoted). Topic: Standard containing general guidelines for information security risk management.Scope: Not publicly available BSI standard, which can be voluntarily implemented. While not legally binding, the text contains direct guidelines for the creation of sound information security practices. The standard is mostly intended as a guiding complementary document to the application of the aforementioned ISO 27001:2005, and is therefore typically applied in conjunction with this standard in risk assessment practices

Information Security Forum

- Standard of Good Practice

Cybercrime

Computer crime, or cybercrime, is crime that involves a computer and a network. The computer may have been used in the commission of a crime, or it may be the target. Debarati Halder and K. Jaishankar define cybercrimes as: "Offences that are committed against individuals or groups of individuals with a criminal motive to intentionally harm the reputation of the victim or cause physical or mental harm, or loss, to the victim directly or indirectly, using modern telecommunication networks such as Internet (Chat rooms, emails, notice boards and groups) and mobile phones (SMS/MMS)". Such crimes may threaten a nation's security and financial health. Issues surrounding these types of crimes have become high-profile, particularly those surrounding hacking, copyright infringement, child pornography, and child grooming. There are also problems of privacy when confidential information is intercepted or disclosed, lawfully or otherwise. Debarati Halder and K. Jaishankar further define cybercrime from the perspective of gender and defined 'cybercrime against women' as "Crimes targeted against women with a motive to intentionally harm the victim psychologically and physically, using modern telecommunication networks such as internet and mobile phones". Internationally, both governmental and non-state actors engage in cybercrimes, including espionage, financial theft, and other cross-border crimes. Activity crossing international borders and involving the interests of at least one nation state is sometimes referred to as cyberwarfare. The international legal system is attempting to hold actors accountable for their actions through the International Criminal Court.

A report (sponsored by McAfee) estimates that the annual damage to the global economy is at $445 billion; however, a Microsoft report shows that such survey-based estimates are "hopelessly flawed" and exaggerate the true losses by orders of magnitude. Approximately $1.5 billion was lost in 2012 to online credit and debit card fraud in the US. In 2016, a study by Juniper Research estimated that the costs of cybercrime could be as high as 2.1 trillion by 2019.

Most measures show that the problem of cybercrime continues to worsen. However, Eric Jardine argues that the frequency, cost and severity of cybercrime cannot be well understood as counts expressed in absolute terms. Instead, these numbers need to be normalized around the growing size of cyberspace, in the same way that crime statistics in the physical world are expressed as a proportion of a population (i.e., 1.5 murders per 100,000 people). Jardine argues that, since cyberspace has been rapidly increasing in size each year, absolute numbers (i.e., a count saying there are 100,000 cyberattacks in 2015) present a worse picture of the security of cyberspace than numbers normalized around the actual size of the Internet ecosystem (i.e., a rate of cybercrime). His proposed intuition is that if cyberspace continues to grow, you should actually expect cybercrime counts to continue to increase because there are more users and activity online, but that as a proportion of the size of the ecosystem crime might actually be becoming less of a problem.

Classification

Computer crime encompasses a broad range of activities.

Fraud and Financial Crimes

Computer fraud is any dishonest misrepresentation of fact intended to let another to do or refrain from doing something which causes loss. In this context, the fraud will result in obtaining a benefit by:

- Altering in an unauthorized way. This requires little technical expertise and is common form of theft by employees altering the data before entry or entering false data, or by entering unauthorized instructions or using unauthorized processes;

- Altering, destroying, suppressing, or stealing output, usually to conceal unauthorized transactions. This is difficult to detect;

- Altering or deleting stored data;

Other forms of fraud may be facilitated using computer systems, including bank fraud, carding, identity theft, extortion, and theft of classified information.

A variety of internet scams, many based on phishing and social engineering, target consumers and businesses.

Cyber Terrorism

Government officials and information technology security specialists have documented a significant increase in Internet problems and server scans since early 2001. But there is a growing concern among federal officials that such intrusions are part of an organized effort by cyberterrorists, foreign intelligence services, or other groups to map potential security holes in critical systems. A cyberterrorist is someone who intimidates or coerces a government or organization to advance his or her political or social objectives by launching a computer-based attack against computers, networks, or the information stored on them.

Cyberterrorism in general, can be defined as an act of terrorism committed through the use of cyberspace or computer resources (Parker 1983). As such, a simple propaganda in the Internet, that there will be bomb attacks during the holidays can be considered cyberterrorism. There are also hacking activities directed towards individuals, families, organized by groups within networks, tending to cause fear among people, demonstrate power, collecting information relevant for ruining peoples' lives, robberies, blackmailing etc.

Cyberextortion

Cyberextortion occurs when a website, e-mail server, or computer system is subjected to or threatened with repeated denial of service or other attacks by malicious hackers. These hackers demand money in return for promising to stop the attacks and to offer "protection". According to the Federal Bureau of Investigation, cyberextortionists are increasingly attacking corporate websites and networks, crippling their ability to operate and demanding payments to restore their service. More than 20 cases are reported each month to the FBI and many go unreported in order to keep the victim's name out of the public domain. Perpetrators typically use a distributed denial-of-service attack.

An example of cyberextortion was the attack on Sony Pictures of 2014.

Cyberwarfare

Sailors analyze, detect and defensively respond to unauthorized activity within U.S. Navy information systems and computer networks

The U.S. Department of Defense (DoD) notes that the cyberspace has emerged as a national-level concern through several recent events of geo-strategic significance. Among those are included, the attack on Estonia's infrastructure in 2007, allegedly by Russian hackers. "In August 2008, Russia again allegedly conducted cyberattacks, this time in a coordinated and synchronized kinetic and non-kinetic campaign against the country of Georgia. Fearing that such attacks may become the norm in future warfare among nation-states, the concept of cyberspace operations impacts and will be adapted by warfighting military commanders in the future.

Computer as a Target

These crimes are committed by a selected group of criminals. Unlike crimes using the computer as a tool, these crimes require the technical knowledge of the perpetrators. As such, as technology evolves, so too does the nature of the crime. These crimes are relatively new, having been in existence for only as long as computers have—which explains how unprepared society and the world in general is towards combating these crimes. There are numerous crimes of this nature committed daily on the internet:

Crimes that primarily target computer networks or devices include:

- Computer viruses

- Denial-of-service attacks

- Malware (malicious code)

Computer as a Tool

When the individual is the main target of cybercrime, the computer can be considered as the tool rather than the target. These crimes generally involve less technical expertise. Human weaknesses are generally exploited. The damage dealt is largely psychological and intangible, making legal action against the variants more difficult. These are the crimes which have existed for centuries in the offline world. Scams, theft, and the likes have existed even before the development in high-tech equipment. The same criminal has simply been given a tool which increases his potential pool of victims and makes him all the harder to trace and apprehend.

Crimes that use computer networks or devices to advance other ends include:

- Fraud and identity theft (although this increasingly uses malware, hacking and/or phishing, making it an example of both "computer as target" and "computer as tool" crime)

- Information warfare

- Phishing scams

- Spam

- Propagation of illegal obscene or offensive content, including harassment and threats

The unsolicited sending of bulk email for commercial purposes (spam) is unlawful in some jurisdictions.

Phishing is mostly propagated via email. Phishing emails may contain links to other websites that are affected by malware. Or, they may contain links to fake online banking or other websites used to steal private account information.

Obscene or Offensive Content

The content of websites and other electronic communications may be distasteful, obscene or offensive for a variety of reasons. In some instances these communications may be legal.

The extent to which these communications are unlawful varies greatly between countries, and even within nations. It is a sensitive area in which the courts can become involved in arbitrating between groups with strong beliefs.

One area of Internet pornography that has been the target of the strongest efforts at curtailment is child pornography.

Harassment

Whereas content may be offensive in a non-specific way, harassment directs obscenities and derogatory comments at specific individuals focusing for example on gender, race, religion, nationality, sexual orientation. This often occurs in chat rooms, through newsgroups, and by sending hate e-mail to interested parties. Harassment on the internet also includes revenge porn.

Various aspects needed to be considered when understanding harassment online.

There are instances where committing a crime using a computer can lead to an enhanced sentence. For example, in the case of United States v. Neil Scott Kramer, Kramer was served an enhanced sentence according to the U.S. Sentencing Guidelines Manual §2G1.3(b)(3) for his use of a cell phone to "persuade, induce, entice, coerce, or facilitate the travel of, the minor to engage in prohibited sexual conduct." Kramer argued that this claim was insufficient because his charge included persuading through a computer device and his cellular phone technically is not a computer. Although Kramer tried to argue this point, U.S. Sentencing Guidelines Manual states that the term computer "means an electronic, magnetic, optical, electrochemically, or other high speed data processing device performing logical, arithmetic, or storage functions, and includes any data storage facility or communications facility directly related to or operating in conjunction with such device."

Connecticut was the U.S. state to pass a statute making it a criminal offense to harass someone by computer. Michigan, Arizona, and Virginia and South Carolina have also passed laws banning harassment by electronic means.

Harassment as defined in the U.S. computer statutes is typically distinct from cyberbullying, in that the former usually relates to a person's "use a computer or computer network to communicate obscene, vulgar, profane, lewd, lascivious, or indecent language, or make any suggestion or proposal of an obscene nature, or threaten any illegal or immoral act," while the latter need not involve anything of a sexual nature.

Although freedom of speech is protected by law in most democratic societies (in the US this is done by the First Amendment), it does not include all types of speech. In fact spoken or written "true threat" speech/text is criminalized because of "intent to harm or intimidate", that also applies for online or any type of network related threats in written text or speech. The US Supreme Court definition of "true threat" is "statements where the speaker means to communicate a serious expression of an intent to commit an act of unlawful violence to a particular individual or group".

Drug Trafficking

Darknet markets are used to buy and sell recreational drugs online. Some drug traffickers use encrypted messaging tools to communicate with drug mules. The dark web site Silk Road was a major online marketplace for drugs before it was shut down by law enforcement (then reopened under new management, and then shut down by law enforcement again).

Documented Cases

One of the highest profiled banking computer crime occurred during a course of three years beginning in 1970. The chief teller at the Park Avenue branch of New York's Union Dime Savings Bank embezzled over $1.5 million from hundreds of accounts.

A hacking group called MOD (Masters of Deception), allegedly stole passwords and technical data from Pacific Bell, Nynex, and other telephone companies as well as several big credit agencies and two major universities. The damage caused was extensive, one company, Southwestern Bell suffered losses of $370,000 alone.

In 1983, a nineteen-year-old UCLA student used his PC to break into a Defense Department international communications system.

Between 1995 and 1998 the Newscorp satellite pay to view encrypted SKY-TV service was hacked several times during an ongoing technological arms race between a pan-European hacking group and Newscorp. The original motivation of the hackers was to watch Star Trek re-runs in Germany; which was something which Newscorp did not have the copyright to allow.

On 26 March 1999, the Melissa worm infected a document on a victim's computer, then automatically sent that document and a copy of the virus spread via e-mail to other people.

In February 2000, an individual going by the alias of MafiaBoy began a series denial-of-service attacks against high-profile websites, including Yahoo!, Amazon.com, Dell, Inc., E*TRADE, eBay, and CNN. About fifty computers at Stanford University, and also computers at the University of California at Santa Barbara, were amongst the zombie computers sending pings in DDoS attacks. On 3 August 2000, Canadian federal prosecutors charged MafiaBoy with 54 counts of illegal access to computers, plus a total of ten counts of mischief to data for his attacks.

The Russian Business Network (RBN) was registered as an internet site in 2006. Initially, much of its activity was legitimate. But apparently the founders soon discovered that it was more profitable to host illegitimate activities and started hiring its services to criminals. The RBN has been described by VeriSign as "the baddest of the bad". It offers web hosting services and internet access to all kinds of criminal and objectionable activities, with an individual activities earning up to $150 million in one year. It specialized in and in some cases monopolized personal identity theft for resale. It is the originator of MPack and an alleged operator of the now defunct Storm botnet.

On 2 March 2010, Spanish investigators arrested 3 in infection of over 13 million computers around the world. The "botnet" of infected computers included PCs inside more than half of the Fortune 1000 companies and more than 40 major banks, according to investigators.

In August 2010 the international investigation Operation Delego, operating under the aegis of the

Department of Homeland Security, shut down the international pedophile ring Dreamboard. The website had approximately 600 members, and may have distributed up to 123 terabytes of child pornography (roughly equivalent to 16,000 DVDs). To date this is the single largest U.S. prosecution of an international child pornography ring; 52 arrests were made worldwide.

On March 1, 2011 at Lassiter High School, two students were accused of impersonation of a staff member via cybercrime, but both claimed they were uninvolved. The offense was made a felony in the Cobb County School District two months after the impersonation had happened. Shortly afterwards, the head of the LHS School Board said "The teacher just wouldn't do this at all". The case ended on May 9, and no evidence was found.

In June 2012 LinkedIn and eHarmony were attacked, compromising 65 million password hashes. 30,000 passwords were cracked and 1.5 million EHarmony passwords were posted online.

December 2012 Wells Fargo website experienced a denial of service attack. Potentially compromising 70 million customers and 8.5 million active viewers. Other banks thought to be compromised: Bank of America, J. P. Morgan U.S. Bank, and PNC Financial Services.

In January 2012 Zappos.com experienced a security breach after as many as 24 million customers' credit card numbers, personal information, billing and shipping addresses had been compromised.

April 23, 2013 saw the Associated Press' Twitter account's hacking to release a hoax tweet about fictional attacks in the White House that left President Obama injured. This erroneous tweet resulted in a brief plunge of 130 points from the Dow Jones Industrial Average, removal of $136 billion from S&P 500 index, and the temporary suspension of their Twitter account. The Dow Jones later restored its session gains.

Combating Computer Crime

Diffusion of Cybercrime

The broad diffusion of cybercriminal activities is an issue in computer crimes detection and prosecution. According to Jean-Loup Richet (Research Fellow at ESSEC ISIS), technical expertise and accessibility no longer act as barriers to entry into cybercrime. Indeed, hacking is much less complex than it was a few years ago, as hacking communities have greatly diffused their knowledge through the Internet. Blogs and communities have hugely contributed to information sharing: beginners could benefit from older hackers' knowledge and advice. Furthermore, Hacking is cheaper than ever: before the cloud computing era, in order to spam or scam one needed a dedicated server, skills in server management, network configuration and maintenance, knowledge of Internet service provider standards, etc. By comparison, a mail software-as-a-service is a scalable, inexpensive, bulk, and transactional e-mail-sending service for marketing purposes and could be easily set up for spam. Jean-Loup Richet explains that cloud computing could be helpful for a cybercriminal as a way to leverage his attack – brute-forcing a password, improve the reach of a botnet, or facilitating a spamming campaign.

Investigation

A computer can be a source of evidence. Even where a computer is not directly used for criminal purposes, it may contain records of value to criminal investigators in the form of a logfile.

In most countries Internet Service Providers are required, by law, to keep their logfiles for a predetermined amount of time. For example; a European wide Data Retention Directive (applicable to all EU member states) states that all E-mail traffic should be retained for a minimum of 12 months.

Legislation

Due to easily exploitable laws, cybercriminals use developing countries in order to evade detection and prosecution from law enforcement. In developing countries, such as the Philippines, laws against cybercrime are weak or sometimes nonexistent. These weak laws allow cybercriminals to strike from international borders and remain undetected. Even when identified, these criminals avoid being punished or extradited to a country, such as the United States, that has developed laws that allow for prosecution. While this proves difficult in some cases, agencies, such as the FBI, have used deception and subterfuge to catch criminals. For example, two Russian hackers had been evading the FBI for some time. The FBI set up a fake computing company based in Seattle, Washington. They proceeded to lure the two Russian men into the United States by offering them work with this company. Upon completion of the interview, the suspects were arrested outside of the building. Clever tricks like this are sometimes a necessary part of catching cybercriminals when weak legislation makes it impossible otherwise.

President Barack Obama released in an executive order in April 2015 to combat cybercrime. The executive order allows the United States to freeze assets of convicted cybercriminals and block their economic activity within the United States. This is some of the first solid legislation that combats cybercrime in this way.

The European Union adopted directive 2013/40/EU. All offences of the directive, and other definitions and procedural institutions are also in the Council of Europe's Convention on Cybercrime.

Penalties

Penalties for computer related crimes in New York State can range from a fine and a short period of jail time for a Class A misdemeanor such as unauthorized use of a computer up to computer tampering in the first degree which is a Class C felony and can carry 3 to 15 years in prison.

However, some hackers have been hired as information security experts by private companies due to their inside knowledge of computer crime, a phenomenon which theoretically could create perverse incentives. A possible counter to this is for courts to ban convicted hackers from using the Internet or computers, even after they have been released from prison – though as computers and the Internet become more and more central to everyday life, this type of punishment may be viewed as more and more harsh and draconian. However, nuanced approaches have been developed that manage cyberoffender behavior without resorting to total computer and/or Internet bans. These approaches involve restricting individuals to specific devices which are subject to computer monitoring and/or computer searches by probation and/or parole officers.

Awareness

As technology advances and more people rely on the internet to store sensitive information such as banking or credit card information, criminals are going to attempt to steal that information.

Cyber-crime is becoming more of a threat to people across the world. Raising awareness about how information is being protected and the tactics criminals use to steal that information is im-portant in today's world. According to the FBI's Internet Crime Complaint Center in 2014 there were 269,422 complaints filed. With all the claims combined there was a reported total loss of $800,492,073. But yet cyber-crime doesn't seem to be on the average person's radar. There are 1.5 million cyber-attacks annually, that means that there are over 4,000 attacks a day, 170 attacks every hour, or nearly three attacks every minute. Anybody who uses the internet for any reason can be a victim, which is why it is important to be aware of how one is being protected while online.

Agencies

- Australian High Tech Crime Centre

- National White Collar Crime Center

ITIL Security Management

ITIL security management (originally Information Technology Infrastructure Library)de-scribes the structured fitting of security into an organization. ITIL security management is based on the ISO 27001 standard. "ISO/IEC 27001:2005 covers all types of organizations (e.g. commercial enterprises, government agencies, not-for profit organizations). ISO/IEC 27001:2005 specifies the requirements for establishing, implementing, operating, monitor-ing, reviewing, maintaining and improving a documented Information Security Management System within the context of the organization's overall business risks. It specifies require-ments for the implementation of security controls customized to the needs of individual or-ganizations or parts thereof. ISO/IEC 27001:2005 is designed to ensure the selection of ade-quate and proportionate security controls that protect information assets and give confidence to interested parties."

A basic concept of security management is information security. The primary goal of information security is to control access to information. The value of the information is what must be protected. These values are include confidentiality, integrity and availability. Inferred aspects are privacy, anonymity and verifiability.

The goal of Security Management comes in two parts:

- Security requirements defined in service level agreements (SLA) and other external re-quirements that are specified in underpinning contracts, legislation and possible internal or external imposed policies.

- Basic security that guarantees management continuity. This is necessary to achieve simpli-fied service-level management for information security.

SLAs define security requirements, along with legislation (if applicable) and other contracts. These requirements can act as key performance indicators (KPIs) that can be used for process management and for interpreting the results of the security management process.

The security management process relates to other ITIL-processes. However, in this particular section the most obvious relations are the relations to the service level management, incident management and change Management processes.

Security Management

Security management is a continuous process that can be compared to W. Edwards Deming's Quality Circle (Plan, Do, Check, Act).

The inputs are requirements that are formed by clients. The requirements are translated into security services and security metrics. Both the client and the plan sub-process affect the SLA. The SLA is an input for both the client and the process. The provider develops security plans for the organization. These plans contain policies and operational level agreements. The security plans (Plan) are then implemented (Do) and the implementation is then evaluated (Check). After the evaluation, the plans and the plan implementation are maintained (Act).

The activities, results/products and the process are documented. External reports are written and sent to the clients. The clients are then able to adapt their requirements based on the information received through the reports. Furthermore, the service provider can adjust their plan or the implementation based on their findings in order to satisfy all the requirements stated in the SLA (including new requirements).

Control

The first activity in the security management process is the "Control" sub-process. The Control sub-process organizes and manages the security management process itself. The Control sub-process defines the processes, the allocation of responsibility for the policy statements and the management framework.

The security management framework defines the sub-processes for: the development of security plans, the implementation of the security plans, the evaluation and how the results of the evaluations are translated into action plans. Furthermore, the management framework defines how should be reported to clients.

The activities that take place in the Control process are summed up in the following table, which contains the name of the (sub) activity and a short definition of the activity.

Activities	Sub-Activities	Descriptions
Control	Implement policies	This process outlines the specific requirements and rules that have to be met in order to implement security management. The process ends with *policy statement*.
	Set up the security organization	This process sets up the organizations for information security. For example in this process the structure the responsibilities are set up. This process ends with *security management framework*.
	Reporting	In this process the whole targeting process is documented in a specific way. This process ends with *reports*.

The meta-modeling technique was used in order to model the activities of the control sub-process. The following figure is the meta-process model of the control sub-process. It is based on a UML activity diagram and it gives an overview of the activities of the Control sub-process. The grey rectangle represents the control sub-process and the smaller beam shapes inside of the grey rectangle represent the activities that take place inside the control sub-process. The beams with a black shadow indicate that the activity is a closed (complex) activity. This means that the activity consists of a collection of (sub) activities but these activities are not expanded because they are not relevant in this particular context. The white beam without shadow indicates that the reporting activity is a standard activity. This means that reporting does not contain (sub) activities.

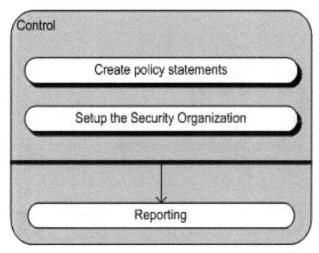

Figure 2.1.1: Meta-process model Control sub-process

Furthermore, it is noticeable that the first two activities are not linked with an arrow and that there is a black stripe with an arrow leading to the reporting activity. This means that the two first activities are not sequential. They are unordered activities and after these two activities have taken place the reporting activity will sequentially follow.

The Following Table (Table 2.1.2) is a Concept Definition Table.

Concept	Description
CONTROL DOCUMENTS	CONTROL is a description of how SECURITY MANAGEMENT will be organized and how it will be managed.
POLICY STATEMENTS	POLICY STATEMENTS are documents that outlines specific requirements or rules that must be met. In the information security realm, policies are usually point-specific, covering a single area. For example, an "Acceptable Use" policy would cover the rules and regulations for appropriate use of the computing facilities.
SECURITY MANAGEMENT FRAMEWORK	SECURITY MANAGEMENT FRAMEWORK is an established management framework to initiate and control the implementation of information security within your organization and to manage ongoing information security provision.

Table 2.1.2: Concept and definition control sub-process Security management

The meta-data model of the control sub-process is based on a UML class diagram. In figure 2.1.2 is the meta-data model of the control sub-process.

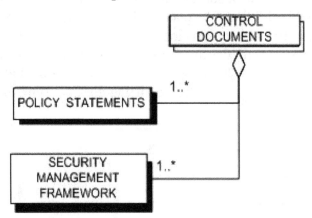

Figure 2.1.2: Meta-process model control sub-process

The CONTROL rectangle with a white shadow is an open complex concept. This means that the CONTROL rectangle consists of a collection of (sub) concepts and these concepts are expanded in this particular context.

The following picture (figure 2.1.3) is the process-data model of the control sub-process. This picture shows the integration of the two models. The dotted arrows indicate which concepts are created or adjusted in the corresponding activities.

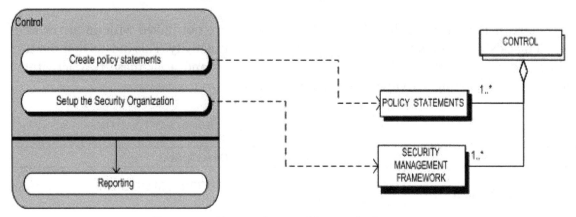

Figure 2.1.3: Process-data model control sub-process

Plan

The Plan sub-process contains activities that in cooperation with the Service Level Management lead to the (information) Security section in the SLA. Furthermore, the Plan sub-process contains activities that are related to the underpinning contracts which are specific for (information) security.

In the Plan sub-process the goals formulated in the SLA are specified in the form of Operational

Level Agreements (OLA). These OLA's can be defined as security plans for a specific internal organization entity of the service provider.

Besides the input of the SLA, the Plan sub-process also works with the policy statements of the service provider itself. As said earlier these policy statements are defined in the control sub-process.

The Operational Level Agreements for information security are set up and implemented based on the ITIL process. This means that there has to be cooperation with other ITIL processes. For example if the security management wishes to change the IT infrastructure in order to achieve maximum security, these changes will only be done through the Change Management process. The Security Management will deliver the input (Request for change) for this change. The change Manager is responsible for the Change Management Process itself.

Table 2.3.1 Shows the Activity Plan the (sub) Activities and their Definition.

Activities	Sub-Activities	Descriptions
Plan	Create Security section for SLA	This process contains activities that lead to the security agreements paragraph in the service level agreements. At the end of this process the *Security* section of the service level agreement is created.
	Create underpinning Contracts	This process contains activities that lead to UNDERPINNING CONTRACTS. These contracts are specific for security.
	Create Operational level agreements	The general formulated goals in the SLA are specified in operational level agreements. These agreements can be seen as security plans for specific organization units.
	Reporting	In this process the whole Create plan process is documented in a specific way. This process ends with REPORTS.

Table 2.2.1: (Sub) activities and descriptions Plan sub-process ITIL Security Management

As well as for the Control sub-process the Plan sub-process has been modeled using the meta-modeling technique. On the right side of figure 2.2.1 the meta-process model of the Plan sub-process is given.

As you can see the Plan sub-process consists of a combination of unordered and ordered (sub) activities. Furthermore, it is noticeable that the sub-process contains three complex activities which are all closed activities and one standard activity. Table 2.2.1 consists of concepts that are created or adjusted during the plan sub-process. The table also gives a definition of these concepts.

Concept	Description
PLAN	Formulated schemes for the security agreements.
Security section of the security level agreements	The security agreements paragraph in the written agreements between a Service Provider and the customer(s) that documents agreed Service Levels for a service.
UNDERPINNING CONTRACTS	A contract with an external supplier covering delivery of services that support the IT organisation in their delivery of services.
OPERATIONAL LEVEL AGREEMENTS	An internal agreement covering the delivery of services which support the IT organization in their delivery of services.

Table 2.2.2: Concept and definition Plan sub-process Security management

Just as the Control sub-process the Plan sub-process is modeled using the meta-modeling technique. The left side of figure 2.2.1 is the meta-data model of the Plan sub-process.

The Plan rectangle is an open (complex) concept which has an aggregation type of relationship with two closed (complex) concepts and one standard concept. The two closed concepts are not expanded in this particular context.

The following picture (figure 2.2.1) is the process-data diagram of the Plan sub-process. This picture shows the integration of the two models. The dotted arrows indicate which concepts are created or adjusted in the corresponding activities of the Plan sub-process.

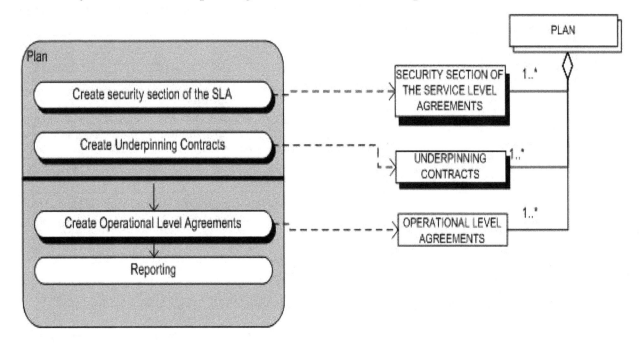

Figure 2.2.1: Process-data model Plan sub-process

Implementation

The Implementation sub-process makes sure that all measures, as specified in the plans, are properly implemented. During the Implementation sub-process no (new) measures are defined nor changed. The definition or change of measures will take place in the Plan sub-process in cooperation with the Change Management Process.

The activities that take place in the implementation sub-process are summed up in the following table (table 2.3.1). The table contains the name of the (sub) activity and a short definition of the activity.

Activities	Sub-Activities	Descriptions
Implement	Classifying and managing of IT applications	Process of formally grouping *configuration items* by type, e.g., software, hardware, documentation, environment, application. Process of formally identifying changes by type e.g., project scope change request, validation change request, infrastructure change request this process leads to *asset classification and control documents*.
	Implement personnel security	Here measures are adopted in order to give personnel safety and confidence and measures to prevent a crime/fraud. The process ends with *personnel security*.
	Implement security management	In this process specific security requirements and/or security rules that must be met are outlined and documented. The process ends with *security policies*.
	Implement access control	In this process specific access security requirements and/or access security rules that must be met are outlined and documented. The process ends with *access control*.
	Reporting	In this process the whole *implement as planned process* is documented in a specific way. This process ends with *reports*.

Table 2.3.1: (Sub) activities and descriptions Implementation sub-process ITIL Security Management

The left side of figure 2.3.1 is the meta-process model of the Implementation phase. The four labels with a black shadow mean that these activities are closed concepts and they are not expanded in this context. It is also noticeable that there are no arrows connecting these four activities this means that these activities are unordered and the reporting will be carried out after the completion of al the four activities.

During the implementation phase there are a number of concepts that are created and /or adjusted. See table 2.3.2 for an overview of the most common concepts and their description.

Concept	Description
Implementation	Accomplished security management according to the security management plan.
Asset classification and control documents	A comprehensive inventory of assets with responsibility assigned to ensure that effective security protection is maintained.
Personnel security	Well defined job descriptions for all staff outlining security roles and responsibilities.
Security policies	Security policies are documents that outlines specific security requirements or security rules that must be met.
Access control	Network management to ensure that only those with the appropriate responsibility have access to information in the networks and the protection of the supporting infrastructure.

Table 2.3.2: Concept and definition Implementation sub-process Security management

The concepts created and/or adjusted are modeled using the meta-modeling technique. The right side of figure 2.3.1 is the meta-data model of the implementation sub-process.

The implementation documents are an open concept and is expanded upon in this context. It consists of four closed concepts which are not expanded because they are irrelevant in this particular context.

In order to make the relations between the two models clearer the integration of the two models are illustrated in figure 2.3.1. The dotted arrows running from the activities to the concepts illustrate which concepts are created/ adjusted in the corresponding activities.

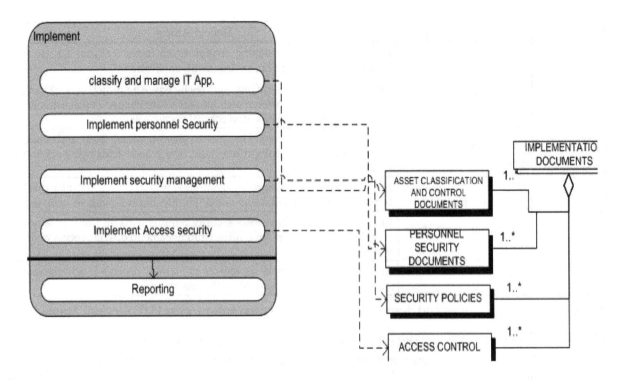

Figure 2.3.1: Process-data model Implementation sub-process

Evaluation

The evaluation of the implementation and the plans is very important. The evaluation is necessary to measure the success of the implementation and the Security plans. The evaluation is also very important for the clients (and possibly third parties). The results of the Evaluation sub-process are used to maintain the agreed measures and the implementation itself. Evaluation results can lead to new requirements and so lead to a Request for Change. The request for change is then defined and it is then send to the Change Management process.

Mainly there are three sorts of evaluation; the Self-assessment; internal audit, and external audit.

The self-assessment is mainly carried out in the organization of the processes. The internal audits are carried out by internal IT-auditors and the external audits are carried out by external independent IT-auditors. Besides, the evaluations already mentioned an evaluation based on the communicated security incidents will also take place. The most important activities for this evaluation are the security monitoring of IT-systems; verify if the security legislation and the implementation of the security plans are complied; trace and react to undesirable use of the IT-supplies.

The activities that take place in the evaluation sub-process are summed up in the following table (Table 2.4.1). The table contains the name of the (sub) activity and a short definition of the activity.

Activities	Sub-Activities	Descriptions
Evaluate	Self-assessment	In this process an examination of the implemented security agreements is done by the organization of the process itself. The result of this process is SELF ASSESSMENT DOCUMENTS.
	Internal Audit	In this process an examination of the implemented security agreements is done by an internal EDP auditor. The result of this process is INTERNAL AUDIT.
	External audit	In this process an examination of the implemented security agreements is done by an external EDP auditor. The result of this process is EXTERNAL AUDIT.
	Evaluation based on security incidents	In this process an examination of the implemented security agreements is done based on security events which is not part of the standard operation of a service and which causes, or may cause, an interruption to, or a reduction in, the quality of that service. The result of this process is SECURITY INCIDENTS.
	Reporting	In this process the whole Evaluate implementation process is documented in a specific way. This process ends with REPORTS.

Table 2.4.1: (Sub) activities and descriptions Evaluation sub-process ITIL Security Management

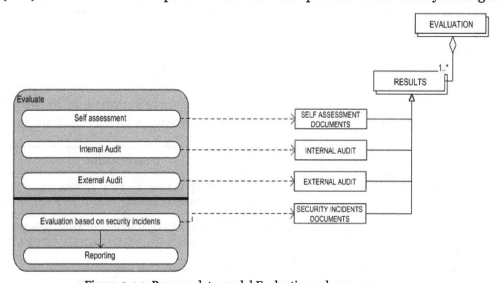

Figure 2.4.1: Process-data model Evaluation sub-process

The process-data diagram illustrated in the figure 2.4.1 consists of a meta-process model and a meta-data model. The Evaluation sub-process was modeled using the meta-modeling technique. The dotted arrows running from the meta-process diagram (left) to the meta-data diagram (right) indicate which concepts are created/ adjusted in the corresponding activities. All of the activities in the evaluation phase are standard activities. For a short description of the Evaluation phase concepts see Table 2.4.2 where the concepts are listed and defined.

Concept	Description
EVALUATION	Evaluated/checked implementation.
RESULTS	The outcome of the evaluated implementation.
SELF ASSESSMENT DOCUMENTS	Result of the examination of the security management by the organization of the process itself.
INTERNAL AUDIT	Result of the examination of the security management by the internal EDP auditor.
EXTERNAL AUDIT	Result of the examination of the security management by the external EDP auditor.
SECURITY INCIDENTS DOCUMENTS	Results of evaluating security events which is not part of the standard operation of a service and which causes, or may cause, an interruption to, or a reduction in, the quality of that service.

Table 2.4.2: Concept and definition evaluation sub-process Security management

Maintenance

It is necessary for the security to be maintained. Because of changes in the IT-infrastructure and changes in the organization itself security risks are bound to change over time. The maintenance of the security concerns both the maintenance of the security section of the service level agreements and the more detailed security plans.

The maintenance is based on the results of the Evaluation sub-process and insight in the changing risks. These activities will only produce proposals. The proposals serve as inputs for the plan sub-process and will go through the whole cycle or the proposals can be taken in the maintenance of the service level agreements. In both cases the proposals could lead to activities in the action plan. The actual changes will be carried by the Change Management process.

The activities that take place in the maintain sub-process are summed up in the following table (Table 2.5.1). The table contains the name of the (sub) activity and a short definition of the activity.

Activities	Sub-Activities	Descriptions
Maintain	Maintenance of Service level agreements	This is a process to keep the service level agreements in proper condition. The process ends with MAINTAINED SERVICE LEVEL AGREEMENTS.
	Maintenance of operational level agreements	This is a process to keep the operational level agreements in proper condition. The process ends with MAINTAINED OPERATIONAL LEVEL AGREEMENTS.
	Request for change to SLA and/or OLA	Request for a change to the SLA and/or OLA is formulated. This process ends with a REQUEST FOR CHANGE.
	Reporting	In this process the whole maintain implemented security policies process is documented in a specific way. This process ends with REPORTS.

Table 2.5.1: (Sub) activities and descriptions Maintenance sub-process ITIL Security Management

Figure 2.5.1 is the process-data diagram of the implementation sub-process. This picture shows the integration of the meta-process model (left) and the meta-data model (right). The dotted arrows indicate which concepts are created or adjusted in the activities of the implementation phase.

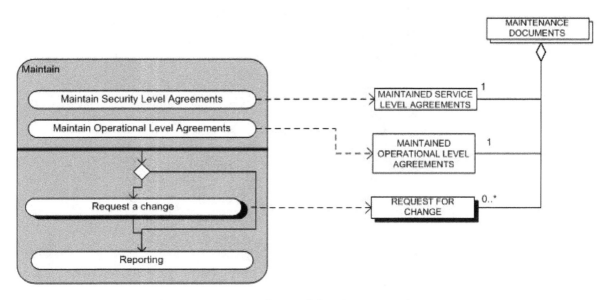

Figure 2.5.1: Process-data model Maintenance sub-process

The maintenance sub-process starts with the maintenance of the service level agreements and the maintenance of the operational level agreements. After these activities take place (in no particular order) and there is a request for a change the request for change activity will take place and after the request for change activity is concluded the reporting activity starts. If there is no request for a change then the reporting activity will start directly after the first two activities. The concepts in the meta-data model are created/ adjusted during the maintenance phase. For a list of the concepts and their definition take a look at table 2.5.2.

Concept	Description
MAINTENANCE DOCUMENTS	Agreements kept in proper condition.
MAINTAINED SERVICE LEVEL AGREEMENTS	Service Level Agreements(security paragraph) kept in proper condition.
MAINTAINED OPERATIONAL LEVEL AGREEMENTS	Operational Level Agreements kept in proper condition.
REQUEST FOR CHANGE	Form, or screen, used to record details of a request for a change to the SLA/OLA.

Table 2.5.2: Concept and definition Plan sub-process Security management

Complete Process-data Model

The following picture shows the complete process-data model of the Security Management process. This means that the complete meta-process model and the complete meta-data model and the integrations of the two models of the Security Management process are shown.

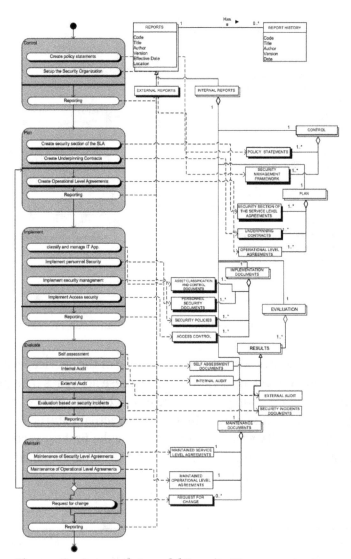

Figure 2.6.1: Process-data model Security Management process

Relations with Other ITIL Processes

The security Management Process, as stated in the introduction, has relations with almost all other ITIL-processes. These processes are:

- IT Customer Relationship Management

- Service Level Management

- Availability Management

- Capacity Management

- IT Service Continuity Management

- Configuration Management

- Release Management

- Incident Management & Service Desk

- Problem Management

- Change Management (ITSM)

Within these processes there are a couple of activities concerning security that have to take place. These activities are done as required. The concerning process and its process manager are responsible for these activities. However, the Security Management will give indications to the concerning process on how these (security specific) activities should be structured.

Example

Internal E-mail Policies.

The use of internal e-mail in an organization has a lot of security risks. So if an organization chooses to use e-mail as a means of communication, it is highly recommended that the organization implements a well thought out e-mail security plan/policies. In this example the ITIL security Management approach is used to implement e-mail policies in an organization.

First of all, the Security management team is formed and the guidelines of how the process should be carried out are formulated and made clear to all employees and providers concerned. These actions are carried out in the Control phase of the Security Management process.

The next step in the process to implement e-mail policies is the Planning phase. In the Planning phase, the policies are formulated. Besides the policies that are already written in the Service Level Agreements, the policies that are specific to e-mail security are formulated and added to the service level agreements. At the end of this phase the entire plan is formulated and is ready to be implemented.

The following phase in the process is the actual implementation of the e-mail policies, which is done according to the plan which was formulated in the preceding phase (Plan phase).

After the actual implementation the e-mail policies will be evaluated. In order to evaluate the implemented policies the organization will perform self-assessments, or have internal or external auditors review the policies for design and operating effectiveness.

The last phase is the maintenance phase. In the maintenance phase the implemented e-mail policies are maintained. The organization now knows which policies are properly implemented and are properly followed, which policies need more work in order to help the security plan of the organization, and if there are new policies that have to be implemented. At the end of this process the Request for Change are formulated (if needed) and the e-mail policies are properly maintained.

In order for the organization to keep its security plan up-to-date the organization will have to perform the security management process continuously. There is no end to this process; an organization can always better its security.

References

- Katsicas, Sokratis K. (2009). "35". In Vacca, John. Computer and Information Security Handbook. Morgan Kaufmann Publications. Elsevier Inc. p. 605. ISBN 978-0-12-374354-1.

- ISACA (2006). CISA Review Manual 2006. Information Systems Audit and Control Association. p. 85. ISBN 1-933284-15-3.

- Warren G. Kruse, Jay G. Heiser (2002). Computer forensics: incident response essentials. Addison-Wesley. p. 392. ISBN 0-201-70719-5.

- * Halder, D., & Jaishankar, K. (2011) Cyber crime and the Victimization of Women: Laws, Rights, and Regulations. Hershey, PA, USA: IGI Global. ISBN 978-1-60960-830-9

- "Cyber Warfare And The Crime Of Aggression: The Need For Individual Accountability On Tomorrow's Battlefield". Law.duke.edu. Retrieved 2011-11-10.

- "DHS: Secretary Napolitano and Attorney General Holder Announce Largest U.S. Prosecution of International Criminal Network Organized to Sexually Exploit Children". Dhs.gov. Retrieved 2011-11-10.

5

Cryptography: A Comprehensive Study

Encryption ensures that only the person meant to receive the data can make sense of it. Cryptography studies the techniques used for secure data communication. This chapter provides an in-depth study of the discipline while delving into topics like copyright infringement, enterprise information security architecture, network security, digital rights management etc.

Cryptography

Cryptography or cryptology is the practice and study of techniques for secure communication in the presence of third parties called adversaries. More generally, cryptography is about constructing and analyzing protocols that prevent third parties or the public from reading private messages; various aspects in information security such as data confidentiality, data integrity, authentication, and non-repudiation are central to modern cryptography. Modern cryptography exists at the intersection of the disciplines of mathematics, computer science, and electrical engineering. Applications of cryptography include ATM cards, computer passwords, and electronic commerce.

German Lorenz cipher machine, used in World War II to encrypt very-high-level general staff messages

Cryptography prior to the modern age was effectively synonymous with *encryption*, the conversion of information from a readable state to apparent nonsense. The originator of an encrypted message (Alice) shared the decoding technique needed to recover the original information only with intended recipients (Bob), thereby precluding unwanted persons (Eve) from doing the same. The cryptography literature often uses Alice ("A") for the sender, Bob ("B") for the intended recipient, and Eve ("eavesdropper") for the adversary. Since the development of rotor cipher machines in World War I and the advent of computers in World War II, the methods used to carry out cryptology have become increasingly complex and its application more widespread.

Modern cryptography is heavily based on mathematical theory and computer science practice; cryptographic algorithms are designed around computational hardness assumptions, making such algorithms hard to break in practice by any adversary. It is theoretically possible to break such a system, but it is infeasible to do so by any known practical means. These schemes are therefore termed computationally secure; theoretical advances, e.g., improvements in integer factorization algorithms, and faster computing technology require these solutions to be continually adapted. There exist information-theoretically secure schemes that provably cannot be broken even with unlimited computing power—an example is the one-time pad—but these schemes are more difficult to implement than the best theoretically breakable but computationally secure mechanisms.

The growth of cryptographic technology has raised a number of legal issues in the information age. Cryptography's potential for use as a tool for espionage and sedition has led many governments to classify it as a weapon and to limit or even prohibit its use and export. In some jurisdictions where the use of cryptography is legal, laws permit investigators to compel the disclosure of encryption keys for documents relevant to an investigation. Cryptography also plays a major role in digital rights management and copyright infringement of digital media.

Terminology

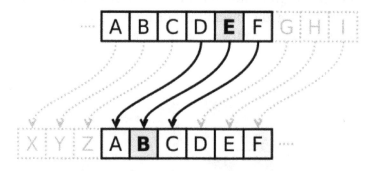

Alphabet shift ciphers are believed to have been used by Julius Caesar over 2,000 years ago. This is an example with k=3. In other words, the letters in the alphabet are shifted three in one direction to encrypt and three in the other direction to decrypt.

Until modern times, cryptography referred almost exclusively to *encryption*, which is the process of converting ordinary information (called plaintext) into unintelligible text (called ciphertext). Decryption is the reverse, in other words, moving from the unintelligible ciphertext back to plaintext. A *cipher* (or *cypher*) is a pair of algorithms that create the encryption and the reversing decryption. The detailed operation of a cipher is controlled both by the algorithm and in each instance by a "key". The key is a secret (ideally known only to the communicants), usually a short string of characters, which is needed to decrypt the ciphertext. Formally, a "cryptosystem" is the ordered list of elements of finite possible plaintexts, finite possible cyphertexts, finite possible keys, and the encryption and decryption algorithms which correspond to each key. Keys are important both formally and in actual practice, as ciphers without variable keys can be trivially broken with only the knowledge of the cipher used and are therefore useless (or even counter-productive) for most purposes. Historically, ciphers were often used directly for encryption or decryption without additional procedures such as authentication or integrity checks. There are two kinds of cryptosystems: symmetric and asymmetric. In symmetric systems the same key (the secret key) is used to encrypt and decrypt a message. Data manipulation in symmetric systems is faster than asymmetric systems as they generally use shorter key lengths. Asymmetric systems use a public key to encrypt a message and a private key to decrypt it. Use of asymmetric systems enhances the security of communication. Examples of asymmetric systems include RSA (Rivest-Shamir-Adleman), and ECC (Elliptic Curve Cryptography). Symmetric models include the commonly used AES (Advanced Encryption Standard) which replaced the older DES (Data Encryption Standard).

In colloquial use, the term "code" is often used to mean any method of encryption or concealment of meaning. However, in cryptography, *code* has a more specific meaning. It means the replacement of a unit of plaintext (i.e., a meaningful word or phrase) with a code word (for example, "wallaby" replaces "attack at dawn").

Cryptanalysis is the term used for the study of methods for obtaining the meaning of encrypted information without access to the key normally required to do so; i.e., it is the study of how to crack encryption algorithms or their implementations.

Some use the terms *cryptography* and *cryptology* interchangeably in English, while others (including US military practice generally) use *cryptography* to refer specifically to the use and practice of cryptographic techniques and *cryptology* to refer to the combined study of cryptography and cryptanalysis. English is more flexible than several other languages in which *cryptology* (done by cryptologists) is always used in the second sense above. RFC 2828 advises that steganography is sometimes included in cryptology.

The study of characteristics of languages that have some application in cryptography or cryptology (e.g. frequency data, letter combinations, universal patterns, etc.) is called cryptolinguistics.

History of Cryptography and Cryptanalysis

Before the modern era, cryptography was concerned solely with message confidentiality (i.e., encryption)—conversion of messages from a comprehensible form into an incomprehensible one and back again at the other end, rendering it unreadable by interceptors or eavesdroppers without secret knowledge (namely the key needed for decryption of that message). Encryption attempted to ensure secrecy in communications, such as those of spies, military leaders, and diplomats. In recent decades, the field has expanded beyond confidentiality concerns to include techniques for message integrity checking, sender/receiver identity authentication, digital signatures, interactive proofs and secure computation, among others.

Classic Cryptography

The earliest forms of secret writing required little more than writing implements since most people could not read. More literacy, or literate opponents, required actual cryptography. The main classical cipher types are transposition ciphers, which rearrange the order of letters in a message (e.g., 'hello world' becomes 'ehlol owrdl' in a trivially simple rearrangement scheme), and substitution ciphers, which systematically replace letters or groups of letters with other letters or groups of letters (e.g., 'fly at once' becomes 'gmz bu podf' by replacing each letter with the one following it in the Latin alphabet). Simple versions of either have never offered much confidentiality from enterprising opponents. An early substitution cipher was the Caesar cipher, in which each letter in the plaintext was replaced by a letter some fixed number of positions further down the alphabet. Suetonius reports that Julius Caesar used it with a shift of three to communicate with his generals. Atbash is an example of an early Hebrew cipher. The earliest known use of cryptography is some carved ciphertext on stone in Egypt (ca 1900 BCE), but this may have been done for the amusement of literate observers rather than as a way of concealing information.

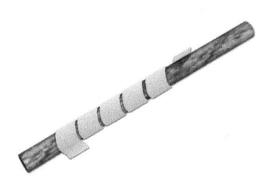

Reconstructed ancient Greek *scytale*, an early cipher device

The Greeks of Classical times are said to have known of ciphers (e.g., the scytale transposition cipher claimed to have been used by the Spartan military). Steganography (i.e., hiding even the existence of a message so as to keep it confidential) was also first developed in ancient times. An early example, from Herodotus, was a message tattooed on a slave's shaved head and concealed under the regrown hair. More modern examples of steganography include the use of invisible ink, microdots, and digital watermarks to conceal information.

In India, the 2000-year-old Kamasutra of Vātsyāyana speaks of two different kinds of ciphers called Kautiliyam and Mulavediya. In the Kautiliyam, the cipher letter substitutions are based on phonetic relations, such as vowels becoming consonants. In the Mulavediya, the cipher alphabet consists of pairing letters and using the reciprocal ones.

First page of a book by Al-Kindi which discusses encryption of messages

Ciphertexts produced by a classical cipher (and some modern ciphers) will reveal statistical information about the plaintext, and that information can often be used to break the cipher. After the discovery of frequency analysis, perhaps by the Arab mathematician and polymath Al-Kindi (also known as *Alkindus*) in the 9th century, nearly all such ciphers could be broken by an informed attacker. Such classical ciphers still enjoy popularity today, though mostly as puzzles. Al-Kindi wrote a book on cryptography entitled *Risalah fi Istikhraj al-Mu'amma* (*Manuscript for the Deciphering Cryptographic Messages*), which described the first known use of frequency analysis cryptanalysis techniques.

16th-century book-shaped French cipher machine, with arms of Henri II of France

Language letter frequencies may offer little help for some extended historical encryption techniques such as homophonic cipher that tend to flatten the frequency distribution. For those ciphers, language letter group (or n-gram) frequencies may provide an attack.

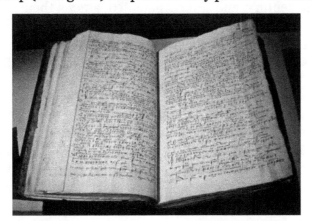

Enciphered letter from Gabriel de Luetz d'Aramon, French Ambassador to the Ottoman Empire, after 1546, with partial decipherment

Essentially all ciphers remained vulnerable to cryptanalysis using the frequency analysis technique until the development of the polyalphabetic cipher, most clearly by Leon Battista Alberti around the year 1467, though there is some indication that it was already known to Al-Kindi. Alberti's innovation was to use different ciphers (i.e., substitution alphabets) for various parts of a message (perhaps for each successive plaintext letter at the limit). He also invented what was probably the first automatic cipher device, a wheel which implemented a partial realization of his invention. In the polyalphabetic Vigenère cipher, encryption uses a *key word*, which controls letter substitution depending on which letter of the key word is used. In the mid-19th century Charles Babbage showed that the Vigenère cipher was vulnerable to Kasiski examination, but this was first published about ten years later by Friedrich Kasiski.

Although frequency analysis can be a powerful and general technique against many ciphers, encryption has still often been effective in practice, as many a would-be cryptanalyst was unaware of the technique. Breaking a message without using frequency analysis essentially required knowledge of the cipher used and perhaps of the key involved, thus making espionage, bribery, burglary, defection, etc., more attractive approaches to the cryptanalytically uninformed. It was finally explicitly recognized in the 19th century that secrecy of a cipher's algorithm is not a sensible nor practical safeguard of message security; in fact, it was further realized that any adequate cryptographic scheme (including ciphers) should remain secure even if the adversary fully understands the cipher algorithm itself. Security of the key used should alone be sufficient for a good cipher to maintain confidentiality under an attack. This fundamental principle was first explicitly stated in 1883 by Auguste Kerckhoffs and is generally called Kerckhoffs's Principle; alternatively and more bluntly, it was restated by Claude Shannon, the inventor of information theory and the fundamentals of theoretical cryptography, as *Shannon's Maxim*—'the enemy knows the system'.

Different physical devices and aids have been used to assist with ciphers. One of the earliest may have been the scytale of ancient Greece, a rod supposedly used by the Spartans as an aid for a transposition cipher. In medieval times, other aids were invented such as the cipher grille, which was also used for a kind of steganography. With the invention of polyalphabetic ciphers came more sophisticated aids such as Alberti's own cipher disk, Johannes Trithemius' tabula recta scheme, and Thomas Jefferson's multi cylinder (not publicly known, and reinvented independently by Bazeries around 1900). Many mechanical encryption/decryption devices were invented early in the 20th century, and several patented, among them rotor machines—famously including the Enigma machine used by the German government and military from the late 1920s and during World War II. The ciphers implemented by better quality examples of these machine designs brought about a substantial increase in cryptanalytic difficulty after WWI.

Computer Era

Cryptanalysis of the new mechanical devices proved to be both difficult and laborious. In the United Kingdom, cryptanalytic efforts at Bletchley Park during WWII spurred the development of more efficient means for carrying out repetitive tasks. This culminated in the development of the Colossus, the world's first fully electronic, digital, programmable computer, which assisted in the decryption of ciphers generated by the German Army's Lorenz SZ40/42 machine.

Just as the development of digital computers and electronics helped in cryptanalysis, it made possible much more complex ciphers. Furthermore, computers allowed for the encryption of any kind of data representable in any binary format, unlike classical ciphers which only encrypted written language texts; this was new and significant. Computer use has thus supplanted linguistic cryptography, both for cipher design and cryptanalysis. Many computer ciphers can be characterized by their operation on binary bit sequences (sometimes in groups or blocks), unlike classical and mechanical schemes, which generally manipulate traditional characters (i.e., letters and digits) directly. However, computers have also assisted cryptanalysis, which has compensated to some extent for increased cipher complexity. Nonetheless, good modern ciphers have stayed ahead of cryptanalysis; it is typically the case that use of a quality cipher is very efficient (i.e., fast and requiring few resources, such as memory or CPU capability), while breaking it requires an effort many orders of magnitude larger, and vastly larger than that required for any classical cipher, making cryptanalysis so inefficient and impractical as to be effectively impossible.

Extensive open academic research into cryptography is relatively recent; it began only in the mid-1970s. In recent times, IBM personnel designed the algorithm that became the Federal (i.e., US) Data Encryption Standard; Whitfield Diffie and Martin Hellman published their key agreement algorithm; and the RSA algorithm was published in Martin Gardner's *Scientific American* column. Since then, cryptography has become a widely used tool in communications, computer networks, and computer security generally. Some modern cryptographic techniques can only keep their keys secret if certain mathematical problems are intractable, such as the integer factorization or the discrete logarithm problems, so there are deep connections with abstract mathematics. There are very few cryptosystems that are proven to be unconditionally secure. The one-time pad is one. There are a few important ones that are proven secure under certain unproven assumptions. For example, the infeasibility of factoring extremely large integers is the basis for believing that RSA is secure, and some other systems, but even there, the proof is usually lost due to practical considerations. There are systems similar to RSA, such as one by Michael O. Rabin that is provably secure provided factoring n = pq is impossible, but the more practical system RSA has never been proved secure in this sense. The discrete logarithm problem is the basis for believing some other cryptosystems are secure, and again, there are related, less practical systems that are provably secure relative to the discrete log problem.

As well as being aware of cryptographic history, cryptographic algorithm and system designers must also sensibly consider probable future developments while working on their designs. For instance, continuous improvements in computer processing power have increased the scope of brute-force attacks, so when specifying key lengths, the required key lengths are similarly advancing. The potential effects of quantum computing are already being considered by some cryptographic system designers; the announced imminence of small implementations of these machines may be making the need for this preemptive caution rather more than merely speculative.

Essentially, prior to the early 20th century, cryptography was chiefly concerned with linguistic and lexicographic patterns. Since then the emphasis has shifted, and cryptography now makes extensive use of mathematics, including aspects of information theory, computational complexity, statistics, combinatorics, abstract algebra, number theory, and finite mathematics generally. Cryptography is also a branch of engineering, but an unusual one since it deals with active, intelligent, and malevolent opposition; other kinds of engineering (e.g., civil or chemical engineering) need deal only with neutral natural forces. There is also active research examining the relationship between cryptographic problems and quantum physics (quantum cryptography and quantum computer).

Modern Cryptography

The modern field of cryptography can be divided into several areas of study. The chief ones are discussed here.

Symmetric-key Cryptography

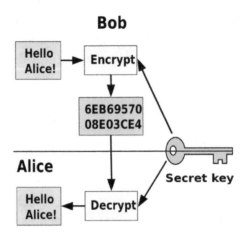

Symmetric-key cryptography, where a single key is used for encryption and decryption

Symmetric-key cryptography refers to encryption methods in which both the sender and receiver share the same key (or, less commonly, in which their keys are different, but related in an easily computable way). This was the only kind of encryption publicly known until June 1976.

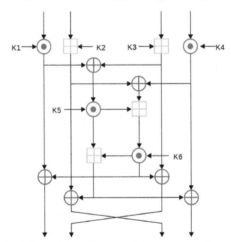

One round (out of 8.5) of the IDEA cipher, used in some versions of PGP for high-speed encryption of, for instance, e-mail

Symmetric key ciphers are implemented as either block ciphers or stream ciphers. A block cipher enciphers input in blocks of plaintext as opposed to individual characters, the input form used by a stream cipher.

The Data Encryption Standard (DES) and the Advanced Encryption Standard (AES) are block cipher designs that have been designated cryptography standards by the US government (though DES's designation was finally withdrawn after the AES was adopted). Despite its deprecation as an official standard, DES (especially its still-approved and much more secure triple-DES variant) remains quite popular; it is used across a wide range of applications, from ATM encryption to e-mail privacy and secure remote access. Many other block ciphers have been designed and released, with considerable variation in quality. Many have been thoroughly broken, such as FEAL.

Stream ciphers, in contrast to the 'block' type, create an arbitrarily long stream of key material, which is combined with the plaintext bit-by-bit or character-by-character, somewhat like the one-time pad. In a stream cipher, the output stream is created based on a hidden internal state that changes as the cipher operates. That internal state is initially set up using the secret key material. RC4 is a widely used stream cipher. Block ciphers can be used as stream ciphers.

Cryptographic hash functions are a third type of cryptographic algorithm. They take a message of any length as input, and output a short, fixed length hash, which can be used in (for example) a digital signature. For good hash functions, an attacker cannot find two messages that produce the same hash. MD4 is a long-used hash function that is now broken; MD5, a strengthened variant of MD4, is also widely used but broken in practice. The US National Security Agency developed the Secure Hash Algorithm series of MD5-like hash functions: SHA-0 was a flawed algorithm that the agency withdrew; SHA-1 is widely deployed and more secure than MD5, but cryptanalysts have identified attacks against it; the SHA-2 family improves on SHA-1, but it isn't yet widely deployed; and the US standards authority thought it "prudent" from a security perspective to develop a new standard to "significantly improve the robustness of NIST's overall hash algorithm toolkit." Thus, a hash function design competition was meant to select a new U.S. national standard, to be called SHA-3, by 2012. The competition ended on October 2, 2012 when the NIST announced that Keccak would be the new SHA-3 hash algorithm.

Message authentication codes (MACs) are much like cryptographic hash functions, except that a secret key can be used to authenticate the hash value upon receipt; this additional complication blocks an attack scheme against bare digest algorithms, and so has been thought worth the effort.

Public-key Cryptography

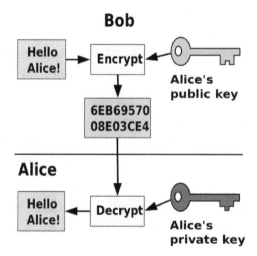

Public-key cryptography, where different keys are used for encryption and decryption

Symmetric-key cryptosystems use the same key for encryption and decryption of a message, though a message or group of messages may have a different key than others. A significant disadvantage of symmetric ciphers is the key management necessary to use them securely. Each distinct pair of communicating parties must, ideally, share a different key, and perhaps each ciphertext exchanged as well. The number of keys required increases as the square of the number of network members, which very quickly requires complex key management schemes to keep them all consistent and secret. The difficulty of securely establishing a secret key between two communicating parties, when a secure channel does not already exist between them, also presents a chicken-and-egg problem which is a considerable practical obstacle for cryptography users in the real world.

Whitfield Diffie and Martin Hellman, authors of the first published paper on public-key cryptography

In a groundbreaking 1976 paper, Whitfield Diffie and Martin Hellman proposed the notion of *public-key* (also, more generally, called *asymmetric key*) cryptography in which two different but mathematically related keys are used—a *public* key and a *private* key. A public key system is so constructed that calculation of one key (the 'private key') is computationally infeasible from the other (the 'public key'), even though they are necessarily related. Instead, both keys are generated secretly, as an interrelated pair. The historian David Kahn described public-key cryptography as "the most revolutionary new concept in the field since polyalphabetic substitution emerged in the Renaissance".

In public-key cryptosystems, the public key may be freely distributed, while its paired private key must remain secret. In a public-key encryption system, the *public key* is used for encryption, while the *private* or *secret key* is used for decryption. While Diffie and Hellman could not find such a system, they showed that public-key cryptography was indeed possible by presenting the Diffie–Hellman key exchange protocol, a solution that is now widely used in secure communications to allow two parties to secretly agree on a shared encryption key.

Diffie and Hellman's publication sparked widespread academic efforts in finding a practical public-key encryption system. This race was finally won in 1978 by Ronald Rivest, Adi Shamir, and Len Adleman, whose solution has since become known as the RSA algorithm.

The Diffie–Hellman and RSA algorithms, in addition to being the first publicly known examples of high quality public-key algorithms, have been among the most widely used. Others include the Cramer–Shoup cryptosystem, ElGamal encryption, and various elliptic curve techniques.

To much surprise, a document published in 1997 by the Government Communications Headquarters (GCHQ), a British intelligence organization, revealed that cryptographers at GCHQ had anticipated several academic developments. Reportedly, around 1970, James H. Ellis had conceived the principles of asymmetric key cryptography. In 1973, Clifford Cocks invented a solution that essentially resembles the RSA algorithm. And in 1974, Malcolm J. Williamson is claimed to have developed the Diffie–Hellman key exchange.

Padlock icon from the Firefox Web browser, which indicates that TLS, a public-key cryptography system, is in use.

Public-key cryptography can also be used for implementing digital signature schemes. A digital signature is reminiscent of an ordinary signature; they both have the characteristic of being easy for a user to produce, but difficult for anyone else to forge. Digital signatures can also be permanently tied to the content of the message being signed; they cannot then be 'moved' from one document to another, for any attempt will be detectable. In digital signature schemes, there are two algorithms: one for *signing*, in which a secret key is used to process the message (or a hash of the message, or both), and one for *verification*, in which the matching public key is used with the message to check the validity of the signature. RSA and DSA are two of the most popular digital signature schemes. Digital signatures are central to the operation of public key infrastructures and many network security schemes (e.g., SSL/TLS, many VPNs, etc.).

Public-key algorithms are most often based on the computational complexity of "hard" problems, often from number theory. For example, the hardness of RSA is related to the integer factorization problem, while Diffie–Hellman and DSA are related to the discrete logarithm problem. More recently, elliptic curve cryptography has developed, a system in which security is based on number theoretic problems involving elliptic curves. Because of the difficulty of the underlying problems, most public-key algorithms involve operations such as modular multiplication and exponentiation, which are much more computationally expensive than the techniques used in most block ciphers, especially with typical key sizes. As a result, public-key cryptosystems are commonly hybrid cryptosystems, in which a fast high-quality symmetric-key encryption algorithm is used for the message itself, while the relevant symmetric key is sent with the message, but encrypted using a public-key algorithm. Similarly, hybrid signature schemes are often used, in which a cryptographic hash function is computed, and only the resulting hash is digitally signed.

Cryptanalysis

Variants of the Enigma machine, implemented a complex electro-mechanical polyalphabetic cipher.

Variants of the Enigma machine, used by Germany's military and civil authorities from the late 1920s through World War II, implemented a complex electro-mechanical polyalphabetic cipher. Breaking and reading of the Enigma cipher at Poland's Cipher Bureau, for 7 years before the war, and subsequent decryption at Bletchley Park, was important to Allied victory.

The goal of cryptanalysis is to find some weakness or insecurity in a cryptographic scheme, thus permitting its subversion or evasion.

It is a common misconception that every encryption method can be broken. In connection with his WWII work at Bell Labs, Claude Shannon proved that the one-time pad cipher is unbreakable, provided the key material is truly random, never reused, kept secret from all possible attackers, and of equal or greater length than the message. Most ciphers, apart from the one-time pad, can be broken with enough computational effort by brute force attack, but the amount of effort needed may be exponentially dependent on the key size, as compared to the effort needed to make use of the cipher. In such cases, effective security could be achieved if it is proven that the effort required (i.e., "work factor", in Shannon's terms) is beyond the ability of any adversary. This means it must be shown that no efficient method (as opposed to the time-consuming brute force method) can be found to break the cipher. Since no such proof has been found to date, the one-time-pad remains the only theoretically unbreakable cipher.

There are a wide variety of cryptanalytic attacks, and they can be classified in any of several ways. A common distinction turns on what Eve (an attacker) knows and what capabilities are available. In a ciphertext-only attack, Eve has access only to the ciphertext (good modern cryptosystems are usually effectively immune to ciphertext-only attacks). In a known-plaintext attack, Eve has access to a ciphertext and its corresponding plaintext (or to many such pairs). In a chosen-plaintext attack, Eve may choose a plaintext and learn its corresponding ciphertext (perhaps many times); an example is gardening, used by the British during WWII. In a chosen-ciphertext attack, Eve may be able to *choose* ciphertexts and learn their corresponding plaintexts. Finally in a man-in-the-middle attack Eve gets in between Alice (the sender) and Bob (the recipient), accesses and modifies the traffic and then forwards it to the recipient. Also important, often overwhelmingly so, are mistakes (generally in the design or use of one of the protocols involved).

Poznań monument (*center*) to Polish cryptologists whose breaking of Germany's Enigma machine ciphers, beginning in 1932, altered the course of World War II

Cryptanalysis of symmetric-key ciphers typically involves looking for attacks against the block ciphers or stream ciphers that are more efficient than any attack that could be against a perfect cipher. For example, a simple brute force attack against DES requires one known plaintext and 2^{55} decryptions, trying approximately half of the possible keys, to reach a point at which chances are better than even that the key sought will have been found. But this may not be enough assurance; a linear cryptanalysis attack against DES requires 2^{43} known plaintexts and approximately 2^{43} DES operations. This is a considerable improvement on brute force attacks.

Public-key algorithms are based on the computational difficulty of various problems. The most famous of these is integer factorization (e.g., the RSA algorithm is based on a problem related to integer factoring), but the discrete logarithm problem is also important. Much public-key cryptanalysis concerns numerical algorithms for solving these computational problems, or some of them, efficiently (i.e., in a practical time). For instance, the best known algorithms for solving the elliptic curve-based version of discrete logarithm are much more time-consuming than the best known algorithms for factoring, at least for problems of more or less equivalent size. Thus, other things being equal, to achieve an equivalent strength of attack resistance, factoring-based encryption techniques must use larger keys than elliptic curve techniques. For this reason, public-key cryptosystems based on elliptic curves have become popular since their invention in the mid-1990s.

While pure cryptanalysis uses weaknesses in the algorithms themselves, other attacks on cryptosystems are based on actual use of the algorithms in real devices, and are called *side-channel attacks*. If a cryptanalyst has access to, for example, the amount of time the device took to encrypt a number of plaintexts or report an error in a password or PIN character, he may be able to use a timing attack to break a cipher that is otherwise resistant to analysis. An attacker might also study the pattern and length of messages to derive valuable information; this is known as traffic analysis and can be quite useful to an alert adversary. Poor administration of a cryptosystem, such as permitting too short keys, will make any system vulnerable, regardless of other virtues. And, of course, social engineering, and other attacks against the personnel who work with cryptosystems or the messages they handle (e.g., bribery, extortion, blackmail, espionage, torture, ...) may be the most productive attacks of all.

Cryptographic Primitives

Much of the theoretical work in cryptography concerns cryptographic *primitives*—algorithms with basic cryptographic properties—and their relationship to other cryptographic problems. More complicated cryptographic tools are then built from these basic primitives. These primitives provide fundamental properties, which are used to develop more complex tools called *cryptosystems* or *cryptographic protocols*, which guarantee one or more high-level security properties. Note however, that the distinction between cryptographic *primitives* and cryptosystems, is quite arbitrary; for example, the RSA algorithm is sometimes considered a cryptosystem, and sometimes a primitive. Typical examples of cryptographic primitives include pseudorandom functions, one-way functions, etc.

Cryptosystems

One or more cryptographic primitives are often used to develop a more complex algorithm, called a cryptographic system, or *cryptosystem*. Cryptosystems (e.g., El-Gamal encryption) are designed to provide particular functionality (e.g., public key encryption) while guaranteeing certain security properties (e.g., chosen-plaintext attack (CPA) security in the random oracle model). Cryptosystems use the properties of the underlying cryptographic primitives to support the system's security properties. Of course, as the distinction between primitives and cryptosystems is somewhat arbitrary, a sophisticated cryptosystem can be derived from a combination of several more primitive cryptosystems. In many cases, the cryptosystem's structure involves back and forth communication among two or more parties in space (e.g., between the sender of a secure message and its receiver) or across time (e.g., cryptographically protected backup data). Such cryptosystems are sometimes called *cryptographic protocols*.

Some widely known cryptosystems include RSA encryption, Schnorr signature, El-Gamal encryption, PGP, etc. More complex cryptosystems include electronic cash systems, signcryption systems, etc. Some more 'theoretical' cryptosystems include interactive proof systems, (like zero-knowledge proofs), systems for secret sharing, etc.

Until recently, most security properties of most cryptosystems were demonstrated using empirical techniques or using ad hoc reasoning. Recently, there has been considerable effort to develop formal techniques for establishing the security of cryptosystems; this has been generally called *provable security*. The general idea of provable security is to give arguments about the computational difficulty needed to compromise some security aspect of the cryptosystem (i.e., to any adversary).

The study of how best to implement and integrate cryptography in software applications is itself a distinct field.

Legal Issues

Prohibitions

Cryptography has long been of interest to intelligence gathering and law enforcement agencies. Secret communications may be criminal or even treasonous. Because of its facilitation of privacy, and the diminution of privacy attendant on its prohibition, cryptography is also of considerable interest to civil rights supporters. Accordingly, there has been a history of controversial legal issues surrounding cryptography, especially since the advent of inexpensive computers has made widespread access to high quality cryptography possible.

In some countries, even the domestic use of cryptography is, or has been, restricted. Until 1999, France significantly restricted the use of cryptography domestically, though it has since relaxed many of these rules. In China and Iran, a license is still required to use cryptography. Many countries have tight restrictions on the use of cryptography. Among the more restrictive are laws in Belarus, Kazakhstan, Mongolia, Pakistan, Singapore, Tunisia, and Vietnam.

In the United States, cryptography is legal for domestic use, but there has been much conflict over legal issues related to cryptography. One particularly important issue has been the export of cryptography and cryptographic software and hardware. Probably because of the importance of cryptanalysis in World War II and an expectation that cryptography would continue to be important for national security, many Western governments have, at some point, strictly regulated export of cryptography. After World War II, it was illegal in the US to sell or distribute encryption technology overseas; in fact, encryption was designated as auxiliary military equipment and put on the United States Munitions List. Until the development of the personal computer, asymmetric key algorithms (i.e., public key techniques), and the Internet, this was not especially problematic. However, as the Internet grew and computers became more widely available, high-quality encryption techniques became well known around the globe.

Export Controls

In the 1990s, there were several challenges to US export regulation of cryptography. After the source code for Philip Zimmermann's Pretty Good Privacy (PGP) encryption program found its way onto the Internet in June 1991, a complaint by RSA Security (then called RSA Data Security, Inc.) resulted in a lengthy criminal investigation of Zimmermann by the US Customs Service and the FBI, though no charges were ever filed. Daniel J. Bernstein, then a graduate student at UC Berkeley, brought a lawsuit against the US government challenging some aspects of the restrictions based on free speech grounds. The 1995 case Bernstein v. United States ultimately resulted in a 1999 decision that printed source code for cryptographic algorithms and systems was protected as free speech by the United States Constitution.

In 1996, thirty-nine countries signed the Wassenaar Arrangement, an arms control treaty that deals with the export of arms and "dual-use" technologies such as cryptography. The treaty stipulated that the use of cryptography with short key-lengths (56-bit for symmetric encryption, 512-bit for RSA) would no longer be export-controlled. Cryptography exports from the US became less strictly regulated as a consequence of a major relaxation in 2000; there are no longer very many restrictions on key sizes in US-exported mass-market software. Since this relaxation in US export restrictions, and because most personal computers connected to the Internet include US-sourced web browsers such as Firefox or Internet Explorer, almost every Internet user worldwide has potential access to quality cryptography via their browsers (e.g., via Transport Layer Security). The Mozilla Thunderbird and Microsoft Outlook E-mail client programs similarly can transmit and receive emails via TLS, and can send and receive email encrypted with S/MIME. Many Internet users don't realize that their basic application software contains such extensive cryptosystems. These browsers and email programs are so ubiquitous that even governments whose intent is to regulate civilian use of cryptography generally don't find it practical to do much to control distribution or use of cryptography of this quality, so even when such laws are in force, actual enforcement is often effectively impossible.

NSA Involvement

Another contentious issue connected to cryptography in the United States is the influence of the National Security Agency on cipher development and policy. The NSA was involved with the design of DES during its development at IBM and its consideration by the National Bureau of Standards as a possible Federal Standard for cryptography. DES was designed to be resistant to differential cryptanalysis, a powerful and general cryptanalytic technique known to the NSA and IBM, that became publicly known only when it was rediscovered in the late 1980s. According to Steven Levy, IBM discovered differential cryptanalysis, but kept the technique secret at the NSA's request. The technique became publicly known only when Biham and Shamir re-discovered and announced it some years later. The entire affair illustrates the difficulty of determining what resources and knowledge an attacker might actually have.

NSA headquarters in Fort Meade, Maryland

Another instance of the NSA's involvement was the 1993 Clipper chip affair, an encryption microchip intended to be part of the Capstone cryptography-control initiative. Clipper was widely criticized by cryptographers for two reasons. The cipher algorithm (called Skipjack) was then classified (declassified in 1998, long after the Clipper initiative lapsed). The classified cipher caused concerns that the NSA had deliberately made the cipher weak in order to assist its intelligence efforts. The whole initiative was also criticized based on its violation of Kerckhoffs's Principle, as the scheme included a special escrow key held by the government for use by law enforcement, for example in wiretaps.

Digital Rights Management

Cryptography is central to digital rights management (DRM), a group of techniques for technologically controlling use of copyrighted material, being widely implemented and deployed at the behest of some copyright holders. In 1998, U.S. President Bill Clinton signed the Digital Millennium Copyright Act (DMCA), which criminalized all production, dissemination, and use of certain cryptanalytic techniques and technology (now known or later discovered); specifically, those that could be used to circumvent DRM technological schemes. This had a noticeable impact on the cryptography research community since an argument can be made that *any* cryptanalytic research violated, or might violate, the DMCA. Similar statutes have since been enacted in several countries and regions, including the implementation in the EU Copyright Directive. Similar restrictions are called for by treaties signed by World Intellectual Property Organization member-states.

The United States Department of Justice and FBI have not enforced the DMCA as rigorously as had been feared by some, but the law, nonetheless, remains a controversial one. Niels Ferguson, a well-respected cryptography researcher, has publicly stated that he will not release some of his research into an Intel security design for fear of prosecution under the DMCA. Both Alan Cox (longtime number 2 in Linux kernel development) and Edward Felten (and some of his students at Princeton) have encountered problems related to the Act. Dmitry Sklyarov was arrested during a visit to the US from Russia, and jailed for five months pending trial for alleged violations of the DMCA arising from work he had done in Russia, where the work was legal. In 2007, the cryptographic keys responsible for Blu-ray and HD DVD content scrambling were discovered and released onto the Internet. In both cases, the MPAA sent out numerous DMCA takedown notices, and there was a massive Internet backlash triggered by the perceived impact of such notices on fair use and free speech.

Forced Disclosure of Encryption Keys

In the United Kingdom, the Regulation of Investigatory Powers Act gives UK police the powers to force suspects to decrypt files or hand over passwords that protect encryption keys. Failure to comply is an offense in its own right, punishable on conviction by a two-year jail sentence or up to five years in cases involving national security. Successful prosecutions have occurred under the Act; the first, in 2009, resulted in a term of 13 months' imprisonment. Similar forced disclosure laws in Australia, Finland, France, and India compel individual suspects under investigation to hand over encryption keys or passwords during a criminal investigation.

In the United States, the federal criminal case of United States v. Fricosu addressed whether a search warrant can compel a person to reveal an encryption passphrase or password. The Electronic Frontier Foundation (EFF) argued that this is a violation of the protection from self-incrimination given by the Fifth Amendment. In 2012, the court ruled that under the All Writs Act, the defendant was required to produce an unencrypted hard drive for the court.

In many jurisdictions, the legal status of forced disclosure remains unclear.

The 2016 FBI–Apple encryption dispute concerns the ability of courts in the United States to compel manufacturers' assistance in unlocking cell phones whose contents are cryptographically protected.

As a potential counter-measure to forced disclosure some cryptographic software supports plausible deniability, where the encrypted data is indistinguishable from unused random data (for example such as that of a drive which has been securely wiped).

Enterprise information Security Architecture

Enterprise information security architecture (EISA) is a part of enterprise architecture focusing on information security throughout the enterprise. The name implies a difference that may not exist between small/medium-sized businesses and larger organizations.

Overview

Enterprise information security architecture (EISA) is the practice of applying a comprehensive and rigorous method for describing a current and/or future structure and behavior for an organization's security processes, information security systems, personnel and organizational sub-units, so that they align with the organization's core goals and strategic direction. Although often associated strictly with information security technology, it relates more broadly to the security practice of business optimization in that it addresses business security architecture, performance management and security process architecture as well.

Enterprise information security architecture is becoming a common practice within the financial institutions around the globe. The primary purpose of creating an enterprise information security architecture is to ensure that business strategy and IT security are aligned. As such, enterprise information security architecture allows traceability from the business strategy down to the underlying technology.

Enterprise Information Security Architecture Topics

Positioning

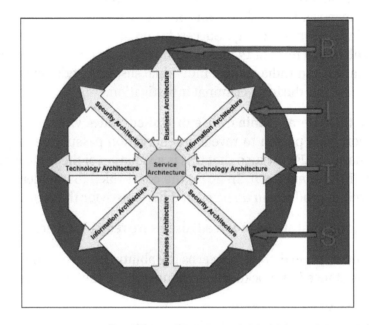

Enterprise information security architecture was first formally positioned by Gartner in their whitepaper called *"Incorporating Security into the Enterprise Architecture Process"*. This was published on 24 January 2006. Since this publication, security architecture has moved from being a silo based architecture to an enterprise focused solution that incorporates business, information and technology. The picture below represents a one-dimensional view of enterprise architecture as a service-oriented architecture. It also reflects the new addition to the enterprise architecture family called "Security". Business architecture, information architecture and technology architecture used to be called BIT for short. Now with security as part of the architecture family it has become BITS.

Security architectural change imperatives now include things like

- Business roadmaps
- Legislative and legal requirements
- Technology roadmaps
- Industry trends
- Risk trends
- Visionaries

Goals

- Provide structure, coherence and cohesiveness.

- Must enable business-to-security alignment.

- Defined top-down beginning with business strategy.

- Ensure that all models and implementations can be traced back to the business strategy, specific business requirements and key principles.

- Provide abstraction so that complicating factors, such as geography and technology religion, can be removed and reinstated at different levels of detail only when required.

- Establish a common "language" for information security within the organization

Methodology

The practice of enterprise information security architecture involves developing an architecture security framework to describe a series of "current", "intermediate" and "target" reference architectures and applying them to align programs of change. These frameworks detail the organizations, roles, entities and relationships that exist or should exist to perform a set of business processes. This framework will provide a rigorous taxonomy and ontology that clearly identifies what processes a business performs and detailed information about how those processes are executed and secured. The end product is a set of artifacts that describe in varying degrees of detail exactly what and how a business operates and what security controls are required. These artifacts are often graphical.

Given these descriptions, whose levels of detail will vary according to affordability and other practical considerations, decision makers are provided the means to make informed decisions about where to invest resources, where to realign organizational goals and processes, and what policies and procedures will support core missions or business functions.

A strong enterprise information security architecture process helps to answer basic questions like:

- What is the information security risk posture of the organization?

- Is the current architecture supporting and adding value to the security of the organization?

- How might a security architecture be modified so that it adds more value to the organization?

- Based on what we know about what the organization wants to accomplish in the future, will the current security architecture support or hinder that?

Implementing enterprise information security architecture generally starts with documenting the organization's strategy and other necessary details such as where and how it operates. The process then cascades down to documenting discrete core competencies, business processes, and how the organization interacts with itself and with external parties such as customers, suppliers, and government entities.

Having documented the organization's strategy and structure, the architecture process then flows down into the discrete information technology components such as:

- Organization charts, activities, and process flows of how the IT Organization operates

- Organization cycles, periods and timing

- Suppliers of technology hardware, software, and services

- Applications and software inventories and diagrams

- Interfaces between applications - that is: events, messages and data flows

- Intranet, Extranet, Internet, eCommerce, EDI links with parties within and outside of the organization

- Data classifications, Databases and supporting data models

- Hardware, platforms, hosting: servers, network components and security devices and where they are kept

- Local and wide area networks, Internet connectivity diagrams

Wherever possible, all of the above should be related explicitly to the organization's strategy, goals, and operations. The enterprise information security architecture will document the current state of the technical security components listed above, as well as an ideal-world desired future state (Reference Architecture) and finally a "Target" future state which is the result of engineering tradeoffs and compromises vs. the ideal. Essentially the result is a nested and interrelated set of models, usually managed and maintained with specialised software available on the market.

Such exhaustive mapping of IT dependencies has notable overlaps with both metadata in the general IT sense, and with the ITIL concept of the configuration management database. Maintaining the accuracy of such data can be a significant challenge.

Along with the models and diagrams goes a set of best practices aimed at securing adaptability, scalability, manageability etc. These systems engineering best practices are not unique to enterprise information security architecture but are essential to its success nonetheless. They involve such things as componentization, asynchronous communication between major components, standardization of key identifiers and so on.

Successful application of enterprise information security architecture requires appropriate positioning in the organization. The analogy of city-planning is often invoked in this connection, and is instructive.

An intermediate outcome of an architecture process is a comprehensive inventory of business security strategy, business security processes, organizational charts, technical security inventories, system and interface diagrams, and network topologies, and the explicit relationships between them. The inventories and diagrams are merely tools that support decision making. But this is not sufficient. It must be a living process.

The organization must design and implement a process that ensures continual movement from the current state to the future state. The future state will generally be a combination of one or more

- Closing gaps that are present between the current organization strategy and the ability of the IT security dimensions to support it

- Closing gaps that are present between the desired future organization strategy and the ability of the security dimensions to support it

- Necessary upgrades and replacements that must be made to the IT security architecture based on supplier viability, age and performance of hardware and software, capacity issues, known or anticipated regulatory requirements, and other issues not driven explicitly by the organization's functional management.

- On a regular basis, the current state and future state are redefined to account for evolution of the architecture, changes in organizational strategy, and purely external factors such as changes in technology and customer/vendor/government requirements, and changes to both internal and external threat landscapes over time.

High-level Security Architecture Framework

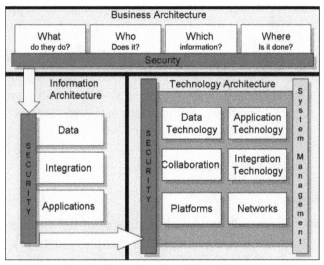

Huxham Security Framework

Enterprise information security architecture frameworks is only a subset of enterprise architecture frameworks. If we had to simplify the conceptual abstraction of enterprise information security architecture within a generic framework, the picture on the right would be acceptable as a high-level conceptual security architecture framework.

Other open enterprise architecture frameworks are:

- SABSA framework and methodology

- The U.S. Department of Defense (DoD) Architecture Framework (DoDAF)

- Extended Enterprise Architecture Framework (E2AF) from the Institute For Enterprise Architecture Developments.

- Federal Enterprise Architecture of the United States Government (FEA)

- Capgemini's Integrated Architecture Framework

- The UK Ministry of Defence (MOD) Architecture Framework (MODAF)

- NIH Enterprise Architecture Framework

- Open Security Architecture

- Information Assurance Enterprise Architectural Framework (IAEAF)

- Service-Oriented Modeling Framework (SOMF)

- The Open Group Architecture Framework (TOGAF)

- Zachman Framework

Relationship to Other IT Disciplines

Enterprise information security architecture is a key component of the information security technology governance process at any organization of significant size. More and more companies are implementing a formal enterprise security architecture process to support the governance and management of IT.

However, as noted in the opening paragraph of this article it ideally relates more broadly to the practice of business optimization in that it addresses business security architecture, performance management and process security architecture as well. Enterprise Information Security Architecture is also related to IT security portfolio management and metadata in the enterprise IT sense.

Network Security

Network security consists of the policies and practices adopted to prevent and monitor unauthorized access, misuse, modification, or denial of a computer network and network-accessible resources. Network security involves the authorization of access to data in a network, which is controlled by the network administrator. Users choose or are assigned an ID and password or other authenticating information that allows them access to information and programs within their authority. Network security covers a variety of computer networks, both public and private, that are used in everyday jobs; conducting transactions and communications among businesses, government agencies and individuals. Networks can be private, such as within a company, and others which might be open to public access. Network security is involved in organizations, enterprises, and other types of institutions. It does as its title explains: It secures the network, as well as protecting and overseeing operations being done. The most common and simple way of protecting a network resource is by assigning it a unique name and a corresponding password.

Network Security concepts

Network security starts with authenticating, commonly with a username and a password. Since this requires just one detail authenticating the user name—i.e., the password—this is sometimes termed one-factor authentication. With two-factor authentication, something the user 'has' is also used (e.g., a security token or 'dongle', an ATM card, or a mobile phone); and with three-factor authentication, something the user 'is' also used (e.g., a fingerprint or retinal scan).

Once authenticated, a firewall enforces access policies such as what services are allowed to be accessed by the network users. Though effective to prevent unauthorized access, this component may fail to check potentially harmful content such as computer worms or Trojans being transmitted over the network. Anti-virus software or an intrusion prevention system (IPS) help detect and inhibit the action of such malware. An anomaly-based intrusion detection system may also monitor the network like wireshark traffic and may be logged for audit purposes and for later high-level analysis.

Communication between two hosts using a network may be encrypted to maintain privacy.

Honeypots, essentially decoy network-accessible resources, may be deployed in a network as surveillance and early-warning tools, as the honeypots are not normally accessed for legitimate purposes. Techniques used by the attackers that attempt to compromise these decoy resources are studied during and after an attack to keep an eye on new exploitation techniques. Such analysis may be used to further tighten security of the actual network being protected by the honeypot. A honeypot can also direct an attacker's attention away from legitimate servers. A honeypot encourages attackers to spend their time and energy on the decoy server while distracting their attention from the data on the real server. Similar to a honeypot, a honeynet is a network set up with intentional vulnerabilities. Its purpose is also to invite attacks so that the attacker's methods can be studied and that information can be used to increase network security. A honeynet typically contains one or more honeypots.

Security Management

Security management for networks is different for all kinds of situations. A home or small office may only require basic security while large businesses may require high-maintenance and advanced software and hardware to prevent malicious attacks from hacking and spamming.

Types of Attacks

Networks are subject to attacks from malicious sources. Attacks can be from two categories: "Passive" when a network intruder intercepts data traveling through the network, and "Active" in which an intruder initiates commands to disrupt the network's normal operation.

Types of attacks include:

- Passive
  - o Network
    - ☐ Wiretapping
    - ☐ Port scanner

☐ Idle scan

- Active

  o Denial-of-service attack

  o DNS spoofing

  o Man in the middle

  o ARP poisoning

  o VLAN hopping

  o Smurf attack

  o Buffer overflow

  o Heap overflow

  o Format string attack

  o SQL injection

  o Phishing

  o Cross-site scripting

  o CSRF

  o Cyber-attack

Digital Rights Management

Digital rights management (DRM) schemes are various access control technologies that are used to restrict usage of proprietary hardware and copyrighted works. DRM technologies try to control the use, modification, and distribution of copyrighted works (such as software and multimedia content), as well as systems within devices that enforce these policies.

The use of digital rights management is not universally accepted. Proponents of DRM argue that it is necessary to prevent intellectual property from being copied freely, just as physical locks are needed to prevent personal property from being stolen, that it can help the copyright holder maintain artistic control, and that it can ensure continued revenue streams. Those opposed to DRM contend there is no evidence that DRM helps prevent copyright infringement, arguing instead that it serves only to inconvenience legitimate customers, and that DRM helps big business stifle innovation and competition. Furthermore, works can become permanently inaccessible if the DRM scheme changes or if the service is discontinued. DRM can also restrict users from exercising their legal rights under the copyright law, such as backing up copies of CDs or DVDs, lending materials out through a library, accessing works in the public domain, or using copyrighted materials for research and education under the fair use doctrine, and under French law. The Electronic Frontier Foundation (EFF) and the Free Software Foundation (FSF) consider the use of DRM systems to be an anti-competitive practice.

Worldwide, many laws have been created which criminalize the circumvention of DRM, communication about such circumvention, and the creation and distribution of tools used for such circumvention. Such laws are part of the United States' Digital Millennium Copyright Act, and the European Union's Copyright Directive, (the French DADVSI is an example of a member state of the European Union ("EU") implementing the directive).

The term *DRM* is also sometimes referred to as "copy protection", "technical protection measures", "copy prevention", or "copy control", although the correctness of doing so is disputed.

Introduction

The advent of digital media and analog-to-digital conversion technologies (especially those that are usable on mass-market general-purpose personal computers) has vastly increased the concerns of copyright-owning individuals and organizations. These concerns are particularly prevalent within the music and movie industries, because these sectors are partly or wholly dependent on the revenue generated from such works. While analog media inevitably loses quality with each copy generation, and in some cases even during normal use, digital media files may be duplicated an unlimited number of times with no degradation in the quality of subsequent copies.

The advent of personal computers as household appliances has made it convenient for consumers to convert media (which may or may not be copyrighted) originally in a physical, analog or broadcast form into a universal, digital form (this process is called ripping) for portability or viewing later. This, combined with the Internet and popular file-sharing tools, has made unauthorized distribution of copies of copyrighted digital media (also called digital piracy) much easier.

DRM technologies enable content publishers to enforce their own access policies on content, such as restrictions on copying or viewing. These technologies have been criticized for restricting individuals from copying or using the content legally, such as by fair use. DRM is in common use by the entertainment industry (e.g., audio and video publishers). Many online music stores, such as Apple's iTunes Store, and e-book publishers and vendors, such as OverDrive, also use DRM, as do cable and satellite service operators, to prevent unauthorized use of content or services. However, Apple dropped DRM from all iTunes music files around 2009.

In recent years the industry expanded the usage of DRM to even traditional hardware products, examples are Keurig's coffeemakers, Philips' light bulbs, mobile device power chargers, and John Deere's tractors. For instance, tractor companies try to prevent the DIY repairing by the owning farmers under usage of DRM-laws as DMCA.

Common DRM Techniques

Digital Rights Management Techniques include:

- Restrictive Licensing Agreements: The access to digital materials, copyright and public domain is controlled. Some restrictive licenses are imposed on consumers as a condition of entering a website or when downloading software.

- Encryption, Scrambling of expressive material and embedding of a tag: This technology is designed to control access and reproduction of information. This includes backup copies for personal use.

Technologies

DRM and Computer Games

Limited Install Activations

Computer games sometimes use DRM technologies to limit the number of systems the game can be installed on by requiring authentication with an online server. Most games with this restriction allow three or five installs, although some allow an installation to be 'recovered' when the game is uninstalled. This not only limits users who have more than three or five computers in their homes (seeing as the rights of the software developers allow them to limit the number of installations), but can also prove to be a problem if the user has to unexpectedly perform certain tasks like upgrading operating systems or reformatting the computer's hard drive, tasks which, depending on how the DRM is implemented, count a game's subsequent reinstall as a new installation, making the game potentially unusable after a certain period even if it is only used on a single computer.

In mid-2008, the publication of *Mass Effect* marked the start of a wave of titles primarily making use of SecuROM for DRM and requiring authentication with a server. The use of the DRM scheme in 2008's *Spore* backfired and there were protests, resulting in a considerable number of users seeking an unlicensed version instead. This backlash against the three-activation limit was a significant factor in *Spore* becoming the most pirated game in 2008, with TorrentFreak compiling a "top 10" list with *Spore* topping the list. However, Tweakguides concluded that the presence of intrusive DRM does not appear to increase the cracking of a game, noting that other games on the list such as *Call of Duty 4*, *Assassin's Creed* and *Crysis* use SafeDisc DRM, which has no install limits and no online activation. Additionally, other video games that use intrusive DRM such as *BioShock*, *Crysis Warhead*, and *Mass Effect*, do not appear on the list.

Persistent Online Authentication

Many mainstream publishers continued to rely on online DRM throughout the later half of 2008 and early 2009, including Electronic Arts, Ubisoft, Valve, and Atari, *The Sims 3* being a notable exception in the case of Electronic Arts. Ubisoft broke with the tendency to use online DRM in late 2008, with the release of *Prince of Persia* as an experiment to "see how truthful people really are" regarding the claim that DRM was inciting people to use illegal copies. Although Ubisoft has not commented on the results of the "experiment", Tweakguides noted that two torrents on Mininova had over 23,000 people downloading the game within 24 hours of its release.

Ubisoft formally announced a return to online authentication on 9 February 2010, through its Uplay online gaming platform, starting with *Silent Hunter 5*, *The Settlers 7*, and *Assassin's Creed II*. *Silent Hunter 5* was first reported to have been compromised within 24 hours of release, but users of the cracked version soon found out that only early parts of the game were playable. The Uplay system works by having the installed game on the local PCs incomplete and then continuously downloading parts of the game-code from Ubisoft's servers as the game progresses. It was more than a month after the PC release in the first week of April that software was released that could bypass Ubisoft's DRM in *Assassin's Creed II*. The software did this by emulating a Ubisoft server for the game. Later that month, a real crack was released that was able to remove the connection requirement altogether.

In early March 2010, the Uplay servers suffered a period of inaccessibility due to a large-scale DDoS attack, causing around 5% of game owners to become locked out of playing their game. The company later credited owners of the affected games with a free download, and there has been no further downtime.

Other developers, such as Blizzard Entertainment are also shifting to a strategy where most of the game logic is on the "side" or taken care of by the servers of the game maker. Blizzard uses this strategy for its game Diablo III and Electronic Arts used this same strategy with their reboot of SimCity, the necessity of which has been questioned.

Software Tampering

Bohemia Interactive have used a form of technology since *Operation Flashpoint: Cold War Crisis*, wherein if the game copy is suspected of being unauthorized, annoyances like guns losing their accuracy or the players being turned into a bird are introduced.

Croteam, the company that released *Serious Sam 3: BFE* in November 2011, implemented a different form of DRM wherein, instead of displaying error messages that stop the illicit version of the game from running, it causes a special invincible foe in the game to appear and constantly attack the player until he or she is killed.

Product Keys

One of the oldest and least complicated DRM protection methods for the computer games is a product key, a typically alphanumerical serial number used to represent a license to a particular piece of software. During the installation process for the software, the user is asked to input the key; if the key correctly corresponds to a valid license (typically via internal algorithms), the key is accepted, and installation can continue. In modern practice, product keys are typically combined with other DRM practices (such as online "activation"), as the software could be cracked to run without a product key, or "keygen" programs could be developed to generate keys that would be accepted.

DRM and Documents

Enterprise digital rights management (E-DRM or ERM) is the application of DRM technology to the control of access to corporate documents such as Microsoft Word, PDF, and AutoCAD files, emails, and intranet web pages rather than to the control of consumer media. E-DRM, now more commonly referenced as IRM (Information Rights Management), is generally intended to prevent the unauthorized use (such as industrial or corporate espionage or inadvertent release) of proprietary documents. IRM typically integrates with content management system software but corporations such as Samsung Electronics also develop their own custom DRM systems.

DRM has been used by organizations such as the British Library in its secure electronic delivery service to permit worldwide access to substantial numbers of rare (and in many cases unique) documents which, for legal reasons, were previously only available to authorized individuals actually visiting the Library's document centre at Boston Spa in England.

DRM and E-books

Electronic books read on a personal computer, or an e-book reader or e-reader app typically use DRM technology to limit copying, printing, and sharing of e-books. E-books (alternatively spelled "ebooks") are usually limited to be used on a limited number of reading devices, and some e-publishers prevent any copying or printing. Some commentors believe DRM makes e-book publishing complex.

As of August 2012, there are five main e-book formats: EPUB, KF8, Mobipocket, PDF, and Topaz. The Amazon Kindle uses KF8, Mobipocket, and Topaz; it also supports native PDF format e-books and native PDF files. Other e-book readers mostly use EPUB format e-books, but with differing DRM schemes.

There are four main e-book DRM schemes in common use today, one each from Adobe, Amazon, Apple, and the Marlin Trust Management Organization (MTMO).

- Adobe's ADEPT DRM is applied to EPUBs and PDFs, and can be read by several third-party e-book readers, as well as Adobe Digital Editions (ADE) software. Barnes & Noble uses a DRM technology provided by Adobe, applied to EPUBs and the older PDB (Palm OS) format e-books. In 2014, Adobe announced a new DRM scheme to replace the old one, to become available as soon as March 2014.

- Amazon's DRM is an adaption of the original Mobipocket encryption and is applied to Amazon's .azw4, KF8, and Mobipocket format e-books. Topaz format e-books have their own encryption system.

- Apple's FairPlay DRM is applied to EPUBs and can currently only be read by Apple's iBooks app on iOS devices and Mac OS computers.

- The Marlin DRM was developed and is maintained in an open industry group known as the Marlin Developer Community (MDC) and is licensed by MTMO. (Marlin was founded by five companies, Intertrust, Panasonic, Philips, Samsung, and Sony.) The Kno online textbook publisher uses Marlin to protect e-books it sells in the EPUB format. These books can be read on the Kno App for iOS and Android.

In one instance of DRM that caused a rift with consumers, Amazon.com in July 2009, remotely deleted purchased copies of George Orwell's *Animal Farm* (1945) and *Nineteen Eighty-Four* (1949) from customers' Amazon Kindles after providing them a refund for the purchased products. Commentors have widely described these actions as Orwellian and have compared Amazon to Big Brother from Orwell's *Nineteen Eighty-Four*. After Amazon CEO Jeff Bezos issued a public apology, the Free Software Foundation wrote that this was just one more example of the excessive power Amazon has to remotely censor what people read through its software, and called upon Amazon to free its e-book reader and drop DRM. Amazon then revealed the reason behind its deletion: the e-books in question were unauthorized reproductions of Orwell's works, which were not within the public domain and to which the company that published and sold them on Amazon's service had no rights.

Websites - such as library.nu (shut down by court order on February 15, 2012), BookFi, Book-Finder, Library Genesis, and Science Hub - have emerged which allow downloading e-books by violating copyright.

DRM and Film

An early example of a DRM system is the Content Scrambling System (CSS) employed by the DVD Forum on film DVDs circa 1996. CSS uses an encryption algorithm to encrypt content on the DVD disc. Manufacturers of DVD players must license this technology and implement it in their devices so that they can decrypt the encrypted content to play it. The CSS license agreement includes restrictions on how the DVD content is played, including what outputs are permitted and how such permitted outputs are made available. This keeps the encryption intact as the video material is played out to a TV.

In 1999, Jon Lech Johansen released an application called DeCSS, which allowed a CSS-encrypted DVD to play on a computer running the Linux operating system, at a time when no licensed DVD player application for Linux had yet been created. The legality of DeCSS is questionable: one of the authors has been the subject of a lawsuit, and reproduction of the keys themselves is subject to restrictions as illegal numbers.

Also in 1999, Microsoft released Windows Media DRM, which read instructions from media files in a rights management language that stated what the user may do with the media. The language can define how many times the media file can be played, and whether or not it can be burned to a CD, forwarded, printed, or saved to the local disk. Later versions of Windows Media DRM also allow producers to declare whether or not the user may transfer the media file to other devices, to implement music subscription services that make downloaded files unplayable after subscriptions are cancelled, and to implement regional lockout.

The Microsoft operating system, Windows Vista, contains a DRM system called the Protected Media Path, which contains the Protected Video Path (PVP). PVP tries to stop DRM-restricted content from playing while unsigned software is running, in order to prevent the unsigned software from accessing the content. Additionally, PVP can encrypt information during transmission to the monitor or the graphics card, which makes it more difficult to make unauthorized recordings.

Advanced Access Content System (AACS) is a DRM system for HD DVD and Blu-ray Discs developed by the AACS Licensing Administrator, LLC (AACS LA), a consortium that includes Disney, IBM, Intel, Microsoft, Matsushita (Panasonic), Sony, Toshiba, and Warner Brothers. In December 2006, hackers published a process key online, which enabled unrestricted access to AACS-protected HD DVD content. After the cracked keys were revoked, further cracked keys were released.

Marlin (DRM) is a technology that is developed and maintained in an open industry group known as the Marlin Developer Community (MDC) and licensed by the Marlin Trust Management Organization (MTMO). Founded in 2005, by five companies: Intertrust, Panasonic, Philips, Samsung, and Sony, Marlin DRM has been deployed in multiple places around the world. In Europe, Philips

NetTVs implement Marlin DRM. Also in Europe, Marlin DRM is required in such industry groups as the Open IPTV Forum and national initiatives such as HDForum in France, Tivu in Italy, and YouView in the UK, and which are starting to see broad deployments. In Japan, the acTVila IPTV service uses Marlin to encrypt video streams, which are permitted to be recorded on a DVR in the home.

OMA DRM is a system invented by the Open Mobile Alliance, whose members represent information technology companies (e.g., IBM and Microsoft), mobile phone network operators (e.g., Cingular, Deutsche Telekom, Orange, O2, and Vodafone), mobile phone manufacturers (e.g., LG, Motorola, Samsung, and Sony), mobile system manufacturers (e.g., Ericsson and Openwave).

DRM and Music

Audio CDs

Discs with DRM schemes are not standards-compliant Compact Discs (CDs) but are rather CD-ROM media. Therefore, they all lack the CD logotype found on discs which follow the standard (known as Red Book). These CDs cannot be played on all CD players or personal computers. Personal computers running Microsoft Windows sometimes even crash when attempting to play the CDs.

In 2005, Sony BMG introduced new DRM technology which installed DRM software on users' computers without clearly notifying the user or requiring confirmation. Among other things, the installed software included a rootkit, which created a severe security vulnerability others could exploit. When the nature of the DRM involved was made public much later, Sony BMG initially minimized the significance of the vulnerabilities its software had created, but was eventually compelled to recall millions of CDs, and released several attempts to patch the surreptitiously included software to at least remove the rootkit. Several class action lawsuits were filed, which were ultimately settled by agreements to provide affected consumers with a cash payout or album downloads free of DRM.

Sony BMG's DRM software actually had only a limited ability to prevent copying, as it affected only playback on Windows computers, not on other equipment. Even on the Windows platform, users regularly bypassed the restrictions. And, while the Sony BMG DRM technology created fundamental vulnerabilities in customers' computers, parts of it could be trivially bypassed by holding down the "shift" key while inserting the CD, or by disabling the autorun feature. In addition, audio tracks could simply be played and re-recorded, thus completely bypassing all the DRM (this is known as the analog hole). Sony BMG's first two attempts at releasing a patch which would remove the DRM software from users' computers failed.

In January 2007, EMI stopped publishing audio CDs with DRM, stating that "the costs of DRM do not measure up to the results." Following EMI, Sony BMG was the last publisher to abolish DRM completely, and audio CDs containing DRM are no longer released by the four largest commercial record label companies.

Internet Music

Many internet music stores employ DRM to restrict usage of music purchased and downloaded.

- Prior to 2009, Apple's iTunes Store utilized the FairPlay DRM system for music. Apple did not license its DRM to other companies, so only Apple devices and Apple's QuickTime media player could play iTunes music. In May 2007, EMI tracks became available in *iTunes Plus* format at a higher price point. These tracks were higher quality (256 kbit/s) and DRM free. In October 2007, the cost of iTunes Plus tracks was lowered to US$0.99. In April 2009, all iTunes music became available completely DRM-free. (Videos sold and rented through iTunes, as well as iOS Apps, however, were to continue using Apple's FairPlay DRM.)

- Napster music store offers a subscription-based approach to DRM alongside permanent purchases. Users of the subscription service can download and stream an unlimited amount of music transcoded to Windows Media Audio (WMA) while subscribed to the service. But when the subscription period lapses, all the downloaded music is unplayable until the user renews his or her subscription. Napster also charges users who wish to use the music on their portable device an additional $5 per month. In addition, Napster gives users the option of paying an additional $0.99 per track to burn it to CD or for the song to never expire. Music bought through Napster can be played on players carrying the Microsoft PlaysForSure logo (which, notably, do not include iPods or even Microsoft's own Zune). As of June 2009, Napster is offering DRM free MP3 music, which can be played on iPhones and iPods.

- Wal-Mart Music Downloads, another music download store, charges $0.94 per track for all non-sale downloads. All Wal-Mart downloads are able to be played on any Windows PlaysForSure marked product. The music does play on the SanDisk's Sansa mp3 player, for example, but must be copied to the player's internal memory. It cannot be played through the player's microSD card slot, which is a problem that many users of the mp3 player experience.

- Sony operated a music download service called "Connect" which used Sony's proprietary OpenMG DRM technology. Music downloaded from this store (usually via Sony's SonicStage software) was only playable on computers running Microsoft Windows and Sony hardware (including the PSP and some Sony Ericsson phones).

- Kazaa is one of a few services offering a subscription-based pricing model. However, music downloads from the Kazaa website are DRM-protected, and can only be played on computers or portable devices running Windows Media Player, and only as long as the customer remains subscribed to Kazaa.

The various services are currently not interoperable, though those that use the same DRM system (for instance the several Windows Media DRM format stores, including Napster, Kazaa and Yahoo Music) all provide songs that can be played side-by-side through the same player program. Almost all stores require client software of some sort to be downloaded, and some also need plug-ins. Several colleges and universities, such as Rensselaer Polytechnic Institute, have made arrangements with assorted Internet music suppliers to provide access (typically DRM-restricted) to music files for their students, to less than universal popularity, sometimes making payments from student activity fee funds. One of the problems is that the music becomes unplayable after leaving school unless the student continues to pay individually. Another is that few of these vendors are compatible with the most common portable music player, the Apple iPod. The Gowers Review of Intellectual Property (to HMG in the UK; 141 pages, 40+ specific recommendations) has taken note of the incompatibilities, and suggests (Recommendations 8—12) that there be explicit fair dealing exceptions to copyright allowing libraries to copy and format-shift between DRM schemes, and further allowing end users to do the same privately. If adopted, some acrimony may decrease.

Although DRM is prevalent for Internet music, some online music stores such as eMusic, Dogmazic, Amazon, and Beatport, do not use DRM despite encouraging users to avoid sharing music. Major labels have begun releasing more music without DRM. Eric Bangeman suggests in Ars Technica that this is because the record labels are "slowly beginning to realize that they can't have DRMed music and complete control over the online music market at the same time... One way to break the cycle is to sell music that is playable on any digital audio player. eMusic does exactly that, and their surprisingly extensive catalog of non-DRMed music has vaulted it into the number two online music store position behind the iTunes Store." Apple's Steve Jobs called on the music industry to eliminate DRM in an open letter titled Thoughts on Music. Apple's iTunes Store will start to sell DRM-free 256 kbit/s (up from 128 kbit/s) AAC encoded music from EMI for a premium price (this has since reverted to the standard price).

In March 2007, Musicload.de, one of Europe's largest internet music retailers, announced their position strongly against DRM. In an open letter, Musicload stated that three out of every four calls to their customer support phone service are as a result of consumer frustration with DRM.

Mobile Ring Tones

The Open Mobile Alliance created a standard for interoperable DRM on mobile devices. The first version of OMA DRM consisted of a simple rights management language and was widely used to protect mobile phone ringtones from being copied from the phone to other devices. Later versions expanded the rights management language to similar expressiveness as Fairplay, but did not become widely used.

DRM and Television

The CableCard standard is used by cable television providers in the United States to restrict content to services to which the customer has subscribed.

The broadcast flag concept was developed by Fox Broadcasting in 2001, and was supported by the MPAA and the U.S. Federal Communications Commission (FCC). A ruling in May 2005, by a United States courts of appeals held that the FCC lacked authority to impose it on the TV industry in the US. It required that all HDTVs obey a stream specification determining whether a stream can be recorded. This could block instances of fair use, such as time-shifting. It achieved more success elsewhere when it was adopted by the Digital Video Broadcasting Project (DVB), a consortium of about 250 broadcasters, manufacturers, network operators, software developers, and regulatory bodies from about 35 countries involved in attempting to develop new digital TV standards.

An updated variant of the broadcast flag has been developed in the Content Protection and Copy Management group under DVB (DVB-CPCM). Upon publication by DVB, the technical specification was submitted to European governments in March 2007. As with much DRM, the CPCM system is intended to control use of copyrighted material by the end-user, at the direction of the copyright holder. According to Ren Bucholz of the EFF, which paid to be a member of the consortium, "You won't even know ahead of time whether and how you will be able to record and make use of particular programs or devices". The DVB claims that the system will harmonize copyright holders' control across different technologies, thereby making things easier for end users. The normative sections have now all been approved for publication by the DVB Steering Board, and will be published by ETSI as a formal European Standard as ETSI TS 102 825-X where X refers to the Part number of specification. Nobody has yet stepped forward to provide a Compliance and Robustness regime for the standard (though several are rumoured to be in development), so it is not presently possible to fully implement a system, as there is nowhere to obtain the necessary device certificates.

Metadata

Sometimes, metadata is included in purchased media which records information such as the purchaser's name, account information, or email address. Also included may be the file's publisher, author, creation date, download date, and various notes. This information is not embedded in the played content, like a watermark, but is kept separate, but within the file or stream.

As an example, metadata is used in media purchased from Apple's iTunes Store for DRM-free as well as DRM-restricted versions of their music or videos. This information is included as MPEG standard metadata.

Watermarks

Digital watermarks are features of media that are added during production or distribution. Digital watermarks involve data that is arguably steganographically embedded within the audio or video data.

Watermarks can be used for different purposes that may include:

- recording the copyright owner
- recording the distributor
- recording the distribution chain
- identifying the purchaser of the music

Watermarks are not complete DRM mechanisms in their own right, but are used as part of a system for copyright enforcement, such as helping provide prosecution evidence for purely legal avenues of rights management, rather than direct technological restriction. Some programs used to edit video and/or audio may distort, delete, or otherwise interfere with watermarks. Signal/modulator-carrier chromatography may also separate watermarks from original audio or detect them as glitches. Additionally, comparison of two separately obtained copies of audio using simple, home-grown algorithms can often reveal watermarks. New methods of detection are currently under investigation by both industry and non-industry researchers.

Streaming Media Services

Since the late-2000s the trend in media consumption has been towards renting content using online streaming services, for example Spotify for music and Netflix for video content. Copyright holders often require that these services protect the content they licence using DRM mechanisms.

Laws Regarding DRM

Article 11 of the 1996 WIPO Copyright Treaty (WCT), requires nations party to the treaties to enact laws against DRM circumvention, and has been implemented in most member states of the World Intellectual Property Organization. The American implementation is the Digital Millennium Copyright Act (DMCA), while in Europe the treaty has been implemented by the 2001 European directive on copyright, which requires member states of the European Union to implement legal protections for technological prevention measures. In 2006, the lower house of the French parliament adopted such legislation as part of the controversial DADVSI law, but added that protected DRM techniques should be made interoperable, a move which caused widespread controversy in the United States. The Tribunal de grande instance de Paris concluded in 2006, that the complete blocking of any possibilities of making private copies was an impermissible behaviour under French copyright law.

Digital Millennium Copyright Act

The Digital Millennium Copyright Act (DMCA) is an amendment to United States copyright law, passed unanimously on May 14, 1998, which criminalizes the production and dissemination of technology that lets users circumvent technical copy-restriction methods.

Reverse engineering of existing systems is expressly permitted under the Act under specific con-ditions. Under the reverse engineering safe harbor, circumvention necessary to achieve interop-erability with other software is specifically authorized. Open-source software to decrypt content scrambled with the Content Scrambling System and other encryption techniques presents an intractable problem with the application of the Act. Much depends on the intent of the actor. If the decryption is done for the purpose of achieving interoperability of open source operating systems with proprietary operating systems, the circumvention would be protected by Section 1201(f) the Act. Cf., Universal City Studios, Inc. v. Corley, 273 F.3d 429 (2d Cir. 2001) at notes 5 and 16. However, dissemination of such software for the purpose of violating or encouraging others to violate copyrights has been held illegal.

The DMCA has been largely ineffective in protecting DRM systems, as software allowing users to circumvent DRM remains widely available. However, those who wish to preserve the DRM systems have attempted to use the Act to restrict the distribution and development of such software, as in the case of DeCSS.

Although the Act contains an exception for research, the exception is subject to vague qualifiers that do little to reassure researchers. Cf., 17 U.S.C. Sec. 1201(g). The DMCA has affected cryptography, because many fear that cryptanalytic research may violate the DMCA. The arrest of Russian programmer Dmitry Sklyarov in 2001, for alleged infringement of the DMCA, was a highly publicized example of the law's use to prevent or penalize development of anti-DRM measures. Sklyarov was arrested in the United States after a presentation at DEF CON, and subsequently spent several months in jail. The DMCA has also been cited as chilling to non-criminal inclined users, such as students of cryptanalysis (including, in a well-known instance, Professor Felten and students at Princeton); security consultants, such as Netherlands based Niels Ferguson, who declined to publish vulnerabilities he discovered in Intel's secure-computing scheme due to fear of being arrested under the DMCA when he travels to the US; and blind or visually impaired users of screen readers or other assistive technologies.

European Union

On 22 May 2001, the European Union passed the EU Copyright Directive, an implementation of the 1996 WIPO Copyright Treaty, that addressed many of the same issues as the DMCA.

On 25 April 2007, the European Parliament supported the first directive of EU, which aims to harmonize criminal law in the member states. It adopted a first reading report on harmonizing the national measures for fighting copyright abuse. If the European Parliament and the Council approve the legislation, the submitted directive will oblige the member states to consider a crime a violation of international copyright committed with commercial purposes. The text suggests numerous measures: from fines to imprisonment, depending on the gravity of the offense. The EP members supported the Commission motion, changing some of the texts. They excluded patent rights from the range of the directive and decided that the sanctions should apply only to offenses with commercial purposes. Copying for personal, non-commercial purposes was also excluded from the range of the directive.

In 2012, the Court of Justice of the European Union ruled in favor of reselling copyrighted games, prohibiting any preventative action that would prevent such transaction. The court said that "The first sale in the EU of a copy of a computer program by the copyright holder or with his consent exhausts the right of distribution of that copy in the EU. A rightholder who has marketed a copy in the territory of a Member State of the EU thus loses the right to rely on his monopoly of exploitation in order to oppose the resale of that copy."

In 2014, the Court of Justice of the European Union ruled that circumventing DRM on game devices may be legal under some circumstances, limiting the legal protection to only cover technological measures intended to prevent or eliminate unauthorised acts of reproduction, communication, public offer or distribution.

International Issues

In Europe, there are several ongoing dialog activities that are characterized by their consensus-building intention:

- Workshop on Digital Rights Management of the World Wide Web Consortium (W3C), January 2001.

- Participative preparation of the European Committee for Standardization/Information Society Standardization System (CEN/ISSS) DRM Report, 2003 (finished).

- DRM Workshops of Directorate-General for Information Society and Media (European

Commission) (finished), and the work of the DRM working groups (finished), as well as the work of the High Level Group on DRM (ongoing).

- The Gowers Review of Intellectual Property is the result of a commission by the British Government from Andrew Gowers, undertaken in December 2005, and published in 2006, with recommendations regarding copyright terms, exceptions, orphaned works, and copyright enforcement.

- Consultation process of the European Commission, DG Internal Market, on the Communication COM(2004)261 by the European Commission on "Management of Copyright and Related Rights" (closed).

- The AXMEDIS project, a European Commission Integrated Project of the FP6, has as its main goal automating content production, copy protection, and distribution, to reduce the related costs, and to support DRM at both B2B and B2C areas, harmonizing them.

- The INDICARE project is an ongoing dialogue on consumer acceptability of DRM solutions in Europe. It is an open and neutral platform for exchange of facts and opinions, mainly based on articles by authors from science and practice.

Israel

Israel is a signatory to, but has not yet ratified, the WIPO Copyright Treaty. Israeli law does not currently expressly prohibit the circumvention of technological measures used to implement digital rights management. The Israeli Ministry of Justice proposed a bill to prohibit such activities in June 2012, but the bill was not passed by the Knesset. In September 2013, the Supreme Court ruled that the current copyright law could not be interpreted to prohibit the circumvention of digital rights management, though the Court left open the possibility that such activities could result in liability under the law of unjust enrichment.

Opposition to DRM

Many organizations, prominent individuals, and computer scientists are opposed to DRM. Two notable DRM critics are John Walker, as expressed for instance, in his article "The Digital Imprimatur: How Big brother and big media can put the Internet genie back in the bottle", and Richard Stallman in his article *The Right to Read* and in other public statements: "DRM is an example of a malicious feature – a feature designed to hurt the user of the software, and therefore, it's something for which there can never be toleration". Stallman also believes that using the word "rights" is misleading and suggests that the word "restrictions", as in "Digital Restrictions Management", be used instead. This terminology has since been adopted by many other writers and critics unconnected with Stallman.

Other prominent critics of DRM include Professor Ross Anderson of Cambridge University, who heads a British organization which opposes DRM and similar efforts in the UK and elsewhere, and Cory Doctorow, a writer and technology blogger.

There have been numerous others who see DRM at a more fundamental level. This is similar to some of the ideas in Michael H. Goldhaber's presentation about "The Attention Economy and the

Net" at a 1997 conference on the "Economics of Digital Information". (sample quote from the "Advice for the Transition" section of that presentation: "If you can't figure out how to afford it without charging, you may be doing something wrong.")

The EFF and similar organizations such as FreeCulture.org also hold positions which are characterized as opposed to DRM.

The Foundation for a Free Information Infrastructure has criticized DRM's effect as a trade barrier from a free market perspective.

The final version of the GNU General Public License version 3, as released by the Free Software Foundation, has a provision that 'strips' DRM of its legal value, so people can break the DRM on GPL software without breaking laws like the DMCA. Also, in May 2006, the FSF launched a "Defective by Design" campaign against DRM.

Creative Commons provides licensing options encouraging the expansion of and building upon creative work without the use of DRM. In addition, the use of DRM by a licensee to restrict the freedoms granted by a Creative Commons license is a breach of the Baseline Rights asserted by each license.

Bill Gates spoke about DRM at CES in 2006. According to him, DRM is not where it should be, and causes problems for legitimate consumers while trying to distinguish between legitimate and illegitimate users.

According to Steve Jobs, Apple opposes DRM music after a public letter calling its music labels to stop requiring DRM on its iTunes Store. As of January 6, 2009, the iTunes Store is DRM-free for songs.

Defective by Design member protesting DRM on May 25, 2007.

The Norwegian consumer rights organization "Forbrukerrådet" complained to Apple Inc. in 2007, about the company's use of DRM in, and in conjunction with, its iPod and iTunes products. Apple was accused of restricting users' access to their music and videos in an unlawful way, and of using EULAs which conflict with Norwegian consumer legislation. The complaint was supported by consumers' ombudsmen in Sweden and Denmark, and is currently being reviewed in the EU.

Similarly, the United States Federal Trade Commission held hearings in March 2009, to review disclosure of DRM limitations to customers' use of media products.

DRM opponents argue that the presence of DRM violates existing private property rights and restricts a range of heretofore normal and legal user activities. A DRM component would control a device a user owns (such as a digital audio player) by restricting how it may act with regards to certain content, overriding some of the user's wishes (for example, preventing the user from burning a copyrighted song to CD as part of a compilation or a review). Doctorow has described this possibility as "the right to make up your own copyright laws".

An example of this restriction to legal user activities may be seen in Microsoft's Windows Vista operating system in which content using a Protected Media Path is disabled or degraded depending on the DRM scheme's evaluation of whether the hardware and its use are 'secure'. All forms of DRM depend on the DRM enabled device (e.g., computer, DVD player, TV) imposing restrictions that (at least by intent) cannot be disabled or modified by the user. Key issues around DRM such as the right to make personal copies, provisions for persons to lend copies to friends, provisions for service discontinuance, hardware agnosticism, software and operating system agnosticism, contracts for public libraries, and customers' protection against one-side amendments of the contract by the publisher have not been fully addressed. It has also been pointed out that it is entirely unclear whether owners of content with DRM are legally permitted to pass on their property as inheritance to another person.

Tools like FairUse4WM have been created to strip Windows Media of DRM restrictions.

Valve Corporation president Gabe Newell also stated "most DRM strategies are just dumb" because they only decrease the value of a game in the consumer's eyes. Newell suggests that the goal should instead be "[creating] greater value for customers through service value". Valve operates Steam, a service which serves as an online store for PC games, as well as a social networking service and a DRM platform.

At the 2012 Game Developers Conference, the CEO of CD Projekt Red, Marcin Iwinski, announced that the company will not use DRM in any of its future releases. Iwinski stated of DRM, "it's just over-complicating things. We release the game. It's cracked in two hours, it was no time for Witcher 2. What really surprised me is that the pirates didn't use the GOG version, which was not protected. They took the SecuROM retail version, cracked it and said 'we cracked it' – meanwhile there's a non-secure version with a simultaneous release. You'd think the GOG version would be the one floating around." Iwinski added after the presentation, "DRM does not protect your game. If there are examples that it does, then people maybe should consider it, but then there are complications with legit users."

Bruce Schneier argues that digital copy prevention is futile: "What the entertainment industry is trying to do is to use technology to contradict that natural law. They want a practical way to make copying hard enough to save their existing business. But they are doomed to fail." He has also described trying to make digital files uncopyable as being like "trying to make water not wet". The creators of StarForce also take this stance, stating that "The purpose of copy protection is not making the game uncrackable – it is impossible."

The Association for Computing Machinery and the Institute of Electrical and Electronics Engineers have historically opposed DRM, even going so far as to name AACS as a technology "most likely to fail" in an issue of IEEE Spectrum.

DRM-free Works

Label proposed by the Free Software Foundation for DRM-free works

In reaction to opposition to DRM, many publishers and artists label their works as "DRM-free". Major companies that have done so include the following:

- Apple Inc. sold DRM content on their iTunes Store when it started 2003, but made music DRM-free after April 2007 and has been labeling all music as "DRM-Free" since January 2009. The music still carries a digital watermark to identify the purchaser. Other works sold on iTunes such as apps, audiobooks, e-books, movies, and TV shows continue to be protected by DRM.

- Since 2014, Comixology, which distributes digital comics, has allowed rights holders to provide the option of a DRM-free download of purchased comics. Publishers which allow this include Dynamite Entertainment, Image Comics, Thrillbent, Top Shelf Productions, and Zenescope Entertainment.

- GOG.com (Good Old Games), a digital distributor started in 2008, specialized in the distribution of PC video games. While most other digital distribution services allow various forms of DRM (or have them embedded), gog.com has a strict non-DRM policy.

- All music sold on Google Play is DRM free.

- Tor Books, a major publisher of science fiction and fantasy books, started selling DRM-free e-books in July 2012. Smaller e-book publishers, such as Baen Books and O'Reilly Media, had already forgone DRM previously.

- Vimeo on Demand is one of the publishers included in the Free Software Foundation's DRM-free guide.

Shortcomings

DRM Server and Internet Outages

Many DRM systems require authentication with an online server. Whenever the server goes down, or a region or country experiences an Internet outage, it effectively locks out people from registering or using the material. This is especially true for a product that requires a persistent online authentication, where, for example, a successful DDoS attack on the server would essentially make all copies of the material unusable.

Methods to Bypass DRM

There are many methods to bypass DRM control on audio, e-book, and video content.

DRM Bypass Methods for Audio and Video Content

One simple method to bypass DRM on audio files is to burn the content to an audio CD and then rip it into DRM-free files. Some software products simplify and automate this burn-rip process by allowing the user to burn music to a CD-RW disc or to a Virtual CD-R drive, then automatically rip and encode the music, and automatically repeat this process until all selected music has been converted, rather than forcing the user to do this one CD (72–80 minutes worth of music) at a time.

Many software programs have been developed that intercept the data stream as it is decrypted out of the DRM-restricted file, and then use this data to construct a DRM-free file. These programs require a decryption key. Programs that do this for Blu-ray Discs, DVDs, and HD DVDs include universal decryption keys in the software itself. Programs that do this for iTunes audio, PlaysForSure songs, and TiVo ToGo recordings, however, rely on the user's own key — that is, they can only process content the user has legally acquired under his or her own account.

Another method is to use software to record the signals being sent through the audio or video cards, or to plug analog recording devices into the analog outputs of the media player. These techniques utilize the "analog hole".

Analog Recording

All forms of DRM for audio and visual material (excluding interactive materials, e.g., videogames) are subject to the *analog hole*, namely that in order for a viewer to play the material, the digital signal must be turned into an analog signal containing light and/or sound for the viewer, and so available to be copied as no DRM is capable of controlling content in this form. In other words, a user could play a purchased audio file while using a separate program to record the sound back into the computer into a DRM-free file format.

All DRM to date can therefore be bypassed by recording this signal and digitally storing and distributing it in a non DRM limited form, by anyone who has the technical means of recording the analog stream. Furthermore, the analog hole cannot be overcome without the additional protection of externally imposed restrictions, such as legal regulations, because the vulnerability is inherent to all analog means of transmission. However, the conversion from digital to analog and back is likely to force a loss of quality, particularly when using lossy digital formats. HDCP is an attempt to plug the analog hole, although it is largely ineffective.

Asus released a soundcard which features a function called "Analog Loopback Transformation" to bypass the restrictions of DRM. This feature allows the user to record DRM-restricted audio via the soundcard's built-in analog I/O connection.

In order to prevent this exploit there has been some discussions between copyright holders and manufacturers of electronics capable of playing such content, to no longer include analog connectivity in their devices. The movement dubbed as "Analog Sunset" has seen a steady decline in analog output options on most Blu-ray devices manufactured after 2010.

DRM on General Computing Platforms

Many of the DRM systems in use are designed to work on general purpose computing hardware, such as desktop PCs, apparently because this equipment is felt to be a major contributor to revenue loss from disallowed copying. Large commercial copyright infringers avoid consumer equipment, so losses from such infringers will not be covered by such provisions.

Such schemes, especially software based ones, can never be wholly secure since the software must include all the information necessary to decrypt the content, such as the decryption keys. An attacker will be able to extract this information, directly decrypt and copy the content, which bypasses the restrictions imposed by a DRM system.

DRM on Purpose-built Hardware

Many DRM schemes use encrypted media which requires purpose-built hardware to hear or see the content. This appears to ensure that only licensed users (those with the hardware) can access the content. It additionally tries to protect a secret decryption key from the users of the system.

While this in principle can work, it is extremely difficult to build the hardware to protect the secret key against a sufficiently determined adversary. Many such systems have failed in the field. Once the secret key is known, building a version of the hardware that performs no checks is often relatively straightforward. In addition user verification provisions are frequently subject to attack, pirate decryption being among the most frequented ones.

A common real-world example can be found in commercial direct broadcast satellite television systems such as DirecTV and Malaysia's Astro. The company uses tamper-resistant smart cards to store decryption keys so that they are hidden from the user and the satellite receiver. However, the system has been compromised in the past, and DirecTV has been forced to roll out periodic updates and replacements for its smart cards.

Watermarks

Watermarks can often be removed, although degradation of video or audio can occur.

Undecrypted Copying Failure

Mass redistribution of hard copies does not necessarily need DRM to be decrypted or removed, as it can be achieved by bit-perfect copying of a legally obtained medium without accessing the decrypted content. Additionally, still-encrypted disk images can be distributed over the Internet and played on legitimately licensed players.

Obsolescence

When standards and formats change, it may be difficult to transfer DRM-restricted content to new media. Additionally, any system that requires contact with an authentication server is vulnerable to that server's becoming unavailable, as happened in 2007, when videos purchased from Major League Baseball (mlb.com) prior to 2006, became unplayable due to a change to the servers that validate the licenses.

Amazon .LIT and PDF E-books

In August 2006, Amazon stopped selling DRMed .LIT and PDF format e-books. Customers were unable to download purchased e-books 30 days after that date, losing access to their purchased content on new devices.

Microsoft Zune

In 2006, when Microsoft introduced their Zune media player, it did not support content that uses Microsoft's own PlaysForSure DRM scheme they had previously been selling. The EFF calls this "a raw deal".

MSN Music

In April 2008, Microsoft sent an email to former customers of the now-defunct MSN Music store that read:

"As of August 31, 2008, we will no longer be able to support the retrieval of license keys for the songs you purchased from MSN Music or the authorization of additional computers. You will need to obtain a license key for each of your songs downloaded from MSN Music on any new computer, and you must do so before August 31, 2008. If you attempt to transfer your songs to additional computers after August 31, 2008, those songs will not successfully play."

However, to avoid a public relations disaster, Microsoft re-issued MSN Music shutdown statement on June 19 and allowed the users to use their licenses until the end of 2011:

"After careful consideration, Microsoft has decided to continue to support the authorization of new computers and devices and delivery of new license keys for MSN Music customers through at least the end of 2011, after which we will evaluate how much this functionality is still being used and what steps should be taken next to support our customers. This means you will continue to be able to listen to your purchased music and transfer your music to new PCs and devices beyond the previously announced August 31, 2008 date."

Yahoo! Music Store

On July 23, 2008, the Yahoo! Music Store emailed its customers to tell them it would be shutting down effective September 30, 2008, and the DRM license key servers would be taken offline.

Walmart

In August 2007, Walmart's online music division started offering (DRM-free) MP3s as an option. Starting in February 2008, they made all sales DRM-free.

On September 26, 2008, the Walmart Music Team notified its customers via email they would be shutting down their DRM servers October 9, 2008, and any DRM-encumbered music acquired from them would no longer be accessible unless backed up to a recordable CDs (a non-DRM format) before that date.

After bad press and negative reaction from customers, on October 9, 2008, Walmart decided not to take its DRM servers offline.

Fictionwise / Overdrive

In January 2009, OverDrive, Inc. informed Fictionwise that they would no longer be providing downloads for purchasers of e-books through Fictionwise as of 31 January 2009. No reason was provided to Fictionwise as to why they were being shut down. This prevented previous purchasers from being able to renew their books on new devices. Fictionwise worked to provide replacement e-books for its customers in alternative, non-DRM formats, but lacked the rights to provide all the books in different formats.

Ads for Adobe PDF

Also in January 2009, Adobe Systems announced that as of March 2009, they would no longer operate the servers that served ads to their PDF reader. Depending on the restriction settings used when PDF documents were created, the content might no longer be readable.

Adobe Content Server 3 for Adobe PDF

In April 2009, Adobe Systems announced that as of March 30, 2009, the Adobe Content 3 server would no longer activate new installations of Adobe Acrobat or Adobe Reader. In addition, the ability to migrate content from Adobe Content Server 3 to Adobe Content Server 4 would cease from mid-December 2009. Anyone who failed to migrate their DRMed PDF files during this nine month window lost access to their content the next time they had to re-install their copy of Adobe Acrobat or Adobe Reader.

Harper Collins E-book Store

In November 2010, Harper Collins announced that as of November 19, 2010, their eBook Store was discontinued; they advised all customers to download and archive their purchases before December 19, 2010, when purchased titles would no longer be accessible, and for books in the secure Mobipocket format, this meant that customers would not be able to read the book on any new devices.

Cyber Read E-book Store

In February 2011, CyberRead announced that they were closing down, and advised all customers to download and archive their purchases. For books in the secure Mobipocket format, this meant that customers would not be able to read the book on any new devices.

Microsoft Reader and .Lit E-books

In August 2011, Microsoft announced: they were discontinuing both Microsoft Reader and the use of the .lit format for e-books at the end of August 2012, the activation servers were now offline, and it was not possible to read DRMed .lit e-books except on an installation made before the servers were taken down.

Fictionwise

In November 2012, Fictionwise announced that they were shutting down. Access to e-book downloads stopped on 31 January 2013. UK and US customers had a limited time-window (up to 26 April 2013) to opt-in to a transfer of (most of) their Fictionwise library to a Barnes & Noble Nook/NOOK UK account. Customers outside the UK and US lost access to new downloads of their books. For books in the secure Mobipocket format, this meant that customers would not be able to read the book on any new devices.

JManga E-book Store

In March 2013, JManga announced that they were closing down and advised all customers that they would lose all access to their content in May 2013.

Waterstones E-book Store

In March 2013, Waterstones announced that they were making changes to their e-book store and advised customers that some of their e-books would become unavailable for download after 18 April 2013. Waterstones advised affected customers to download before then. Any customer who had not kept their own backups and missed this 31-day window lost their e-books.

Books on Board E-book Store

In April 2013, BooksOnBoard announced that they had stopped selling ebooks. Downloads from their website stopped working sometime before June 2016., leading to loss of access to any Mobipocket format ebooks on new devices.

Acetrax Video on Demand

In May 2013, Acetrax announced they were shutting down. Refunds were provided for purchases of HD movies, but for standard definition versions, the only option made available was a limited time option to download to a Windows PC, but the movie would then be locked to that particular installation of Microsoft Media Player. Non-Windows users lost access to their SD movies.

Sony Reader Store

In February 2014, Sony announced that their US e-book store would be closing by the end of March 2014. Accounts were transferred to Kobo, but not all books in Sony accounts could be transferred. In May 2014, Sony announced that their European and Australian e-book stores would be closing on 16 June 2014, with similar arrangements for transfer to Kobo accounts. Customers were advised to download all their e-books before the closing date, because not all books could be transferred.

Diesel eBooks

In March 2014, Diesel announced that their e-book store would be closing by the end of March 2014. Customers were advised to download all their e-books by month end as downloads will not be possible after this date.

Barnes & Noble Non-US/UK Nook Store

In July 2015, Barnes & Noble announced that their non-US/UK e-book stores would be closing in August 2015, losing access to all ebooks purchases. Customers were advised to see if Microsoft would give them refunds for purchases bought through a Microsoft account.

Barnes & Noble UK Nook Store

In March 2016, Barnes & Noble announced that their UK e-book store would be closing by the end of May 2016, with accounts transferred to Sainsbury Digital Entertainment, but not all books in the accounts will be transferred. Customers were advised to download all their e-books before the closing date, because not all books could be transferred. Books previously transferred to nook following the closure of Fictionwise were not transferred.

Waterstones ebook Store

In May 2016, Waterstones announced that their e-book store would be closing, with accounts transferred to Kobo.

Environmental Issues

DRM can accelerate hardware obsolescence, turning it into electronic waste sooner:

- DRM-related restrictions on capabilities of hardware can artificially reduce the range of potential uses of the device (to the point of making a device consisting of general-purpose components usable only for a purpose approved, or with "content" provided, by the vendor), limit upgradeability and repairability. Cf. proprietary abandonware, orphan works, planned obsolescence. Examples:
    - o DVD region code (applies to discs as well as DVD players and drives);
    - o the removal of the OtherOS feature from Sony PlayStation 3 game consoles;

     o   Tivoization, UEFI Secure Boot and similar.

- Users may be forced to buy new devices for compatibility with DRM, i.a. through having to upgrade an operating system to one with different hardware requirements.

Moral and Legitimacy Implications

According to the EFF, "in an effort to attract customers, these music services try to obscure the restrictions they impose on you with clever marketing."

DRM laws are widely flouted: according to Australia Official Music Chart Survey, copyright infringements from all causes are practised by millions of people.

Relaxing Some forms of DRM can be Beneficial

Jeff Raikes, ex-president of the Microsoft Business Division, stated: "If they're going to pirate somebody, we want it to be us rather than somebody else". An analogous argument was made in an early paper by Kathleen Conner and Richard Rummelt. A subsequent study of digital rights management for e-books by Gal Oestreicher-Singer and Arun Sundararajan showed that relaxing some forms of DRM can be beneficial to digital rights holders because the losses from piracy are outweighed by the increases in value to legal buyers.

Also, free distribution, even if unauthorized, can be beneficial to small or new content providers by spreading and popularizing content and therefore generating a larger consumer base by sharing and word of mouth. Several musicians have grown to popularity by posting their music videos on sites like YouTube where the content is free to listen to. This method of putting the product out in the world free of DRM not only generates a greater following but also fuels greater revenue through other merchandise (hats, T-shirts), concert tickets, and of course, more sales of the content to paying consumers.

Can Increase Infringement

While the main intent of DRM is to prevent unauthorized copies of a product, there are mathematical models that suggest that DRM schemes can fail to do their job on multiple levels. Ironically, the biggest failure that can result from DRM is that they have a potential to increase the infringement rate of a product. This goes against the held belief that DRM can always reduce unauthorized distribution. There also seems to be evidence that DRM will reduce profits.

The driving factor behind this is related to how many restrictions DRM imposes on a legal buyer. An ideal DRM would be one which imposes zero restrictions on legal buyers but makes imposing restrictions on infringers. Even if an ideal DRM can be created and used, in certain cases, it can be shown that removing the DRM will result in less unauthorized copying. For the ideal DRM, the reason why profits can increase is because of the demand is elastic. When there are more people legally buying and few people sharing the product, more profits are going to be made.

The mathematical models are strictly applied to the music industry (music CDs, downloadable music). These models could be extended to the other industries such as the gaming industry which show similarities to the music industry model. There are real instances when DRM restrain consumers in the gaming industry. Some DRM games are required to connect to the Internet in order to play them. Good Old Games' head of public relations and marketing, Trevor Longino, in agreement with this, believes that using DRM is less effective than improving a game's value in reducing video game infringement. However, TorrentFreak published a "Top 10 pirated games of 2008" list which shows that intrusive DRM is not the main reason why some games are copied more heavily than others. Popular games such as BioShock, Crysis Warhead, and Mass Effect which use intrusive DRM are strangely absent from the list.

Alternatives to DRM

Several business models have been proposed that offer an alternative to the use of DRM by content providers and rights holders.

"Easy and Cheap"

The first business model that dissuades illegal file sharing is to make the downloading easy and cheap. The use of a noncommercial site makes downloading music complex. If someone misspells the artist's name, the search will leave the consumer dissatisfied. Also, some[which?] illegal file sharing websites lead to many viruses and malware that attach themselves to the files, somewhat in a way of torrent poisoning. Some sites limit the traffic, which can make downloading a song a long and frustrating process. If the songs are all provided on one site, and reasonably priced, consumers will purchase the music legally to overcome the frustrations such as media files appearing empty or failing to play smoothly/correctly occasionally on DRM'ed players and pcs giving a risky feel to the potential "sharer" that can occur downloading illegally.

Comedian Louis C.K. made headlines in 2011, with the release of his concert film *Live at the Beacon Theater* as an inexpensive (US$5), DRM-free download. The only attempt to deter unlicensed copies was a letter emphasizing the lack of corporate involvement and direct relationship between artist and viewer. The film was a commercial success, turning a profit within 12 hours of its release. Some, including the artist himself, have suggested that file sharing rates were lower than normal as a result, making the release an important case study for the digital marketplace.

Webcomic Diesel Sweeties released a DRM-free PDF e-book on author R Stevens's 35th birthday, leading to more than 140,000 downloads in the first month, according to Stevens. He followed this with a DRM-free iBook specifically for the iPad, using Apple's new software, which generated more than 10,000 downloads in three days. That led Stevens to launch a Kickstarter project – "ebook stravaganza 3000" – to fund the conversion of 3,000 comics, written over 12 years, into a single "humongous" e-book to be released both for free and through the iBookstore; launched February 8, 2012, with the goal of raising $3,000 in 30 days, the project met its goal in 45 minutes, and went on to be funded at more than 10 times its original goal. The "payment optional" DRM-free model in this case was adopted on Stevens' view that "there is a class of webcomics reader who would prefer to read in large chunks and, even better, would be willing to spend a little money on it."

Crowdfunding or Pre-order Model

In February 2012, Double Fine asked for an upcoming video game, *Double Fine Adventure*, for crowdfunding on kickstarter.com and offered the game DRM-free for backers. This project exceeded its original goal of $400,000 in 45 days, raising in excess of $2 million. In this case DRM freedom was offered to backers as an incentive for supporting the project before release, with the consumer and community support and media attention from the highly successful Kickstarter drive counterbalancing any loss through file sharing. Also, crowdfunding with the product itself as benefit for the supporters can be seen as pre-order or subscription business model in which one motivation for DRM, the uncertainty if a product will have enough paying customers to outweigh the development costs, is eliminated. After the success of *Double Fine Adventure*, many games were crowd-funded and many of them offered a DRM-free game version for the backers.

Digital Content as Promotion for Traditional Products

Many artists are using the Internet to give away music to create awareness and liking to a new upcoming album. The artists release a new song on the internet for free download, which consumers can download. The hope is to have the listeners buy the new album because of the free download. A common practice used today is releasing a song or two on the internet for consumers to indulge. In 2007, Radiohead released an album named In Rainbows, in which fans could pay any amount they want, or download it for free.

Artistic Freedom Voucher

The Artistic Freedom Voucher (AFV) introduced by Dean Baker is a way for consumers to support "creative and artistic work." In this system, each consumer would have a refundable tax credit of $100 to give to any artist of creative work. To restrict fraud, the artists must register with the government. The voucher prohibits any artist that receives the benefits from copyrighting their material for a certain length of time. Consumers can obtain music for a certain amount of time easily and the consumer decides which artists receive the $100. The money can either be given to one artist or to many, the distribution is up to the consumer.

Historical Note

A very early implementation of DRM was the Software Service System (SSS) devised by the Japanese engineer Ryoichi Mori in 1983 and subsequently refined under the name superdistribution. The SSS was based on encryption, with specialized hardware that controlled decryption and also enabled payments to be sent to the copyright holder. The underlying principle of the SSS and subsequently of superdistribution was that the distribution of encrypted digital products should be completely unrestricted and that users of those products would not just be permitted to redistribute them but would actually be encouraged to do so.

Copyright Infringement

Copyright infringement is the use of works protected by copyright law without permission, infringing certain exclusive rights granted to the copyright holder, such as the right to reproduce, distribute, display or perform the protected work, or to make derivative works. The copyright holder is typically the work's creator, or a publisher or other business to whom copyright has been assigned.

Copyright holders routinely invoke legal and technological measures to prevent and penalize copyright infringement.

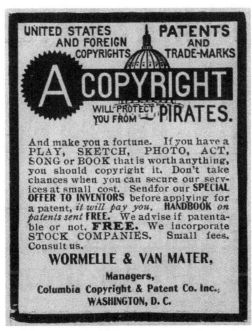

An advertisement for copyright and patent preparation services from 1906,
when copyright registration formalities were still required in the US

Copyright infringement disputes are usually resolved through direct negotiation, a notice and take down process, or litigation in civil court. Egregious or large-scale commercial infringement, especially when it involves counterfeiting, is sometimes prosecuted via the criminal justice system. Shifting public expectations, advances in digital technology, and the increasing reach of the Internet have led to such widespread, anonymous infringement that copyright-dependent industries now focus less on pursuing individuals who seek and share copyright-protected content online, and more on expanding copyright law to recognize and penalize – as "indirect" infringers – the service providers and software distributors which are said to facilitate and encourage individual acts of infringement by others.

Estimates of the actual economic impact of copyright infringement vary widely and depend on many factors. Nevertheless, copyright holders, industry representatives, and legislators have long characterized copyright infringement as **piracy** or **theft** – language which some U.S. courts now regard as pejorative or otherwise contentious.

Terminology

The terms *piracy* and *theft* are often associated with copyright infringement. The original meaning of *piracy* is "robbery or illegal violence at sea", but the term has been in use for centuries as a synonym for acts of copyright infringement. *Theft*, meanwhile, emphasizes the potential commercial harm of infringement to copyright holders. However, copyright is a type of intellectual property, an area of law distinct from that which covers robbery or theft, offenses related only to tangible property. Not all copyright infringement results in commercial loss, and the U.S. Supreme Court ruled in 1985 that infringement does not *easily* equate with theft.

"Piracy"

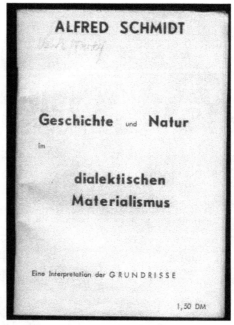

Pirated edition of German philosopher Alfred Schmidt (Amsterdam, ca. 1970)

The practice of labelling the infringement of exclusive rights in creative works as "piracy" predates statutory copyright law. Prior to the Statute of Anne in 1710, the Stationers' Company of London in 1557, received a Royal Charter giving the company a monopoly on publication and tasking it with enforcing the charter. Those who violated the charter were labelled pirates as early as 1603. The term "piracy" has been used to refer to the unauthorized copying, distribution and selling of works in copyright. Article 12 of the 1886 Berne Convention for the Protection of Literary and Artistic Works uses the term "piracy" in relation to copyright infringement, stating "Pirated works may be seized on importation into those countries of the Union where the original work enjoys legal protection." Article 61 of the 1994 Agreement on Trade-Related Aspects of Intellectual Property Rights (TRIPs) requires criminal procedures and penalties in cases of "willful trademark counterfeiting or copyright piracy on a commercial scale." Piracy traditionally refers to acts of copyright infringement intentionally committed for financial gain, though more recently, copyright holders have described online copyright infringement, particularly in relation to peer-to-peer file sharing networks, as "piracy."

Richard Stallman and the GNU Project have criticized the use of the word "piracy" in these situations, saying that publishers use the word to refer to "copying they don't approve of" and that "they [publishers] imply that it is ethically equivalent to attacking ships on the high seas, kidnapping and murdering the people on them."

"Theft"

Copyright holders frequently refer to copyright infringement as theft. In copyright law, infringement does not refer to theft of physical objects that take away the owner's possession, but an instance where a person exercises one of the exclusive rights of the copyright holder without authorization. Courts have distinguished between copyright infringement and theft. For instance, the

United States Supreme Court held in *Dowling v. United States* (1985) that bootleg phonorecords did not constitute stolen property. Instead, "interference with copyright does not easily equate with theft, conversion, or fraud. The Copyright Act even employs a separate term of art to define one who misappropriates a copyright: '[...] an infringer of the copyright.'" The court said that in the case of copyright infringement, the province guaranteed to the copyright holder by copyright law – certain exclusive rights – is invaded, but no control, physical or otherwise, is taken over the copyright, nor is the copyright holder wholly deprived of using the copyrighted work or exercising the exclusive rights held.

Motivation

Some of the motives for engaging in copyright infringement are the following:

- Pricing – unwillingness or inability to pay the price requested by the legitimate sellers

- Unavailability – no legitimate sellers providing the product in the country of the end-user: not yet launched there, already withdrawn from sales, never to be sold there, geographical restrictions on online distribution and international shipping

- Usefulness – the legitimate product comes with various means (DRM, region lock, DVD region code, Blu-ray region code) of restricting legitimate use (backups, usage on devices of different vendors, offline usage) or comes with annoying non-skippable advertisements and anti-piracy disclaimers, which are removed in the unauthorized product making it more desirable for the end-user

- Shopping experience – no legitimate sellers providing the product with the required quality through online distribution and through a shopping system with the required level of user-friendliness

- Anonymity – downloading works does not require identification whereas downloads directly from the website of the copyright owner often require a valid email address and/ or other credentials

Sometimes only partial compliance with license agreements is the cause. For example, in 2013, the US Army settled a lawsuit with Texas-based company Apptricity, which makes software that allows the army to track their soldiers in real time. In 2004, the US Army paid US$4.5 million for a license of 500 users, while allegedly installing the software for more than 9000 users; the case was settled for US$50 million. Major anti-piracy organizations, like the BSA, conduct software licensing audits regularly to ensure full compliance.

Cara Cusumano, director of the Tribeca Film Festival, stated in April 2014: "Piracy is less about people not wanting to pay and more about just wanting the immediacy – people saying, 'I want to watch Spiderman right now' and downloading it". The statement occurred during the third year that the festival used the Internet to present its content, while it was the first year that it featured a showcase of content producers who work exclusively online. Cusumano further explained that downloading behavior is not merely conducted by people who merely want to obtain content for free:

I think that if companies were willing to put that material out there, moving forward, consumers will follow. It's just that they [consumers] want to consume films online and they're ready to consume films that way and we're not necessarily offering them in that way. So it's the distribution models that need to catch up. People will pay for the content.

In response to Cusumano's perspective, Screen Producers Australia executive director Matt Deaner clarified the motivation of the film industry: "Distributors are usually wanting to encourage cinema-going as part of this process [monetizing through returns] and restrict the immediate access to online so as to encourage the maximum number of people to go to the cinema." Deaner further explained the matter in terms of the Australian film industry, stating: "there are currently restrictions on quantities of tax support that a film can receive unless the film has a traditional cinema release."

In a study published in the *Journal of Behavioural and Experimental Economics*, and reported on in early May 2014, researchers from the University of Portsmouth in the UK discussed findings from examining the illegal downloading behavior of 6,000 Finnish people, aged seven to 84. The list of reasons for downloading given by the study respondents included money saving; the ability to access material not on general release, or before it was released; and assisting artists to avoid involvement with record companies and movie studios.

In a public talk between Bill Gates, Warren Buffett, and Brent Schlender at the University of Washington in 1998, Bill Gates commented on piracy as a means to an end, whereby people who use Microsoft software illegally will eventually pay for it, out of familiarity, as a country's economy develops and legitimate products become more affordable to businesses and consumers:

Although about three million computers get sold every year in China, people don't pay for the software. Someday they will, though. And as long as they're going to steal it, we want them to steal ours. They'll get sort of addicted, and then we'll somehow figure out how to collect sometime in the next decade.

Developing World

In Media Piracy in Emerging Economies, the first independent international comparative study of media piracy with center on Brazil, India, Russia, South Africa, Mexico, Turkey and Bolivia, "high prices for media goods, low incomes, and cheap digital technologies" are the chief factors that lead to the global spread of media piracy, especially in emerging markets.

According to the same study, even though digital piracy inflicts additional costs on the production side of media, it also offers the main access to media goods in developing countries. The strong tradeoffs that favor using digital piracy in developing economies dictate the current neglected law enforcements toward digital piracy. In China, the issue of digital infringement is not merely legal, but social – originating from the high demand for cheap and affordable goods as well as the governmental connections of the businesses which produce such goods.

Motivations Due to Censorship

There have been instances where a country's government bans a movie, resulting in the spread of copied videos and DVDs. Romanian-born documentary maker Ilinca Calugareanu wrote a *New York Times* article telling the story of Irina Margareta Nistor, a narrator for state TV under Nicolae Ceauşescu's regime. A visitor from the west gave her bootlegged copies of American movies, which she dubbed for secret viewings through Romania. According to the article, she dubbed more than 3,000 movies and became the country's second-most famous voice after Ceauşescu, even though no one knew her name until many years later.

Existing and Proposed Laws

Demonstration in Sweden in support of file sharing, 2006

Most countries extend copyright protections to authors of works. In countries with copyright legislation, enforcement of copyright is generally the responsibility of the copyright holder. However, in several jurisdictions there are also criminal penalties for copyright infringement.

The Pirate Bay logo, a retaliation to the stereotypical image of piracy

Civil Law

Copyright infringement in civil law is any violation of the exclusive rights of the owner. In U.S. law, those rights include reproduction, the preparation of derivative works, distributing copies by sale or rental, and public performance or display.

In the U.S., copyright infringement is sometimes confronted via lawsuits in civil court, against alleged infringers directly, or against providers of services and software that support unauthorized copying. For example, major motion-picture corporation MGM Studios filed suit against P2P file-sharing services Grokster and Streamcast for their contributory role in copyright infringement. In 2005, the Supreme Court ruled in favor of MGM, holding that such services could be held liable for copyright infringement since they functioned and, indeed, willfully marketed themselves as venues for acquiring copyrighted movies. The *MGM v. Grokster* case did not overturn the earlier *Sony* decision, but rather clouded the legal waters; future designers of software capable of being used for copyright infringement were warned.

In the United States, copyright term has been extended many times over from the original term of 14 years with a single renewal allowance of 14 years, to the current term of the life of the author plus 70 years. If the work was produced under corporate authorship it may last 120 years after creation or 95 years after publication, whichever is sooner.

Article 50 of the Agreement on Trade-Related Aspects of Intellectual Property Rights (TRIPs) requires that signatory countries enable courts to remedy copyright infringement with injunctions and the destruction of infringing products, and award damages. Some jurisdictions only allow actual, provable damages, and some, like the U.S., allow for large statutory damage awards intended to deter would-be infringers and allow for compensation in situations where actual damages are difficult to prove.

In some jurisdictions, copyright or the right to enforce it can be contractually assigned to a third party which did not have a role in producing the work. When this outsourced litigator appears to have no intention of taking any copyright infringement cases to trial, but rather only takes them just far enough through the legal system to identify and exact settlements from suspected infringers, critics commonly refer to the party as a "copyright troll." Such practices have had mixed results in the U.S.

Criminal Law

Punishment of copyright infringement varies case-by-case across countries. Convictions may include jail time and/or severe fines for each instance of copyright infringement. In the United States, willful copyright infringement carries a maximum penalty of $150,000 per instance.

Article 61 of the Agreement on Trade-Related Aspects of Intellectual Property Rights (TRIPs) requires that signatory countries establish criminal procedures and penalties in cases of "willful trademark counterfeiting or copyright piracy on a commercial scale". Copyright holders have demanded that states provide criminal sanctions for all types of copyright infringement.

The first criminal provision in U.S. copyright law was added in 1897, which established a misdemeanor penalty for "unlawful performances and representations of copyrighted dramatic and musical compositions" if the violation had been "willful and for profit." Criminal copyright infringement requires that the infringer acted "for the purpose of commercial advantage or private financial gain." 17 U.S.C. § 506. To establish criminal liability, the prosecutor must first show the basic elements of copyright infringement: ownership of a valid copyright, and the violation of one or more of the copyright holder's exclusive rights. The government must then establish that defendant willfully infringed or, in other words, possessed the necessary *mens rea*. Misdemeanor infringement has a very low threshold in terms of number of copies and the value of the infringed works.

The ACTA trade agreement, signed in May 2011 by the United States, Japan, and the EU, requires that its parties add criminal penalties, including incarceration and fines, for copyright and trademark infringement, and obligated the parties to actively police for infringement.

United States v. LaMacchia 871 F.Supp. 535 (1994) was a case decided by the United States District Court for the District of Massachusetts which ruled that, under the copyright and cybercrime laws effective at the time, committing copyright infringement for non-commercial motives could not be prosecuted under criminal copyright law. The ruling gave rise to what became known as the "LaMacchia Loophole," wherein criminal charges of fraud or copyright infringement would be dismissed under current legal standards, so long as there was no profit motive involved.

The United States No Electronic Theft Act (NET Act), a federal law passed in 1997, in response to LaMacchia, provides for criminal prosecution of individuals who engage in copyright infringement under certain circumstances, even when there is no monetary profit or commercial benefit from the infringement. Maximum penalties can be five years in prison and up to $250,000 in fines. The NET Act also raised statutory damages by 50%. The court's ruling explicitly drew attention to the shortcomings of current law that allowed people to facilitate mass copyright infringement while being immune to prosecution under the Copyright Act.

Proposed laws such as the Stop Online Piracy Act broaden the definition of "willful infringement", and introduce felony charges for unauthorized media streaming. These bills are aimed towards defeating websites that carry or contain links to infringing content, but have raised concerns about domestic abuse and internet censorship.

Noncommercial File Sharing

Legality of Downloading

To an extent, copyright law in some countries permits downloading copyright-protected content for personal, noncommercial use. Examples include Canada and European Union (EU) member states like Poland, The Netherlands, and Spain.

The personal copying exemption in the copyright law of EU member states stems from the EU Copyright Directive of 2001, which is generally devised to allow EU members to enact laws sanctioning making copies without authorization, as long as they are for personal, noncommerical use. The Copyright Directive was not intended to legitimize file-sharing, but rather the common practice of space shifting copyright-protected content from a legally purchased CD (for example) to certain kinds of devices and media, provided rights holders are compensated and no copy protection measures are circumvented. Rights-holder compensation takes various forms, depending on the country, but is generally either a levy on "recording" devices and media, or a tax on the content itself. In some countries, such as Canada, the applicability of such laws to copying onto general-purpose storage devices like computer hard drives, portable media players, and phones, for which no levies are collected, has been the subject of debate and further efforts to reform copyright law.

In some countries, the personal copying exemption explicitly requires that the content being copied was obtained legitimately – i.e., from authorized sources, not file-sharing networks. Other countries, such as the Netherlands, make no such distinction; the exemption there had been assumed, even by the government, to apply to any such copying, even from file-sharing networks. However, in April 2014, the Court of Justice of the European Union ruled that "national legislation which makes no distinction between private copies made from lawful sources and those made from counterfeited or pirated sources cannot be tolerated." Thus, in the Netherlands, for example, downloading from file-sharing networks is no longer legal.

Legality of Uploading

Although downloading or other private copying is sometimes permitted, public distribution – by uploading or otherwise offering to share copyright-protected content – remains illegal in most, if not all countries. For example, in Canada, even though it was once legal to download any copyrighted file as long as it was for noncommercial use, it was still illegal to distribute the copyrighted files (e.g. by uploading them to a P2P network).

Relaxed Penalties

Some countries, like Canada and Germany, have limited the penalties for non-commercial copyright infringement. For example, Germany has passed a bill to limit the fine for individuals accused of sharing music and movies to $200. Canada's Copyright Modernization Act claims that statutory damages for non-commercial copyright infringement are capped at C$5,000 but this only applies to copies that have been made without the breaking of any "digital lock".

On September 20, 2013, the Spanish government approved new laws that took effect at the beginning of 2014. Under the approved legislation, website owners who are earning "direct or indirect profit," such as via advertising links, from infringed content can be imprisoned for up to six years. However, peer-to-peer file-sharing platforms and search engines are exempt from the laws.

DMCA and Anti-circumvention Laws

Title I of the U.S. DMCA, the WIPO Copyright and Performances and Phonograms Treaties Implementation Act has provisions that prevent persons from "circumvent[ing] a technological measure that effectively controls access to a work". Thus if a distributor of copyrighted works has some kind of software, dongle or password access device installed in instances of the work, any attempt to bypass such a copy protection scheme may be actionable – though the US Copyright Office is currently reviewing anticircumvention rulemaking under DMCA – anticircumvention exemptions that have been in place under the DMCA include those in software designed to filter websites that are generally seen to be inefficient (child safety and public library website filtering software) and the circumvention of copy protection mechanisms that have malfunctioned, have caused the instance of the work to become inoperable or which are no longer supported by their manufacturers.

Online Intermediary Liability

Whether Internet intermediaries are liable for copyright infringement by their users is a subject of debate and court cases in a number of countries.

Definition of Intermediary

Internet intermediaries were formerly understood to be internet service providers (ISPs). However, questions of liability have also emerged in relation to other Internet infrastructure intermediaries, including Internet backbone providers, cable companies and mobile communications providers.

In addition, intermediaries are now also generally understood to include Internet portals, software and games providers, those providing virtual information such as interactive forums and comment facilities with or without a moderation system, aggregators of various kinds, such as news aggregators, universities, libraries and archives, web search engines, chat rooms, web blogs, mailing lists, and any website which provides access to third party content through, for example, hyperlinks, a crucial element of the World Wide Web.

Litigation and Legislation Concerning Intermediaries

Early court cases focused on the liability of Internet service providers (ISPs) for hosting, transmitting or publishing user-supplied content that could be actioned under civil or criminal law, such as libel, defamation, or pornography. As different content was considered in different legal systems, and in the absence of common definitions for "ISPs," "bulletin boards" or "online publishers," early law on online intermediaries' liability varied widely from country to country. The first laws on online intermediaries' liability were passed from the mid-1990s onwards.

The debate has shifted away from questions about liability for specific content, including that which may infringe copyright, towards whether online intermediaries should be *generally* responsible for content accessible through their services or infrastructure.

The U.S. Digital Millennium Copyright Act (1998) and the European E-Commerce Directive (2000) provide online intermediaries with limited statutory immunity from liability for copyright infringement. Online intermediaries hosting content that infringes copyright are not liable, so long as they do not know about it and take actions once the infringing content is brought to their attention. In U.S. law this is characterized as "safe harbor" provisions. Under European law, the governing principles for Internet Service Providers are "mere conduit", meaning that they are neutral 'pipes' with no knowledge of what they are carrying; and 'no obligation to monitor' meaning that they cannot be given a general mandate by governments to monitor content. These two principles are a barrier for certain forms of online copyright enforcement and they were the reason behind an attempt to amend the European Telecoms Package in 2009 to support new measures against copyright infringement.

Peer-to-peer Issues

Peer-to-peer file sharing intermediaries have been denied access to safe harbor provisions in relation to copyright infringement. Legal action against such intermediaries, such as Napster, are generally brought in relation to principles of secondary liability for copyright infringement, such as contributory liability and vicarious liability.

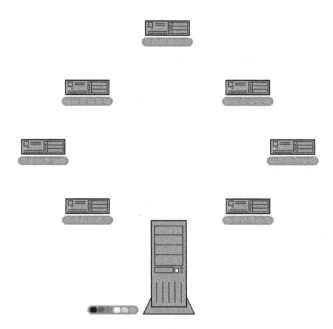

The BitTorrent protocol: In this animation, the colored bars beneath all of the seven clients in the upper region above represent the file, with each color representing an individual piece of the file. After the initial pieces transfer from the seed (large system at the bottom), the pieces are individually transferred from client to client. The original *seeder* only needs to send out one copy of the file for all the clients to receive a copy.

These types of intermediaries do not host or transmit infringing content, themselves, but may be regarded in some courts as encouraging, enabling or facilitating infringement by users. These intermediaries may include the author, publishers and marketers of peer-to-peer networking software, and the websites that allow users to download such software. In the case of the BitTorrent protocol, intermediaries may include the torrent tracker and any websites or search engines which facilitate access to torrent files. Torrent files don't contain copyrighted content, but they may make reference to files that do, and they may point to trackers which coordinate the sharing of those files. Some torrent indexing and search sites, such as The Pirate Bay, now encourage the use of magnet links, instead of direct links to torrent files, creating another layer of indirection; using such links, torrent files are obtained from other peers, rather than from a particular website.

Since the late 1990s, copyright holders have taken legal actions against a number of peer-to-peer intermediaries, such as pir, Grokster, eMule, SoulSeek, BitTorrent and Limewire, and case law on the liability of Internet service providers (ISPs) in relation to copyright infringement has emerged primarily in relation to these cases.

Nevertheless, whether and to what degree any of these types of intermediaries have secondary liability is the subject of ongoing litigation. The decentralised structure of peer-to-peer networks, in particular, does not sit easily with existing laws on online intermediaries' liability. The BitTorrent protocol established an entirely decentralised network architecture in order to distribute large files effectively. Recent developments in peer-to-peer technology towards more complex network configurations are said to have been driven by a desire to avoid liability as intermediaries under existing laws.

Limitations

Copyright law does not grant authors and publishers absolute control over the use of their work. Only certain types of works and certain kinds of uses are protected; only unauthorized uses of protected works can be said to be infringing.

Non-infringing Uses

Article 10 of the Berne Convention mandates that national laws provide for limitations to copyright, so that copyright protection does not extend to certain kinds of uses that fall under what the treaty calls "fair practice," including but not limited to minimal quotations used in journalism and education. The laws implementing these limitations and exceptions for uses that would otherwise be infringing broadly fall into the categories of either fair use or fair dealing. In common law systems, these fair practice statutes typically enshrine principles underlying many earlier judicial precedents, and are considered essential to freedom of speech.

Another example is the practice of compulsory licensing, which is where the law forbids copyright owners from denying a license for certain uses of certain kinds of works, such as compilations and live performances of music. Compulsory licensing laws generally say that for certain uses of certain works, no infringement occurs as long as a royalty, at a rate determined by law rather than private negotiation, is paid to the copyright owner or representative copyright collective. Some fair dealing laws, such as Canada's, include similar royalty requirements.

In Europe, the copyright infringement case Public Relations Consultants Association Ltd v Newspaper Licensing Agency Ltd had two prongs; one concerned whether a news aggregator service infringed the copyright of the news generators; the other concerned whether the temporary web cache created by the web browser of a consumer of the aggregator's service, *also* infringed the copyright of the news generators. The first prong was decided in favor of the news generators; in June 2014 the second prong was decided by the Court of Justice of the European Union (CJEU), which ruled that the temporary web cache of consumers of the aggregator did not infringe the copyright of the news generators.

Non-infringing Types of Works

In order to qualify for protection, a work must be an expression with a degree of originality, and it must be in a fixed medium, such as written down on paper or recorded digitally. The idea itself is not protected. That is, a copy of someone else's original idea is not infringing unless it copies that person's unique, tangible *expression* of the idea. Some of these limitations, especially regarding what qualifies as original, are embodied only in case law (judicial precedent), rather than in statutes.

In the U.S., for example, copyright case law contains a substantial similarity requirement to determine whether the work was copied. Likewise, courts may require computer software to pass an Abstraction-Filtration-Comparison test (AFC Test) to determine if it is too abstract to qualify for protection, or too dissimilar to an original work to be considered infringing. Software-related case law has also clarified that the amount of R&D, effort and expense put into a work's creation doesn't affect copyright protection.

Evaluation of alleged copyright infringement in a court of law may be substantial; the time and costs required to apply these tests vary based on the size and complexity of the copyrighted material. Furthermore, there is no standard or universally accepted test; some courts have rejected the AFC Test, for example, in favor of narrower criteria.

The POSAR test, a recently devised forensic procedure for establishing software copyright infringement cases, is an extension or an enhancement of the AFC test. POSAR, with its added features and additional facilities, offers something more to the legal and the judicial domain than what the AFC test offers. These additional features and facilities make the test more sensitive to the technical and legal requirements of software copyright infringement.

Preventative Measures

The BSA outlined four strategies that governments can adopt to reduce software piracy rates in its 2011 piracy study results:

- "Increase public education and raise awareness about software piracy and IP rights in cooperation with industry and law enforcement."

- "Modernize protections for software and other copyrighted materials to keep pace with new innovations such as cloud computing and the proliferation of networked mobile devices."

- "Strengthen enforcement of IP laws with dedicated resources, including specialized enforcement units, training for law enforcement and judiciary officials, improved cross-border cooperation among law enforcement agencies, and fulfillment of obligations under the World Trade Organization's Agreement on Trade-Related Aspects of Intellectual Property Rights (TRIPS)."

- "Lead by example by using only fully licensed software, implementing software asset management (SAM) programs, and promoting the use of legal software in state-owned enterprises, and among all contractors and suppliers."

Legal

Corporations and legislatures take different types of preventative measures to deter copyright infringement, with much of the focus since the early 1990s being on preventing or reducing digital methods of infringement. Strategies include education, civil & criminal legislation, and international agreements, as well as publicizing anti-piracy litigation successes and imposing forms of digital media copy protection, such as controversial DRM technology and anti-circumvention laws, which limit the amount of control consumers have over the use of products and content they have purchased.

Legislatures have reduced infringement by narrowing the scope of what is considered infringing. Aside from upholding international copyright treaty obligations to provide general limitations and exceptions, nations have enacted compulsory licensing laws applying specifically to digital works and uses. For example, in the U.S., the DMCA, an implementation of the 1996 WIPO Copyright Treaty, considers digital transmissions of audio recordings to be licensed as long as a designated copyright collective's royalty and reporting requirements are met. The DMCA also provides safe harbor for digital service providers whose users are suspected of copyright infringement, thus reducing the likelihood that the providers themselves will be considered directly infringing.

Some copyright owners voluntarily reduce the scope of what is considered infringement by employing relatively permissive, "open" licensing strategies: rather than privately negotiating license terms with individual users who must first seek out the copyright owner and ask for permission, the copyright owner publishes and distributes the work with a prepared license that anyone can use, as long as they adhere to certain conditions. This has the effect of reducing infringement – and the burden on courts – by simply permitting certain types of uses under terms that the copyright owner considers reasonable. Examples include free software licenses, like the GNU General Public License (GPL), and the Creative Commons licenses, which are predominantly applied to visual and literary works.

Protected Distribution

To prevent piracy of films, the standard drill of film distribution is to have a movie first released through movie theaters (theatrical window), on average approximately 16 and a half weeks, before having it released to Blu-Ray and DVD (entering its video window). During the theatrical window, digital versions of films are often transported in data storage devices by couriers rather than by data transmission. The data can be encrypted, with the key being made to work only at specific times in order to prevent leakage between screens. Coded Anti-Piracy marks can be added to films to identify the source of illegal copies and shut them down. As a result of these measures, the only versions of films available for piracy during the theatrical window are usually "cams" made by video recordings of the movie screens, which are of inferior quality compared to the original film version.

Economic Impact of Copyright Infringement

Organizations disagree on the scope and magnitude of copyright infringement's free rider economic effects and public support for the copyright regime.

In relation to computer software, the Business Software Alliance (BSA) claimed in its 2011 piracy study: "Public opinion continues to support intellectual property (IP) rights: Seven PC users in 10 support paying innovators to promote more technological advances."

Following consultation with experts on copyright infringement, the United States Government Accountability Office (GAO) clarified in 2010 that "estimating the economic impact of IP [intellectual property] infringements is extremely difficult, and assumptions must be used due to the absence of data," while "it is difficult, if not impossible, to quantify the net effect of counterfeiting and piracy on the economy as a whole."

The U.S. GAO's 2010 findings regarding the great difficulty of accurately gauging the economic impact of copyright infringement was reinforced within the same report by the body's research into three commonly cited estimates that had previously been provided to U.S. agencies. The GAO report explained that the sources – a Federal Bureau of Investigation (FBI) estimate, a Customs and Border Protection (CBP) press release and a Motor and Equipment Manufacturers Association estimate – "cannot be substantiated or traced back to an underlying data source or methodology."

Deaner explained the importance of rewarding the "investment risk" taken by motion picture studios in 2014:

Usually movies are hot because a distributor has spent hundreds of thousands of dollars promoting the product in print and TV and other forms of advertising. The major Hollywood studios spend millions on this process with marketing costs rivalling the costs of production. They are attempting then to monetise through returns that can justify the investment in both the costs of promotion and production.

Motion Picture Industry Estimates

In 2008, the Motion Picture Association of America (MPAA) reported that its six major member companies lost US$6.1 billion to piracy. A 2009 *Los Angeles Daily News* article then cited a loss figure of "roughly $20 billion a year" for Hollywood studios. According to a 2013 Wall Street Journal article, industry estimates in the United States range between $6.1B to $18.5B per year.

In an early May 2014 *Guardian* article, an annual loss figure of US$20.5 billion was cited for the movie industry. The article's basis is the results of a University of Portsmouth study that only involved Finnish participants, aged between seven and 84. The researchers, who worked with 6,000 participants, stated: "Movie pirates are also more likely to cut down their piracy if they feel they are harming the industry compared with people who illegally download music".

Software Industry Estimates

According to a 2007 BSA and International Data Corporation (IDC) study, the five countries with the highest rates of software piracy were: 1. Armenia (93%); 2. Bangladesh (92%); 3. Azerbaijan (92%); 4. Moldova (92%); and 5. Zimbabwe (91%). According to the study's results, the five countries with the lowest piracy rates were: 1. U.S. (20%); 2. Luxembourg (21%); 3. New Zealand (22%); 4. Japan (23%); and 5. Austria (25%). The 2007 report showed that the Asia-Pacific region was associated with the highest amount of loss, in terms of U.S. dollars, with $14,090,000, followed by the European Union, with a loss of $12,383,000; the lowest amount of U.S. dollars was lost in the Middle East/Africa region, where $2,446,000 was documented.

In its 2011 report, conducted in partnership with IDC and Ipsos Public Affairs, the BSA stated: "Over half of the world's personal computer users – 57 percent – admit to pirating software." The ninth annual "BSA Global Software Piracy Study" claims that the "commercial value of this shadow market of pirated software" was worth US$63.4 billion in 2011, with the highest commercial value of pirated PC software existent in the U.S. during that time period (US$9,773,000). According to the 2011 study, Zimbabwe was the nation with the highest piracy rate, at 92%, while the lowest piracy rate was present in the U.S., at 19%.

The GAO noted in 2010 that the BSA's research up until that year defined "piracy as the difference between total installed software and legitimate software sold, and its scope involved only packaged physical software."

Music Industry Estimates

In 2007, the Institute for Policy Innovation (IPI) reported that music piracy took $12.5 billion from the U.S. economy. According to the study, musicians and those involved in the recording industry are not the only ones who experience losses attributed to music piracy. Retailers have lost over a billion dollars, while piracy has resulted in 46,000 fewer production-level jobs and almost 25,000 retail jobs. The U.S. government was also reported to suffer from music piracy, losing $422 million in tax revenue.

A report from 2013, released by the European Commission Joint Research Centre suggests that illegal music downloads have almost no effect on the number of legal music downloads. The study analyzed the behavior of 16,000 European music consumers and found that although music piracy negatively affects offline music sales, illegal music downloads had a positive effect on legal music purchases. Without illegal downloading, legal purchases were about two percent lower.

The study has received criticism, particularly from The International Federation of the Phonographic Industry, which believes the study is flawed and misleading. One argument against the research is that many music consumers only download music illegally. The IFPI also points out that music piracy affects not only online music sales but also multiple facets of the music industry, which is not addressed in the study.

Criticism of Industry Estimates

The methodology of studies utilized by industry spokespeople has been heavily criticized. Inflated claims for damages and allegations of economic harm are common in copyright disputes. Some studies and figures, including those cited by the MPAA and RIAA with regards to the economic effects of film and music downloads, have been widely disputed as based on questionable assumptions which resulted in statistically unsound numbers.

In one extreme example, the RIAA claimed damages against LimeWire totaling $75 trillion – more than the global GDP – and "respectfully" disagreed with the judge's ruling that such claims were "absurd".

However, this $75 trillion figure is obtained through one specific interpretation of copyright law that would count each song downloaded as an infringement of copyright. After the conclusion of the case, LimeWire agreed to pay $105 million to RIAA.

The judicial system has also found flaws in industry estimates and calculations. In one decision, US District Court Judge James P. Jones found that the "RIAA's request problematically assumes that every illegal download resulted in a lost sale," indicating profit-loss estimates were likely extremely off.

Other critics of industry estimates argue that those who use peer-to-peer sharing services, or practice "piracy" are actually more likely to pay for music. A Jupiter Research study in 2000 found that "Napster users were 45 percent more likely to have increased their music purchasing habits than online music fans who don't use the software were." This indicated that users of peer-to-peer sharing didn't hurt the profits of the music industry, but in fact may have increased it.

Professor Aram Sinnreich, in his book *The Piracy Crusade*, states that the connection between declining music sales and the creation of peer to peer file sharing sites such as Napster is tenuous, based on correlation rather than causation. He argues that the industry at the time was undergoing artificial expansion, what he describes as a "'perfect bubble'—a confluence of economic, political, and technological forces that drove the aggregate value of music sales to unprecedented heights at the end of the twentieth century".

Sinnreich cites multiple causes for the economic bubble, including the CD format replacement cycle; the shift from music specialty stores to wholesale suppliers of music and 'minimum advertised pricing'; and the economic expansion of 1991-2001. He believes that with the introduction of new digital technologies, the bubble burst, and the industry suffered as a result.

Economic Impact of Infringement in Emerging Markets

The 2011 Business Software Alliance Piracy Study Standard, estimates the total commercial value of illegally copied software to be at $59 billion in 2010, with emerging markets accounting for $31.9 billion, over half of the total. Furthermore, mature markets for the first time received less PC shipments than emerging economies in 2010, making emerging markets now responsible for more than half of all computers in use worldwide. In addition with software infringement rates of 68 percent comparing to 24 percent of mature markets, emerging markets thus possess the majority of the global increase in the commercial value of counterfeit software. China continues to have the highest commercial value of such software at $8.9 billion among developing countries and second in the world behind the US at $9.7 billion in 2011. In 2011, the Business Software Alliance announced that 83 percent of software deployed on PCs in Africa has been pirated (excluding South Africa).

Some countries distinguish corporate piracy from private use, which is tolerated as a welfare service. This is the leading reason developing countries refuse to accept or respect copyright laws. Traian Băsescu, the president of Romania, stated that "piracy helped the young generation discover computers. It set off the development of the IT industry in Romania."

Pro-open Culture Organizations

- Free Software Foundation (FSF)
- Electronic Frontier Foundation (EFF)
- Creative Commons (CC)
- Demand Progress
- Fight for the Future
- Pirate Party

Anti-copyright Infringement Organizations

- Business Software Alliance (BSA)
- Canadian Alliance Against Software Theft (CAAST)
- Entertainment Software Association (ESA)
- Federation Against Software Theft (FAST)

- International Intellectual Property Alliance (IIPA)

- Association For the Protection Of Internet Copyright (APIC)

- Copyright Alliance

References

- Gannon, James (2001). Stealing Secrets, Telling Lies: How Spies and Codebreakers Helped Shape the Twentieth Century. Washington, D.C.: Brassey's. ISBN 1-57488-367-4.

- Shannon, Claude; Weaver, Warren (1963). The Mathematical Theory of Communication. University of Illinois Press. ISBN 0-252-72548-4.

- Levy, Steven (2001). Crypto: How the Code Rebels Beat the Government—Saving Privacy in the Digital Age. Penguin Books. p. 56. ISBN 0-14-024432-8. OCLC 244148644.

- Computer Forensics: Investigating Network Intrusions and Cybercrime. Cengage Learning. 2009-09-16. pp. 9–26. ISBN 1435483529.

- Correa, Carlos Maria; Li, Xuan (2009). and source=gbs_navlinks_s Intellectual property enforcement: international perspectives Check |url= value (help). Edward Elgar Publishing. p. 208. ISBN 978-1-84844-663-2.

- Horten, Monica (2012). The Copyright Enforcement Enigma – Internet Politics and the Telecoms Package. Palgrave Macmillan. pp. 104–106. ISBN 9780230321717.

- Virginia Crisp, Gabriel Menotti Gonring (2015). Besides the Screen: Moving Images through Distribution, Promotion and Curation. Palgrave Macmillan. ISBN 9781137471031.

- Sinnreich, Aram (2013). The Piracy Crusade: How the Music Industry's War on Sharing Destroys Markets and Erodes Civil Liberties. University of Massachusetts Press. pp. 94–118. ISBN 978-1-62534-052-8.

- Ranger, Steve (24 March 2015). "The undercover war on your internet secrets: How online surveillance cracked our trust in the web". TechRepublic. Archived from the original on 2016-06-12. Retrieved 2016-06-12.

- Blaze, Matt; Diffie, Whitefield; Rivest, Ronald L.; Schneier, Bruce; Shimomura, Tsutomu; Thompson, Eric; Wiener, Michael (January 1996). "Minimal key lengths for symmetric ciphers to provide adequate commercial security". Fortify. Retrieved 26 March 2015.

- "FIPS PUB 197: The official Advanced Encryption Standard" (PDF). Computer Security Resource Center. National Institute of Standards and Technology. Retrieved 26 March 2015.

- "NIST Selects Winner of Secure Hash Algorithm (SHA-3) Competition". Tech Beat. National Institute of Standards and Technology. October 2, 2012. Retrieved 26 March 2015.

- Wayner, Peter (24 December 1997). "British Document Outlines Early Encryption Discovery". New York Times. Retrieved 26 March 2015.

- Rosenoer, Jonathan (1995). "CRYPTOGRAPHY & SPEECH". CyberLaw. Missing or empty |url= (50. "Case Closed on Zimmermann PGP Investigation". IEEE Computer Society's Technical Committee on Security and Privacy. 14 February 1996. Retrieved 26 March 2015.

- "Bernstein v USDOJ". Electronic Privacy Information Center. United States Court of Appeals for the Ninth Circuit. 6 May 1999. Retrieved 26 March 2015.

- "DUAL-USE LIST - CATEGORY 5 – PART 2 – "INFORMATION SECURITY"" (DOC). Wassenaar Arrangement. Retrieved 26 March 2015.

6

Various Aspects and Forms of Cryptography

Cryptography as a discipline is extensive and this chapter focuses on its various aspects and forms. Confidentiality, authentication, data integrity and non-repudiation are some of the aspects of cryptography explored in this chapter. Based on the type of key used, the forms of cryptography can be broadly divided into symmetric-key algorithm and public-key algorithm, both of which have been studied in detail. Also this chapter scrutinizes topics like Cryptanalysis, Network Security Services, data security etc.

Confidentiality

Confidentiality involves a set of rules or a promise that limits access or places restrictions on certain types of information.

Legal Confidentiality

Lawyers are often required by law to keep confidential anything pertaining to the representation of a client. The duty of confidentiality is much broader than the attorney–client evidentiary privilege, which only covers *communications* between the attorney and the client.

Both the privilege and the duty serve the purpose of encouraging clients to speak frankly about their cases. This way, lawyers will be able to carry out their duty to provide clients with zealous representation. Otherwise, the opposing side may be able to surprise the lawyer in court with something which he did not know about his client, which may weaken the client's position. Also, a distrustful client might hide a relevant fact which he thinks is incriminating, but which a skilled lawyer could turn to the client's advantage (for example, by raising affirmative defenses like self-defense)

However, most jurisdictions have exceptions for situations where the lawyer has reason to believe that the client may kill or seriously injure someone, may cause substantial injury to the financial interest or property of another, or is using (or seeking to use) the lawyer's services to perpetrate a crime or fraud.

In such situations the lawyer has the discretion, but not the obligation, to disclose information designed to prevent the planned action. Most states have a version of this discretionary disclosure rule under Rules of Professional Conduct, Rule 1.6 (or its equivalent).

A few jurisdictions have made this traditionally discretionary duty mandatory.

In some jurisdictions the lawyer must try to convince the client to conform his or her conduct to the boundaries of the law before disclosing any otherwise confidential information.

Note that these exceptions generally do not cover crimes that have already occurred, even in extreme cases where murderers have confessed the location of missing bodies to their lawyers but the police are still looking for those bodies. The U.S. Supreme Court and many state supreme courts have affirmed the right of a lawyer to withhold information in such situations. Otherwise, it would be impossible for any criminal defendant to obtain a zealous defense.

California is famous for having one of the strongest duties of confidentiality in the world; its lawyers must protect client confidences at "every peril to himself [or herself]" under former California Business and Professions Code section 6068(e). Until an amendment in 2004 (which turned subsection (e) into subsection (e)(1) and added subsection (e)(2) to section 6068), California lawyers were not even permitted to disclose that a client was about to commit murder or assault. The Supreme Court of California promptly amended the California Rules of Professional Conduct to conform to the new exception in the revised statute.

Recent legislation in the UK curtails the confidentiality professionals like lawyers and accountants can maintain at the expense of the state. Accountants, for example, are required to disclose to the state any suspicions of fraudulent accounting and, even, the legitimate use of tax saving schemes if those schemes are not already known to the tax authorities.

History of the English Law About Confidentiality

The modern English law of confidence stems from the judgment of the Lord Chancellor, Lord Cottenham, in which he restrained the defendant from publishing a catalogue of private etchings made by Queen Victoria and Prince Albert (Prince Albert v Strange).

However, the jurisprudential basis of confidentiality remained largely unexamined until the case of *Saltman Engineering Co. Ltd. v Campbell Engineering Co. Ltd.*, in which the Court of Appeal upheld the existence of an equitable doctrine of confidence, independent of contract.

In *Coco v A.N.Clark (Engineers) Ltd* R.P.C. 41, Megarry J developed an influential tri-partite analysis of the essential ingredients of the cause of action for breach of confidence:

1. the information must be confidential in quality, and nature.

2. it must be imparted so as to import an obligation of confidence,

3. and there must be an unauthorised use of that information resulting in the detriment of the party communicating it.

The law in its then current state of development was authoritatively summarised by Lord Goff in the Spycatcher case. He identified three qualifications limiting the broad general principle that a duty of confidence arose when confidential information came to the knowledge of a person (the confidant) in circumstances where he had notice that the information was confidential, with the effect that it would be just in all the circumstances that he should be precluded from disclosing the information to others. First, once information had entered the public domain, it could no longer be protected as confidential. Secondly, the duty of confidence applied neither to useless information, nor to trivia. Thirdly, the public interest in the preservation of a confidence might be outweighed by a greater public interest favouring disclosure.

The incorporation into domestic law of Article 8 of the European Convention on Human Rights by the Human Rights Act 1998 has since had a profound effect on the development of the English law of confidentiality. Article 8 provides that everyone has the right to respect for his private and family life, his home and his correspondence. In *Campbell v MGN Ltd*, the House of Lords held that the Daily Mirror had breached Naomi Campbell's confidentiality rights by publishing reports and pictures of her attendance at Narcotics Anonymous meetings. Although their lordships were divided 3–2 as to the result of the appeal and adopted slightly different formulations of the applicable principles, there was broad agreement that, in confidentiality cases involving issues of privacy, the focus shifted from the nature of the relationship between claimant and defendant to (a) an examination of the nature of the information itself and (b) a balancing exercise between the claimant's rights under Article 8 and the defendant's competing rights (for example, under Article 10, to free speech).

It presently remains unclear to what extent and how this judge-led development of a partial law of privacy will impact on the equitable principles of confidentiality as traditionally understood.

Medical Confidentiality

Confidentiality is commonly applied to conversations between doctors and patients. Legal protections prevent physicians from revealing certain discussions with patients, even under oath in court. This physician-patient privilege only applies to secrets shared between physician and patient during the course of providing medical care.

The rule dates back to at least the Hippocratic Oath, which reads: *Whatever, in connection with my professional service, or not in connection with it, I see or hear, in the life of men, which ought not to be spoken of abroad, I will not divulge, as reckoning that all such should be kept secret.*

Traditionally, medical ethics has viewed the duty of confidentiality as a relatively non-negotiable tenet of medical practice.

In the United Kingdom information about an individual's HIV status is kept confidential within the NHS. This is based in law, in the NHS Constitution and in key NHS rules and procedures. It is also outlined in every NHS employee's contract of employment and in professional standards set by regulatory bodies. The National AIDS Trust's Confidentiality in the NHS: Your Information, Your Rights outlines these rights. However, there are a few limited instances when a healthcare worker can share personal information without consent if it is in the public interest. These instances are set out in guidance from the General Medical Council which is the regulatory body for doctors. Sometimes the healthcare worker has to provide the information - if required by law or in response to a court order.

Confidentiality is standard in the United States by HIPAA laws, specifically the Privacy Rule, and various state laws, some more rigorous than HIPAA. However, numerous exceptions to the rules have been carved out over the years. For example, many American states require physicians to report gunshot wounds to the police and impaired drivers to the Department of Motor Vehicles. Confidentiality is also challenged in cases involving the diagnosis of a sexually transmitted disease in a patient who refuses to reveal the diagnosis to a spouse, and in the termination of a pregnancy in an underage patient, without the knowledge of the patient's parents. Many states in the U.S. have laws governing parental notification in underage abortion.

Clinical and Counseling Psychology

The ethical principle of confidentiality requires that information shared by a client with a therapist in the course of treatment is not shared with others. This principle bolsters the therapeutic alliance, as it promotes an environment of trust. There are important exceptions to confidentiality, namely where it conflicts with the clinician's duty to warn or duty to protect. This includes instances of suicidal behavior or homicidal plans, child abuse, elder abuse and dependent adult abuse.

On 26 June 2012 a judge of Oslo District Court apologized for the court's hearing of testimony (on 14 June, regarding contact with Child Welfare Services (Norway)) that was covered by confidentiality (that had not been waived at that point of the trial of Anders Behring Breivik).

Commercial Confidentiality

Some legal jurisdictions recognise a category of commercial confidentiality whereby a business may withhold information on the basis of perceived harm to "commercial interests".

Public Policy Concerns

Confidentiality agreements which "seal" litigation settlements are not uncommon, but this can leave regulators and society ignorant of public hazards. In the U.S. state of Washington, for example, journalists discovered that about two dozen medical malpractice cases had been improperly sealed by judges, leading to improperly weak discipline by the state Department of Health. In the 1990s and early 2000s, the Catholic sexual abuse scandal involved a number of confidentiality agreements with victims. Some states have passed laws which limit confidentiality. For example, in 1990 Florida passed a 'Sunshine in Litigation' law which limits confidentiality from concealing public hazards. Washington state, Texas, Arkansas, and Louisiana have laws limiting confidentiality as well, although judicial interpretation has weakened the application of these types of laws. In the U.S. Congress, a similar federal Sunshine in Litigation Act has been proposed but not passed in 2009, 2011, 2014, and 2015.

Data integrity

Data integrity refers to maintaining and assuring the accuracy and consistency of data over its entire life-cycle, and is a critical aspect to the design, implementation and usage of any system which stores, processes, or retrieves data. The term data integrity is broad in scope and may have widely different meanings depending on the specific context – even under the same general umbrella of computing. This article provides only a broad overview of some of the different types and concerns of data integrity.

Data integrity is the opposite of data corruption, which is a form of data loss. The overall intent of any data integrity technique is the same: ensure data is recorded exactly as intended (such as a database correctly rejecting mutually exclusive possibilities,) and upon later retrieval, ensure the data is the same as it was when it was originally recorded. In short, data integrity aims to prevent unintentional changes to information. Data integrity is not to be confused with data security, the discipline of protecting data from unauthorized parties.

Any unintended changes to data as the result of a storage, retrieval or processing operation, including malicious intent, unexpected hardware failure, and human error, is failure of data integrity. If the changes are the result of unauthorized access, it may also be a failure of data security. Depending on the data involved this could manifest itself as benign as a single pixel in an image appearing a different color than was originally recorded, to the loss of vacation pictures or a business-critical database, to even catastrophic loss of human life in a life-critical system.

Integrity Types

Physical Integrity

Physical integrity deals with challenges associated with correctly storing and fetching the data itself. Challenges with physical integrity may include electromechanical faults, design flaws, material fatigue, corrosion, power outages, natural disasters, acts of war and terrorism, and other special environmental hazards such as ionizing radiation, extreme temperatures, pressures and g-forces. Ensuring physical integrity includes methods such as redundant hardware, an uninterruptible power supply, certain types of RAID arrays, radiation hardened chips, error-correcting memory, use of a clustered file system, using file systems that employ block level checksums such as ZFS, storage arrays that compute parity calculations such as exclusive or or use a cryptographic hash function and even having a watchdog timer on critical subsystems.

Physical integrity often makes extensive use of error detecting algorithms known as error-correcting codes. Human-induced data integrity errors are often detected through the use of simpler checks and algorithms, such as the Damm algorithm or Luhn algorithm. These are used to maintain data integrity after manual transcription from one computer system to another by a human intermediary (e.g. credit card or bank routing numbers). Computer-induced transcription errors can be detected through hash functions.

In production systems these techniques are used together to ensure various degrees of data integrity. For example, a computer file system may be configured on a fault-tolerant RAID array, but might not provide block-level checksums to detect and prevent silent data corruption. As another example, a database management system might be compliant with the ACID properties, but the RAID controller or hard disk drive's internal write cache might not be.

Logical Integrity

This type of integrity is concerned with the correctness or rationality of a piece of data, given a particular context. This includes topics such as referential integrity and entity integrity in a relational database or correctly ignoring impossible sensor data in robotic systems. These concerns involve ensuring that the data "makes sense" given its environment. Challenges include software bugs, design flaws, and human errors. Common methods of ensuring logical integrity include things such as a check constraints, foreign key constraints, program assertions, and other run-time sanity checks.

Both physical and logical integrity often share many common challenges such as human errors and design flaws, and both must appropriately deal with concurrent requests to record and retrieve data, the latter of which is entirely a subject on its own.

Databases

Data integrity contains guidelines for data retention, specifying or guaranteeing the length of time data can be retained in a particular database. It specifies what can be done with data values when their validity or usefulness expires. In order to achieve data integrity, these rules are consistently and routinely applied to all data entering the system, and any relaxation of enforcement could cause errors in the data. Implementing checks on the data as close as possible to the source of input (such as human data entry), causes less erroneous data to enter the system. Strict enforcement of data integrity rules causes the error rates to be lower, resulting in time saved troubleshooting and tracing erroneous data and the errors it causes algorithms.

Data integrity also includes rules defining the relations a piece of data can have, to other pieces of data, such as a *Customer* record being allowed to link to purchased *Products*, but not to unrelated data such as *Corporate Assets*. Data integrity often includes checks and correction for invalid data, based on a fixed schema or a predefined set of rules. An example being textual data entered where a date-time value is required. Rules for data derivation are also applicable, specifying how a data value is derived based on algorithm, contributors and conditions. It also specifies the conditions on how the data value could be re-derived.

Types of Integrity Constraints

Data integrity is normally enforced in a database system by a series of integrity constraints or rules. Three types of integrity constraints are an inherent part of the relational data model: entity integrity, referential integrity and domain integrity:

- *Entity integrity* concerns the concept of a primary key. Entity integrity is an integrity rule which states that every table must have a primary key and that the column or columns chosen to be the primary key should be unique and not null.

- *Referential integrity* concerns the concept of a foreign key. The referential integrity rule states that any foreign-key value can only be in one of two states. The usual state of affairs is that the foreign-key value refers to a primary key value of some table in the database. Occasionally, and this will depend on the rules of the data owner, a foreign-key value can be null. In this case we are explicitly saying that either there is no relationship between the objects represented in the database or that this relationship is unknown.

- *Domain integrity* specifies that all columns in a relational database must be declared upon a defined domain. The primary unit of data in the relational data model is the data item. Such data items are said to be non-decomposable or atomic. A domain is a set of values of the same type. Domains are therefore pools of values from which actual values appearing in the columns of a table are drawn.

- *User-defined integrity* refers to a set of rules specified by a user, which do not belong to the entity, domain and referential integrity categories.

If a database supports these features, it is the responsibility of the database to ensure data integrity as well as the consistency model for the data storage and retrieval. If a database does not support these features it is the responsibility of the applications to ensure data integrity while the database supports the consistency model for the data storage and retrieval.

Having a single, well-controlled, and well-defined data-integrity system increases

- stability (one centralized system performs all data integrity operations)

- performance (all data integrity operations are performed in the same tier as the consistency model)

- re-usability (all applications benefit from a single centralized data integrity system)

- maintainability (one centralized system for all data integrity administration).

As of 2012, since all modern databases support these features, it has become the de facto responsibility of the database to ensure data integrity. Out-dated and legacy systems that use file systems (text, spreadsheets, ISAM, flat files, etc.) for their consistency model lack any kind of data-integrity model. This requires organizations to invest a large amount of time, money and personnel in building data-integrity systems on a per-application basis that needlessly duplicate the existing data integrity systems found in modern databases. Many companies, and indeed many database systems themselves, offer products and services to migrate out-dated and legacy systems to modern databases to provide these data-integrity features. This offers organizations substantial savings in time, money and resources because they do not have to develop per-application data-integrity systems that must be refactored each time the business requirements change.

Examples

An example of a data-integrity mechanism is the parent-and-child relationship of related records. If a parent record owns one or more related child records all of the referential integrity processes are handled by the database itself, which automatically ensures the accuracy and integrity of the data so that no child record can exist without a parent (also called being orphaned) and that no parent loses their child records. It also ensures that no parent record can be deleted while the parent record owns any child records. All of this is handled at the database level and does not require coding integrity checks into each applications.

File Systems

Various research results show that neither widespread filesystems (including UFS, Ext, XFS, JFS and NTFS) nor hardware RAID solutions provide sufficient protection against data integrity problems.

Some filesystems (including Btrfs and ZFS) provide internal data and metadata checksumming, what is used for detecting silent data corruption and improving data integrity. If a corruption is detected that way and internal RAID mechanisms provided by those filesystems are also used, such filesystems can additionally reconstruct corrupted data in a transparent way. This approach allows improved data integrity protection covering the entire data paths, which is usually known as end-to-end data protection.

Data Storage

Apart from data in databases, standards exist to address the integrity of data on storage devices.

Authentication

Authentication is the act of confirming the truth of an attribute of a single piece of data (a datum) claimed true by an entity. In contrast with identification which refers to the act of stating or otherwise indicating a claim purportedly attesting to a person or thing's identity, authentication is the process of actually confirming that identity. It might involve confirming the identity of a person by validating their identity documents, verifying the authenticity of a website with a digital certificate, determining the age of an artifact by carbon dating, or ensuring that a product is what its packaging and labeling claim to be. In other words, authentication often involves verifying the validity of at least one form of identification.

Methods

Authentication is relevant to multiple fields. In art, antiques and anthropology, a common problem is verifying that a given artifact was produced by a certain person or in a certain place or period of history. In computer science, verifying a person's identity is often required to allow access to confidential data or systems.

Authentication can be considered to be of three types:

The first type of authentication is accepting proof of identity given by a credible person who has first-hand evidence that the identity is genuine. When authentication is required of art or physical objects, this proof could be a friend, family member or colleague attesting to the item's provenance, perhaps by having witnessed the item in its creator's possession. With autographed sports memorabilia, this could involve someone attesting that they witnessed the object being signed. A vendor selling branded items implies authenticity, while he or she may not have evidence that every step in the supply chain was authenticated. Centralized authority-based trust relationships back most secure internet communication through known public certificate authorities; decentralized peer-based trust, also known as a web of trust, is used for personal services such as email or files (pretty good privacy, GNU Privacy Guard) and trust is established by known individuals signing each other's cryptographic key at Key signing parties, for instance.

The second type of authentication is comparing the attributes of the object itself to what is known about objects of that origin. For example, an art expert might look for similarities in the style of painting, check the location and form of a signature, or compare the object to an old photograph. An archaeologist, on the other hand, might use carbon dating to verify the age of an artifact, do a chemical and spectroscopic analysis of the materials used, or compare the style of construction or decoration to other artifacts of similar origin. The physics of sound and light, and comparison with a known physical environment, can be used to examine the authenticity of audio recordings, photographs, or videos. Documents can be verified as being created on ink or paper readily available at the time of the item's implied creation.

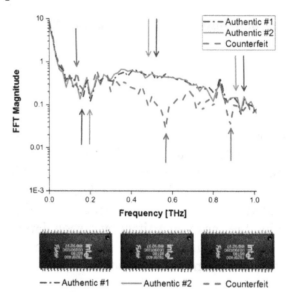

Authentication using spectroscopic material analysis: The differences in constituent materials reveals the counterfeit item.

Attribute comparison may be vulnerable to forgery. In general, it relies on the facts that creating a forgery indistinguishable from a genuine artifact requires expert knowledge, that mistakes are easily made, and that the amount of effort required to do so is considerably greater than the amount of profit that can be gained from the forgery.

In art and antiques, certificates are of great importance for authenticating an object of interest and value. Certificates can, however, also be forged, and the authentication of these poses a problem. For instance, the son of Han van Meegeren, the well-known art-forger, forged the work of his father and provided a certificate for its provenance as well.

Criminal and civil penalties for fraud, forgery, and counterfeiting can reduce the incentive for falsification, depending on the risk of getting caught.

Currency and other financial instruments commonly use this second type of authentication method. Bills, coins, and cheques incorporate hard-to-duplicate physical features, such as fine printing or engraving, distinctive feel, watermarks, and holographic imagery, which are easy for trained receivers to verify.

The third type of authentication relies on documentation or other external affirmations. In criminal courts, the rules of evidence often require establishing the chain of custody of evidence presented. This can be accomplished through a written evidence log, or by testimony from the police detectives and forensics staff that handled it. Some antiques are accompanied by certificates attesting to their authenticity. Signed sports memorabilia is usually accompanied by a certificate of authenticity. These external records have their own problems of forgery and perjury, and are also vulnerable to being separated from the artifact and lost.

In computer science, a user can be given access to secure systems based on user credentials that imply authenticity. A network administrator can give a user a password, or provide the user with a key card or other access device to allow system access. In this case, authenticity is implied but not guaranteed.

Consumer goods such as pharmaceuticals, perfume, fashion clothing can use all three forms of authentication to prevent counterfeit goods from taking advantage of a popular brand's reputation (damaging the brand owner's sales and reputation). As mentioned above, having an item for sale in a reputable store implicitly attests to it being genuine, the first type of authentication. The second type of authentication might involve comparing the quality and craftsmanship of an item, such as an expensive handbag, to genuine articles. The third type of authentication could be the presence of a trademark on the item, which is a legally protected marking, or any other identifying feature which aids consumers in the identification of genuine brand-name goods. With software, companies have taken great steps to protect from counterfeiters, including adding holograms, security rings, security threads and color shifting ink.

Factors and Identity

The ways in which someone may be authenticated fall into three categories, based on what are known as the factors of authentication: something the user *knows*, something the user *has*, and something the user *is*. Each authentication factor covers a range of elements used to authenticate or verify a person's identity prior to being granted access, approving a transaction request, signing a document or other work product, granting authority to others, and establishing a chain of authority.

Security research has determined that for a positive authentication, elements from at least two, and preferably all three, factors should be verified. The three factors (classes) and some of elements of each factor are:

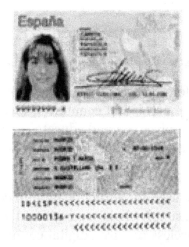

This is a picture of the front (top) and back (bottom) of an ID Card.

- the knowledge factors: Something the user knows (e.g., a password, Partial Password, pass phrase, or personal identification number (PIN), challenge response (the user must answer a question, or pattern), Security question

- the ownership factors: Something the user has (e.g., wrist band, ID card, security token, cell phone with built-in hardware token, software token, or cell phone holding a software token)

- the inherence factors: Something the user is or does (e.g., fingerprint, retinal pattern, DNA sequence (there are assorted definitions of what is sufficient), signature, face, voice, unique bio-electric signals, or other biometric identifier).

Two-factor Authentication

When elements representing two factors are required for authentication, the term *two-factor authentication* is applied — e.g. a bankcard (something the user has) and a PIN (something the user knows). Business networks may require users to provide a password (knowledge factor) and a pseudorandom number from a security token (ownership factor). Access to a very-high-security system might require a mantrap screening of height, weight, facial, and fingerprint checks (several inherence factor elements) plus a PIN and a day code (knowledge factor elements), but this is still a two-factor authentication.

Product Authentication

A Security hologram label on an electronics box for authentication

Counterfeit products are often offered to consumers as being authentic. Counterfeit consumer goods such as electronics, music, apparel, and counterfeit medications have been sold as being legitimate. Efforts to control the supply chain and educate consumers help ensure that authentic products are sold and used. Even security printing on packages, labels, and nameplates, however, is subject to counterfeiting.

A secure key storage device can be used for authentication in consumer electronics, network authentication, license management, supply chain management, etc. Generally the device to be authenticated needs some sort of wireless or wired digital connection to either a host system or a network. Nonetheless, the component being authenticated need not be electronic in nature as an authentication chip can be mechanically attached and read through a connector to the host e.g. an authenticated ink tank for use with a printer. For products and services that these Secure Coprocessors can be applied to, they can offer a solution that can be much more difficult to counterfeit than most other options while at the same time being more easily verified.

Packaging

Packaging and labeling can be engineered to help reduce the risks of counterfeit consumer goods or the theft and resale of products. Some package constructions are more difficult to copy and some have pilfer indicating seals. Counterfeit goods, unauthorized sales (diversion), material substitution and tampering can all be reduced with these anti-counterfeiting technologies. Packages may include authentication seals and use security printing to help indicate that the package and contents are not counterfeit; these too are subject to counterfeiting. Packages also can include anti-theft devices, such as dye-packs, RFID tags, or electronic article surveillance tags that can be activated or detected by devices at exit points and require specialized tools to deactivate. Anti-counterfeiting technologies that can be used with packaging include:

- Taggant fingerprinting – uniquely coded microscopic materials that are verified from a database

- Encrypted micro-particles – unpredictably placed markings (numbers, layers and colors) not visible to the human eye

- Holograms – graphics printed on seals, patches, foils or labels and used at point of sale for visual verification

- Micro-printing – second line authentication often used on currencies

- Serialized barcodes

- UV printing – marks only visible under UV light

- Track and trace systems – use codes to link products to database tracking system

- Water indicators – become visible when contacted with water

- DNA tracking – genes embedded onto labels that can be traced

- Color shifting ink or film – visible marks that switch colors or texture when tilted

- Tamper evident seals and tapes – destructible or graphically verifiable at point of sale

- 2d barcodes – data codes that can be tracked

- RFID chips

Information Content

The authentication of information can pose special problems with electronic communication, such as vulnerability to man-in-the-middle attacks, whereby a third party taps into the communication stream, and poses as each of the two other communicating parties, in order to intercept information from each. Extra identity factors can be required to authenticate each party's identity.

Literary forgery can involve imitating the style of a famous author. If an original manuscript, typewritten text, or recording is available, then the medium itself (or its packaging — anything from a box to e-mail headers) can help prove or disprove the authenticity of the document.

However, text, audio, and video can be copied into new media, possibly leaving only the informational content itself to use in authentication.

Various systems have been invented to allow authors to provide a means for readers to reliably authenticate that a given message originated from or was relayed by them. These involve authentication factors like:

- A difficult-to-reproduce physical artifact, such as a seal, signature, watermark, special stationery, or fingerprint.

- A shared secret, such as a passphrase, in the content of the message.

- An electronic signature; public-key infrastructure is often used to cryptographically guarantee that a message has been signed by the holder of a particular private key.

The opposite problem is detection of plagiarism, where information from a different author is passed off as a person's own work. A common technique for proving plagiarism is the discovery of another copy of the same or very similar text, which has different attribution. In some cases, excessively high quality or a style mismatch may raise suspicion of plagiarism.

Factual Verification

Determining the truth or factual accuracy of information in a message is generally considered a separate problem from authentication. A wide range of techniques, from detective work, to fact checking in journalism, to scientific experiment might be employed.

Video Authentication

It is sometimes necessary to authenticate the veracity of video recordings used as evidence in judicial proceedings. Proper chain-of-custody records and secure storage facilities can help ensure the admissibility of digital or analog recordings by the Court.

Literacy & Literature Authentication

In literacy, authentication is a readers' process of questioning the veracity of an aspect of literature and then verifying those questions via research. The fundamental question for authentication of literature is - Do you believe it? Related to that, an authentication project is therefore a reading and writing activity which students documents the relevant research process (). It builds students' critical literacy. The documentation materials for literature go beyond narrative texts and likely include informational texts, primary sources, and multimedia. The process typically involves both internet and hands-on library research. When authenticating historical fiction in particular, readers considers the extent that the major historical events, as well as the culture portrayed (e.g., the language, clothing, food, gender roles), are believable for the time period. ().

History and State-of-the-art

NSA KAL-55B Tactical Authentication System used by the U.S. military during the Vietnam War. - National Cryptologic Museum

Historically, fingerprints have been used as the most authoritative method of authentication, but recent court cases in the US and elsewhere have raised fundamental doubts about fingerprint reliability. Outside of the legal system as well, fingerprints have been shown to be easily spoofable, with British Telecom's top computer-security official noting that "few" fingerprint readers have not already been tricked by one spoof or another. Hybrid or two-tiered authentication methods offer a compelling solution, such as private keys encrypted by fingerprint inside of a USB device.

In a computer data context, cryptographic methods have been developed which are currently not spoofable if and only if the originator's key has not been compromised. That the originator (or anyone other than an attacker) knows (or doesn't know) about a compromise is irrelevant. It is not known whether these cryptographically based authentication methods are provably secure, since unanticipated mathematical developments may make them vulnerable to attack in future. If that were to occur, it may call into question much of the authentication in the past. In particular, a digitally signed contract may be questioned when a new attack on the cryptography underlying the signature is discovered.

Strong Authentication

The U.S. Government's National Information Assurance Glossary defines strong authentication as

layered authentication approach relying on two or more authenticators to establish the identity of an originator or receiver of information.

The above definition is consistent with that of the European Central Bank, as discussed in the strong authentication entry.

The Fast IDentity Online (FIDO) Alliance has been striving to establish technical specifications for strong authentication.

Authorization

A soldier checks a driver's identification card before allowing her to enter a military base.

The process of authorization is distinct from that of authentication. Whereas authentication is the process of verifying that "you are who you say you are", authorization is the process of verifying that "you are permitted to do what you are trying to do". Authorization thus presupposes authentication.

For example, a client showing proper identification credentials to a bank teller is asking to be authenticated that he really is the one whose identification he is showing. A client whose authentication request is approved becomes authorized to access the accounts of that account holder, but no others.

However note that if a stranger tries to access someone else's account with his own identification credentials, the stranger's identification credentials will still be successfully authenticated because they are genuine and not counterfeit, however the stranger will not be successfully authorized to access the account, as the stranger's identification credentials had not been previously set to be eligible to access the account, even if valid (i.e. authentic).

Similarly when someone tries to log on a computer, they are usually first requested to identify themselves with a login name and support that with a password. Afterwards, this combination is checked against an existing login-password validity record to check if the combination is authentic. If so, the user becomes authenticated (i.e. the identification he supplied in step 1 is valid, or authentic). Finally, a set of pre-defined permissions and restrictions for that particular login name is assigned to this user, which completes the final step, authorization.

Even though authorization cannot occur without authentication, the former term is sometimes used to mean the combination of both.

To distinguish "authentication" from the closely related "authorization", the shorthand notations A1 (authentication), A2 (authorization) as well as AuthN / AuthZ (AuthR) or Au / Az are used in some communities.

Normally delegation was considered to be a part of authorization domain. Recently authentication is also used for various type of delegation tasks. Delegation in IT network is also a new but evolving field.

Access Control

One familiar use of authentication and authorization is access control. A computer system that is supposed to be used only by those authorized must attempt to detect and exclude the unauthorized. Access to it is therefore usually controlled by insisting on an authentication procedure to establish with some degree of confidence the identity of the user, granting privileges established for that identity. One such procedure involves the usage of Layer 8 which allows IT administrators to identify users, control Internet activity of users in the network, set user based policies and generate reports by username. Common examples of access control involving authentication include:

- Asking for photoID when a contractor first arrives at a house to perform work.
- Using captcha as a means of asserting that a user is a human being and not a computer program.
- By using One Time Password (OTP), received on a tele-network enabled device like mobile phone, as an authentication password/PIN
- A computer program using a blind credential to authenticate to another program
- Entering a country with a passport
- Logging in to a computer
- Using a confirmation E-mail to verify ownership of an e-mail address
- Using an Internet banking system
- Withdrawing cash from an ATM

In some cases, ease of access is balanced against the strictness of access checks. For example, the credit card network does not require a personal identification number for authentication of the claimed identity; and a small transaction usually does not even require a signature of the authenticated person for proof of authorization of the transaction. The security of the system is maintained by limiting distribution of credit card numbers, and by the threat of punishment for fraud.

Security experts argue that it is impossible to prove the identity of a computer user with absolute certainty. It is only possible to apply one or more tests which, if passed, have been previously declared to be sufficient to proceed. The problem is to determine which tests are sufficient, and many such are inadequate. Any given test can be spoofed one way or another, with varying degrees of difficulty.

Computer security experts are now also recognising that despite extensive efforts, as a business, research and network community, we still do not have a secure understanding of the requirements for authentication, in a range of circumstances. Lacking this understanding is a significant barrier to identifying optimum methods of authentication. major questions are:

- What is authentication for?

- Who benefits from authentication/who is disadvantaged by authentication failures?

- What disadvantages can effective authentication actually guard against?

Non-repudiation

Non-repudiation refers to a state of affairs where the author of a statement will not be able to successfully challenge the authorship of the statement or validity of an associated contract. The term is often seen in a legal setting wherein the authenticity of a signature is being challenged. In such an instance, the authenticity is being "repudiated".

In Security

In a general sense *non-repudiation* involves associating actions or changes to a unique individual. For a secure area, for example, it may be desirable to implement a key card access system. Non-repudiation would be violated if it were not also a strictly enforced policy to prohibit sharing of the key cards and to immediately report lost or stolen cards. Otherwise determining who performed the action of opening the door cannot be trivially determined. Similarly, for computer accounts, the individual owner of the account must not allow others to use that account, especially, for instance, by giving away their account's password, and a policy should be implemented to enforce this. This prevents the owner of the account from denying actions performed by the account.

In Digital Security

Regarding digital security, the cryptological meaning and application of non-repudiation shifts to mean:

- A service that provides proof of the integrity and origin of data.

- An authentication that can be asserted to be genuine with high assurance.

Proof of data integrity is typically the easiest of these requirements to accomplish. A data hash, such as SHA2, is usually sufficient to establish that the likelihood of data being undetectably changed is extremely low. Even with this safeguard, it is still possible to tamper with data in transit, either through a man-in-the-middle attack or phishing. Due to this flaw, data integrity is best asserted when the recipient already possesses the necessary verification information.

The most common method of asserting the digital origin of data is through digital certificates, a form of public key infrastructure to which digital signatures belong. Note that the public key scheme is not used for encryption in this form; i.e. the goal is not to achieve confidentiality, since a message signed with a private key can be read by anyone using the public key. Verifying the digital origin means that the certified/signed data can be, with reasonable certainty, trusted to be from somebody who possesses the private key corresponding to the signing certificate. If the key is not properly safeguarded by the original owner, digital forgery can become a major concern.

Trusted Third Parties (TTPs)

The ways in which a party may attempt to repudiate a signature present a challenge to the trust-worthiness of the signatures themselves. The standard approach to mitigating these risks is to involve a trusted third party.

The two most common TTPs are forensic analysts and notaries. A forensic analyst specializing in handwriting can look at a signature, compare it to a known valid signature, and make a reasonable assessment of the legitimacy of the first signature. A notary provides a witness whose job is to veri-fy the identity of an individual by checking other credentials and affixing their certification that the party signing is who they claim to be. Further, a notary provides the extra benefit of maintaining independent logs of their transactions, complete with the type of credential checked and another signature that can independently be verified by the preceding forensic analyst. For this double security, notaries are the preferred form of verification.

On the digital side, the only TTP is the repository for public key certificates. This provides the recipient with the ability to verify the origin of an item even if no direct exchange of the public information has ever been made. The digital signature, however, is forensically identical in both legitimate and forged uses - if someone possesses the private key they can create a "real" signature. The protection of the private key is the idea behind the United States Department of Defense's Common Access Card (CAC), which never allows the key to leave the card and therefore necessi-tates the possession of the card in addition to the personal identification number (PIN) code nec-essary to unlock the card for permission to use it for encryption and digital signatures.

Symmetric-key Algorithm

Symmetric-key algorithms are algorithms for cryptography that use the same cryptographic keys for both encryption of plaintext and decryption of ciphertext. The keys may be identical or there may be a simple transformation to go between the two keys. The keys, in practice, represent a shared secret between two or more parties that can be used to maintain a private information link. This requirement that both parties have access to the secret key is one of the main drawbacks of symmetric key encryption, in comparison to public-key encryption (also known as asymmetric key encryption).

Types of Symmetric-key Algorithms

Symmetric-key encryption can use either stream ciphers or block ciphers.

- Stream ciphers encrypt the digits (typically bytes) of a message one at a time.

- Block ciphers take a number of bits and encrypt them as a single unit, padding the plaintext so that it is a multiple of the block size. Blocks of 64 bits was commonly used. The Advanced Encryption Standard (AES) algorithm approved by NIST in December 2001, and the GCM block cipher mode of operation use 128-bit blocks.

Implementations

Examples of popular symmetric algorithms include Twofish, Serpent, AES (Rijndael), Blowfish, CAST5, Grasshopper, RC4, 3DES, Skipjack, Safer+/++ (Bluetooth), and IDEA.

Cryptographic Primitives Based on Symmetric Ciphers

Symmetric ciphers are commonly used to achieve other cryptographic primitives than just encryption.

Encrypting a message does not guarantee that this message is not changed while encrypted. Hence often a message authentication code is added to a ciphertext to ensure that changes to the ciphertext will be noted by the receiver. Message authentication codes can be constructed from symmetric ciphers (e.g. CBC-MAC).

However, symmetric ciphers cannot be used for non-repudiation purposes except by involving additional parties.

Another application is to build hash functions from block ciphers. See one-way compression function for descriptions of several such methods.

Construction of Symmetric Ciphers

Many modern block ciphers are based on a construction proposed by Horst Feistel. Feistel's construction makes it possible to build invertible functions from other functions that are themselves not invertible.

Security of Symmetric Ciphers

Symmetric ciphers have historically been susceptible to known-plaintext attacks, chosen-plaintext attacks, differential cryptanalysis and linear cryptanalysis. Careful construction of the functions for each round can greatly reduce the chances of a successful attack.

Key Generation

When used with asymmetric ciphers for key transfer, pseudorandom key generators are nearly always used to generate the symmetric cipher session keys. However, lack of randomness in those generators or in their initialization vectors is disastrous and has led to cryptanalytic breaks in the past. Therefore, it is essential that an implementation uses a source of high entropy for its initialization.

Reciprocal Cipher

A reciprocal cipher is a cipher where, just as one enters the plaintext into the cryptography system to get the ciphertext, one could enter the ciphertext into the same place in the system to get the plaintext. A reciprocal cipher is also sometimes referred as self-reciprocal cipher. Examples of reciprocal ciphers include:

- Beaufort cipher
- Enigma machine
- ROT13
- XOR cipher
- Vatsyayana cipher

Public-key Cryptography

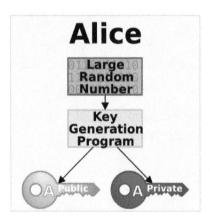

An unpredictable (typically large and random) number is used to begin generation of an acceptable pair of keys suitable for use by an asymmetric key algorithm.

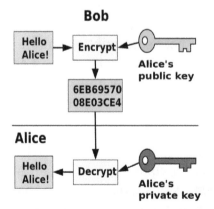

In an asymmetric key encryption scheme, anyone can encrypt messages using the public key, but only the holder of the paired private key can decrypt. Security depends on the secrecy of the private key.

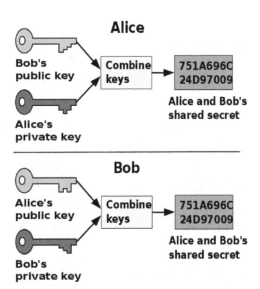

In the Diffie–Hellman key exchange scheme, each party generates a public/private key pair and distributes the public key. After obtaining an authentic copy of each other's public keys, Alice and Bob can compute a shared secret offline. The shared secret can be used, for instance, as the key for a symmetric cipher.

Public-key cryptography, or asymmetric cryptography, is any cryptographic system that uses pairs of keys: *public keys* that may be disseminated widely paired with *private keys* which are known only to the owner. There are two functions that can be achieved: using a public key to authenticate that a message originated with a holder of the paired private key; or encrypting a message with a public key to ensure that only the holder of the paired private key can decrypt it.

In a public-key encryption system, any person can encrypt a message using the public key of the receiver, but such a message can be decrypted only with the receiver's private key. For this to work it must be computationally easy for a user to generate a public and private key-pair to be used for encryption and decryption. The strength of a public-key cryptography system relies on the degree of difficulty (computational impracticality) for a properly generated private key to be determined from its corresponding public key. Security then depends only on keeping the private key private, and the public key may be published without compromising security.

Public-key cryptography systems often rely on cryptographic algorithms based on mathematical problems that currently admit no efficient solution—particularly those inherent in certain integer factorization, discrete logarithm, and elliptic curve relationships. Public key algorithms, unlike symmetric key algorithms, do *not* require a secure channel for the initial exchange of one (or more) secret keys between the parties.

Because of the computational complexity of asymmetric encryption, it is usually used only for small blocks of data, typically the transfer of a symmetric encryption key (e.g. a session key). This symmetric key is then used to encrypt the rest of the potentially long message sequence. The symmetric encryption/decryption is based on simpler algorithms and is much faster.

Message authentication involves hashing the message to produce a "digest," and encrypting the digest with the private key to produce a digital signature. Thereafter anyone can verify this signature by:

1. computing the hash of the message

2. decrypting the signature with the signer's public key

3. comparing the computed digest with the decrypted digest

Equality between the digests confirms the message is unmodified since it was signed, and that the signer, and no one else, intentionally performed the signature operation — presuming the signer's private key has remained secret. The security of such procedure depends on a hash algorithm of such quality that it is computationally impossible to alter or find a substitute message that produces the same digest - but studies have shown that even with the MD5 and SHA-1 algorithms, producing an altered or substitute message is not impossible. The current hashing standard for encryption is SHA-2. The message itself can also be used in place of the digest.

Public-key algorithms are fundamental security ingredients in cryptosystems, applications and protocols. They underpin various Internet standards, such as Transport Layer Security (TLS), S/MIME, PGP, and GPG. Some public key algorithms provide key distribution and secrecy (e.g., Diffie–Hellman key exchange), some provide digital signatures (e.g., Digital Signature Algorithm), and some provide both (e.g., RSA).

Public-key cryptography finds application in, among others, the information technology security discipline, information security. Information security (IS) is concerned with all aspects of protecting electronic information assets against security threats. Public-key cryptography is used as a method of assuring the confidentiality, authenticity and non-repudiability of electronic communications and data storage.

Description

Two of the best-known uses of public-key cryptography are:

- *Public-key encryption*, in which a message is encrypted with a recipient's public key. The message cannot be decrypted by anyone who does not possess the matching private key, who is thus presumed to be the owner of that key and the person associated with the public key. This is used in an attempt to ensure confidentiality.

- *Digital signatures*, in which a message is signed with the sender's private key and can be verified by anyone who has access to the sender's public key. This verification proves that the sender had access to the private key, and therefore is likely to be the person associated with the public key. This also ensures that the message has not been tampered with, as any manipulation of the message will result in changes to the encoded message digest, which otherwise remains unchanged between the sender and receiver.

An analogy to public-key encryption is that of a locked mail box with a mail slot. The mail slot is exposed and accessible to the public – its location (the street address) is, in essence, the public key. Anyone knowing the street address can go to the door and drop a written message through the slot. However, only the person who possesses the key can open the mailbox and read the message.

An analogy for digital signatures is the sealing of an envelope with a personal wax seal. The message can be opened by anyone, but the presence of the unique seal authenticates the sender.

A central problem with the use of public-key cryptography is confidence/proof that a particular public key is authentic, in that it is correct and belongs to the person or entity claimed, and has not been tampered with or replaced by a malicious third party. The usual approach to this problem is to use a public-key infrastructure (PKI), in which one or more third parties – known as certificate authorities – certify ownership of key pairs. PGP, in addition to being a certificate authority structure, has used a scheme generally called the "web of trust", which decentralizes such authentication of public keys by a central mechanism, and substitutes individual endorsements of the link between user and public key. To date, no fully satisfactory solution to the "public key authentication problem" has been found.

History

During the early history of cryptography, two parties would rely upon a key that they would exchange by means of a secure, but non-cryptographic, method such as a face-to-face meeting or a trusted courier. This key, which both parties kept absolutely secret, could then be used to exchange encrypted messages. A number of significant practical difficulties arise with this approach to distributing keys.

In the 1874 book *The Principles of Science* by William Stanley Jevons, he wrote:

"Can the reader say what two numbers multiplied together will produce the number 8616460799? I think it unlikely that anyone but myself will ever know." -William Stanley Jevons

Here he described the relationship of one-way functions to cryptography, and went on to discuss specifically the factorization problem used to create a trapdoor function. In July 1996, mathematician Solomon W. Golomb said: "Jevons anticipated a key feature of the RSA Algorithm for public key cryptography, although he certainly did not invent the concept of public key cryptography." (In 1869, Jevons had also invented a computing machine he called a "Logic Piano".)

Classified Discovery

In 1970, James H. Ellis, a British cryptographer at the UK Government Communications Headquarters (GCHQ), conceived of the possibility of "non-secret encryption", (now called public-key cryptography), but could see no way to implement it. In 1973, his colleague Clifford Cocks implemented what has become known as the RSA encryption algorithm, giving a practical method of "non-secret encryption", and in 1974, another GCHQ mathematician and cryptographer, Malcolm J. Williamson, developed what is now known as Diffie–Hellman key exchange. The scheme was also passed to the NSA. With a military focus, and low computing power, the power of public-key cryptography was unrealised in both organisations:

I judged it most important for military use .... if you can share your key rapidly and electronically, you have a major advantage over your opponent. Only at the end of the evolution from Berners-Lee designing an open internet architecture for CERN, its adaptation and adoption for the Arpanet ... did public key cryptography realise its full potential. -Ralph Benjamin

Their discovery did not become public knowledge for 27 years, until the research was declassified by the British government in 1997.

Public Discovery

In 1976, an asymmetric-key cryptosystem was published by Whitfield Diffie and Martin Hellman who, influenced by Ralph Merkle's work on public-key distribution, disclosed a method of public-key agreement. This method of key exchange, which uses exponentiation in a finite field, came to be known as Diffie–Hellman key exchange. This was the first published practical method for establishing a shared secret-key over an authenticated (but not confidential) communications channel without using a prior shared secret. Merkle's "public-key-agreement technique" became known as Merkle's Puzzles, and was invented in 1974 and published in 1978.

In 1977, a generalization of Cocks' scheme was independently invented by Ron Rivest, Adi Shamir and Leonard Adleman, all then at MIT. The latter authors published their work in 1978, and the algorithm came to be known as RSA, from their initials. RSA uses exponentiation modulo a product of two very large primes, to encrypt and decrypt, performing both public key encryption and public key digital signature. Its security is connected to the extreme difficulty of factoring large integers, a problem for which there is no known efficient general technique. In 1979, Michael O. Rabin published a related cryptosystem that is probably secure as long as the factorization of the public key remains difficult – it remains an assumption that RSA also enjoys this security.

Since the 1970s, a large number and variety of encryption, digital signature, key agreement, and other techniques have been developed in the field of public-key cryptography. The ElGamal cryptosystem, invented by Taher ElGamal relies on the similar and related high level of difficulty of the discrete logarithm problem, as does the closely related DSA, which was developed at the US National Security Agency (NSA) and published by NIST as a proposed standard.

The introduction of elliptic curve cryptography by Neal Koblitz and Victor Miller, independently and simultaneously in the mid-1980s, has yielded new public-key algorithms based on the discrete logarithm problem. Although mathematically more complex, elliptic curves provide smaller key sizes and faster operations for approximately equivalent estimated security.

Typical Use

Public-key cryptography is often used to secure electronic communication over an open networked environment such as the Internet, without relying on a hidden or covert channel, even for key exchange. Open networked environments are susceptible to a variety of communication security problems, such as man-in-the-middle attacks and spoofs. Communication security typically includes requirements that the communication must not be readable during transit (preserving confidentiality), the communication must not be modified during transit (preserving the integrity of the communication), the communication must originate from an identified party (sender authenticity), and the recipient must not be able to repudiate or deny receiving the communication. Combining public-key cryptography with an Enveloped Public Key Encryption (EPKE) method, allows for the secure sending of a communication over an open networked environment.

The distinguishing technique used in public-key cryptography is the use of asymmetric key algorithms, where a key used by one party to perform encryption is not the same as the key used by another in decryption. Each user has a pair of cryptographic keys – a public encryption key and a private decryption key. For example, a key pair used for digital signatures consists of a private signing key and a public verification key. The public key may be widely distributed, while the private key is known only to its proprietor. The keys are related mathematically, but the parameters are chosen so that calculating the private key from the public key is unfeasible.

In contrast, symmetric-key algorithms – variations of which have been used for thousands of years – use a *single* secret key, which must be shared and kept private by both the sender (for encryption) and the receiver (for decryption). To use a symmetric encryption scheme, the sender and receiver must securely share a key in advance.

Because symmetric key algorithms are nearly always much less computationally intensive than asymmetric ones, it is common to exchange a key using a key-exchange algorithm, then transmit data using that key and a symmetric key algorithm. PGP and the SSL/TLS family of schemes use this procedure, and are thus called *hybrid cryptosystems*.

Security

Some encryption schemes can be proven secure on the basis of the presumed difficulty of a mathematical problem, such as factoring the product of two large primes or computing discrete logarithms. Note that "secure" here has a precise mathematical meaning, and there are multiple different (meaningful) definitions of what it means for an encryption scheme to be "secure". The "right" definition depends on the context in which the scheme will be deployed.

The most obvious application of a public key encryption system is confidentiality – a message that a sender encrypts using the recipient's public key can be decrypted only by the recipient's paired private key. This assumes, of course, that no flaw is discovered in the basic algorithm used.

Another application in public-key cryptography is the digital signature. Digital signature schemes can be used for sender authentication and non-repudiation. The sender computes a digital signature for the message to be sent, then sends the signature (together with the message) to the intended receiver. Digital signature schemes have the property that signatures can be computed only with the knowledge of the correct private key. To verify that a message has been signed by a user and has not been modified, the receiver needs to know only the corresponding public key. In some cases (e.g., RSA), a single algorithm can be used to both encrypt and create digital signatures. In other cases (e.g., DSA), each algorithm can only be used for one specific purpose.

To achieve both authentication and confidentiality, the sender should include the recipient's name in the message, sign it using his private key, and then encrypt both the message and the signature using the recipient's public key.

These characteristics can be used to construct many other (sometimes surprising) cryptographic protocols and applications, such as digital cash, password-authenticated key agreement, multi-party key agreement, time-stamping services, non-repudiation protocols, etc.

Practical Considerations

Enveloped Public Key Encryption

Enveloped Public Key Encryption (EPKE) is the method of applying public-key cryptography and ensuring that an electronic communication is transmitted confidentially, has the contents of the communication protected against being modified (communication integrity) and cannot be denied from having been sent (non-repudiation). This is often the method used when securing communication on an open networked environment such by making use of the Transport Layer Security (TLS) or Secure Sockets Layer (SSL) protocols.

EPKE consists of a two-stage process that includes both Public Key Encryption (PKE) and a digital signature. Both Public Key Encryption and digital signatures make up the foundation of Enveloped Public Key Encryption (these two processes are described in full in their own sections).

For EPKE to work effectively, it is required that:

- Every participant in the communication has their own unique pair of keys. The first key that is required is a public key and the second key that is required is a private key.

- Each person's own private and public keys must be mathematically related where the private key is used to decrypt a communication sent using a public key and vice versa. Some well-known asymmetric encryption algorithms are based on the RSA cryptosystem.

- The private key must be kept absolutely private by the owner, though the public key can be published in a public directory such as with a certification authority.

To send a message using EPKE, the sender of the message first signs the message using their own private key, this ensures non-repudiation of the message. The sender then encrypts their digitally signed message using the receiver's public key thus applying a digital envelope to the message. This step ensures confidentiality during the transmission of the message. The receiver of the message then uses their private key to decrypt the message thus removing the digital envelope and then uses the sender's public key to decrypt the sender's digital signature. At this point, if the message has been unaltered during transmission, the message will be clear to the receiver.

Due to the computationally complex nature of RSA-based asymmetric encryption algorithms, the time taken to encrypt large documents or files to be transmitted can be relatively long. To speed up the process of transmission, instead of applying the sender's digital signature to the large documents or files, the sender can rather hash the documents or files using a cryptographic hash function and then digitally sign the generated hash value, therefore enforcing non-repudiation. Hashing is a much faster computation to complete as opposed to using an RSA-based digital signature algorithm alone. The sender would then sign the newly generated hash value and encrypt the original documents or files with the receiver's public key. The transmission would then take place securely and with confidentiality and non-repudiation still intact. The receiver would then verify the signature and decrypt the encrypted documents or files with their private key.

Note: The sender and receiver do not usually carry out the process mentioned above manually though, but rather rely on sophisticated software to automatically complete the EPKE process.

Public Key Encryption

The goal of Public Key Encryption (PKE) is to ensure that the communication being sent is kept confidential during transit.

To send a message using PKE, the sender of the message uses the public key of the receiver to encrypt the contents of the message. The encrypted message is then transmitted electronically to the receiver and the receiver can then use their own matching private key to decrypt the message.

The encryption process of using the receivers public key is useful for preserving the confidentiality of the message as only the receiver has the matching private key to decrypt the message. Therefore, the sender of the message cannot decrypt the message once it has been encrypted using the receivers public key. However, PKE does not address the problem of non-repudiation, as the message could have been sent by anyone that has access to the receivers public key.

Digital Signatures

The goal of a digital signature scheme is to ensure that the sender of the communication that is being sent is known to the receiver and that the sender of the message cannot repudiate a message that they sent. Therefore, the purpose of digital signatures is to ensure the non-repudiation of the message being sent. This is useful in a practical setting where a sender wishes to make an electronic purchase of shares and the receiver wants to be able to prove who requested the purchase. Digital signatures do not provide confidentiality for the message being sent.

The message is signed using the sender's private signing key. The digitally signed message is then sent to the receiver, who can then use the sender's public key to verify the signature.

Certification Authority

In order for Enveloped Public Key Encryption to be as secure as possible, there needs to be a "gatekeeper" of public and private keys, or else anyone could create key pairs and masquerade as the intended sender of a communication, proposing them as the keys of the intended sender. This digital key "gatekeeper" is known as a certification authority. A certification authority is a trusted third party that can issue public and private keys, thus certifying public keys. It also works as a depository to store key chain and enforce the trust factor.

Postal Analogies

An analogy that can be used to understand the advantages of an asymmetric system is to imagine two people, Alice and Bob, who are sending a secret message through the public mail. In this example, Alice wants to send a secret message to Bob, and expects a secret reply from Bob.

With a symmetric key system, Alice first puts the secret message in a box, and locks the box using a padlock to which she has a key. She then sends the box to Bob through regular mail. When Bob receives the box, he uses an identical copy of Alice's key (which he has somehow obtained previously, maybe by a face-to-face meeting) to open the box, and reads the message. Bob can then use the same padlock to send his secret reply.

In an asymmetric key system, Bob and Alice have separate padlocks. First, Alice asks Bob to send his open padlock to her through regular mail, keeping his key to himself. When Alice receives it she uses it to lock a box containing her message, and sends the locked box to Bob. Bob can then unlock the box with his key and read the message from Alice. To reply, Bob must similarly get Alice's open padlock to lock the box before sending it back to her.

The critical advantage in an asymmetric key system is that Bob and Alice never need to send a copy of their keys to each other. This prevents a third party – perhaps, in this example, a corrupt postal worker who opens unlocked boxes – from copying a key while it is in transit, allowing the third party to spy on all future messages sent between Alice and Bob. So, in the public key scenario, Alice and Bob need not trust the postal service as much. In addition, if Bob were careless and allowed someone else to copy *his* key, Alice's messages to *Bob* would be compromised, but Alice's messages to *other people* would remain secret, since the other people would be providing different padlocks for Alice to use.

Another kind of asymmetric key system, called a three-pass protocol, requires neither party to even touch the other party's padlock (or key to get access); Bob and Alice have separate padlocks. First, Alice puts the secret message in a box, and locks the box using a padlock to which only she has a key. She then sends the box to Bob through regular mail. When Bob receives the box, he adds his own padlock to the box, and sends it back to Alice. When Alice receives the box with the two padlocks, she removes her padlock and sends it back to Bob. When Bob receives the box with only his padlock on it, Bob can then unlock the box with his key and read the message from Alice. Note that, in this scheme, the order of decryption is NOT the same as the order of encryption – this is only possible if commutative ciphers are used. A commutative cipher is one in which the order of encryption and decryption is interchangeable, just as the order of multiplication is interchangeable (i.e., $A*B*C = A*C*B = C*B*A$). This method is secure for certain choices of commutative ciphers, but insecure for others (e.g., a simple XOR). For example, let $E_1()$ and $E_2()$ be two encryption functions, and let "M" be the message so that if Alice encrypts it using $E_1()$ and sends $E_1(M)$ to Bob. Bob then again encrypts the message as $E_2(E_1(M))$ and sends it to Alice. Now, Alice decrypts $E_2(E_1(M))$ using $E_1()$. Alice will now get $E_2(M)$, meaning when she sends this again to Bob, he will be able to decrypt the message using $E_2()$ and get "M". Although none of the keys were ever exchanged, the message "M" may well be a key (e.g., Alice's Public key). This three-pass protocol is typically used during key exchange.

Actual Algorithms: Two Linked Keys

Not all asymmetric key algorithms operate in this way. In the most common, Alice and Bob each own *two* keys, one for encryption and one for decryption. In a secure asymmetric key encryption scheme, the private key should not be deducible from the public key. This makes possible public-key encryption, since an encryption key can be published without compromising the security of messages encrypted with that key.

In other schemes, either key can be used to encrypt the message. When Bob encrypts a message with his private key, only his public key will successfully decrypt it, authenticating Bob's authorship of the message. In the alternative, when a message is encrypted with the public key, only the private key can decrypt it. In this arrangement, Alice and Bob can exchange secret messages with no prior secret agreement, each using the other's public key to encrypt, and each using his own to decrypt.

Weaknesses

Among symmetric key encryption algorithms, only the one-time pad can be proven to be secure against any adversary – no matter how much computing power is available. However, there is no public-key scheme with this property, since all public-key schemes are susceptible to a "brute-force key search attack". Such attacks are impractical if the amount of computation needed to succeed – termed the "work factor" by Claude Shannon – is out of reach of all potential attackers. In many cases, the work factor can be increased by simply choosing a longer key. But other algorithms may have much lower work factors, making resistance to a brute-force attack irrelevant. Some special and specific algorithms have been developed to aid in attacking some public key encryption algorithms – both RSA and ElGamal encryption have known attacks that are much faster than the brute-force approach. These factors have changed dramatically in recent decades, both with the decreasing cost of computing power and with new mathematical discoveries.

Aside from the resistance to attack of a particular key pair, the security of the certification hierarchy must be considered when deploying public key systems. Some certificate authority – usually a purpose-built program running on a server computer – vouches for the identities assigned to specific private keys by producing a digital certificate. Public key digital certificates are typically valid for several years at a time, so the associated private keys must be held securely over that time. When a private key used for certificate creation higher in the PKI server hierarchy is compromised, or accidentally disclosed, then a "man-in-the-middle attack" is possible, making any subordinate certificate wholly insecure.

Major weaknesses have been found for several formerly promising asymmetric key algorithms. The 'knapsack packing' algorithm was found to be insecure after the development of a new attack. Recently, some attacks based on careful measurements of the exact amount of time it takes known hardware to encrypt plain text have been used to simplify the search for likely decryption keys. Thus, mere use of asymmetric key algorithms does not ensure security. A great deal of active research is currently underway to both discover, and to protect against, new attack algorithms.

Another potential security vulnerability in using asymmetric keys is the possibility of a "man-in-the-middle" attack, in which the communication of public keys is intercepted by a third party (the "man in the middle") and then modified to provide different public keys instead. Encrypted messages and responses must also be intercepted, decrypted, and re-encrypted by the attacker using the correct public keys for different communication segments, in all instances, so as to avoid suspicion. This attack may seem to be difficult to implement in practice, but it is not impossible when using insecure media (e.g., public networks, such as the Internet or wireless forms of communications) – for example, a malicious staff member at Alice or Bob's Internet Service Provider (ISP) might find it quite easy to carry out. In the earlier postal analogy, Alice would have to have a way to make sure that the lock on the returned packet really belongs to Bob before she removes her lock and sends the packet back. Otherwise, the lock could have been put on the packet by a corrupt postal worker pretending to be Bob, so as to fool Alice.

One approach to prevent such attacks involves the use of a certificate authority, a trusted third party responsible for verifying the identity of a user of the system. This authority issues a tamper-resistant, non-spoofable digital certificate for the participants. Such certificates are signed data blocks stating that this public key belongs to that person, company, or other entity. This approach also has its weaknesses – for example, the certificate authority issuing the certificate must be trusted to have properly checked the identity of the key-holder, must ensure the correctness of the public key when it issues a certificate, must be secure from computer piracy, and must have made arrangements with all participants to check all their certificates before protected communications can begin. Web browsers, for instance, are supplied with a long list of "self-signed identity certificates" from PKI providers – these are used to check the *bona fides* of the certificate authority and then, in a second step, the certificates of potential communicators. An attacker who could subvert any single one of those certificate authorities into issuing a certificate for a bogus public key could then mount a "man-in-the-middle" attack as easily as if the certificate scheme were not used at all. In an alternate scenario rarely discussed, an attacker who penetrated an authority's servers and obtained its store of certificates and keys (public and private) would be able to spoof, masquerade, decrypt, and forge transactions without limit.

Despite its theoretical and potential problems, this approach is widely used. Examples include SSL and its successor, TLS, which are commonly used to provide security for web browser transactions (for example, to securely send credit card details to an online store).

Computational Cost

The public key algorithms known thus far are relatively computationally costly compared with most symmetric key algorithms of apparently equivalent security. The difference factor is the use of typically quite large keys. This has important implications for their practical use. Most are used in hybrid cryptosystems for reasons of efficiency – in such a cryptosystem, a shared secret key ("session key") is generated by one party, and this much briefer session key is then encrypted by each recipient's public key. Each recipient then uses his own private key to decrypt the session key. Once all parties have obtained the session key, they can use a much faster symmetric algorithm to encrypt and decrypt messages. In many of these schemes, the session key is unique to each message exchange, being pseudo-randomly chosen for each message.

Associating Public Keys with Identities

The binding between a public key and its "owner" must be correct, or else the algorithm may function perfectly and yet be entirely insecure in practice. As with most cryptography applications, the protocols used to establish and verify this binding are critically important. Associating a public key with its owner is typically done by protocols implementing a public key infrastructure – these allow the validity of the association to be formally verified by reference to a trusted third party in the form of either a hierarchical certificate authority (e.g., X.509), a local trust model (e.g., SPKI), or a web of trust scheme, like that originally built into PGP and GPG, and still to some extent usable with them. Whatever the cryptographic assurance of the protocols themselves, the association between a public key and its owner is ultimately a matter of subjective judgment on the part of the trusted third party, since the key is a mathematical entity, while the owner – and the connection between owner and key – are not. For this reason, the formalism of a public key infrastructure must provide for explicit statements of the policy followed when making this judgment. For example, the complex and never fully implemented X.509 standard allows a certificate authority to identify its policy by means of an object identifier, which functions as an index into a catalog of registered policies. Policies may exist for many different purposes, ranging from anonymity to military classifications.

Relation to Real World Events

A public key will be known to a large and, in practice, unknown set of users. All events requiring revocation or replacement of a public key can take a long time to take full effect with all who must be informed (i.e., all those users who possess that key). For this reason, systems that must react to events in real time (e.g., safety-critical systems or national security systems) should not use public-key encryption without taking great care. There are four issues of interest:

Privilege of Key Revocation

A malicious (or erroneous) revocation of some (or all) of the keys in the system is likely, or in the second case, certain, to cause a complete failure of the system. If public keys can be revoked individually, this is a possibility. However, there are design approaches that can reduce the practical chance of this occurring. For example, by means of certificates, we can create what is called a "compound principal" – one such principal could be "Alice and Bob have Revoke Authority". Now, only Alice and Bob (in concert) can revoke a key, and neither Alice nor Bob can revoke keys alone. However, revoking a key now requires both Alice *and* Bob to be available, and this creates a problem of reliability. In concrete terms, from a security point of view, there is now a "single point of failure" in the public key revocation system. A successful Denial of Service attack against either Alice or Bob (or both) will block a required revocation. In fact, any partition of authority between Alice and Bob will have this effect, regardless of how it comes about.

Because the principle allowing revocation authority for keys is very powerful, the mechanisms used to control it should involve both as many participants as possible (to guard against malicious attacks of this type), while at the same time as few as possible (to ensure that a key can be revoked without dangerous delay). Public key certificates that include an expiration date are unsatisfactory in that the expiration date may not correspond with a real-world revocation but at least such certificates need not all be tracked down system-wide, nor must all users be in constant contact with the system at all times.

Distribution of a New Key

After a key has been revoked, or when a new user is added to a system, a new key must be distributed in some predetermined manner. Assume that Carol's key has been revoked (e.g., by exceeding its expiration date, or because of a compromise of Carol's matching private key). Until a new key has been distributed, Carol is effectively "out of contact". No one will be able to send her messages without violating system protocols (i.e., without a valid public key, no one can encrypt messages to her), and messages from her cannot be signed, for the same reason. Or, in other words, the "part of the system" controlled by Carol is, in essence, unavailable. Security requirements have been ranked higher than system availability in such designs.

One could leave the power to create (and certify) keys (as well as to revoke them) in the hands of each user – the original PGP design did so – but this raises problems of user understanding and operation. For security reasons, this approach has considerable difficulties – if nothing else, some users will be forgetful, or inattentive, or confused. On the one hand, a message revoking a public key certificate should be spread as fast as possible, while on the other hand, parts of the system might be rendered inoperable *before* a new key can be installed. The time window can be reduced to zero by always issuing the new key together with the certificate that revokes the old one, but this requires co-location of authority to both revoke keys and generate new keys.

It is most likely a system-wide failure if the (possibly combined) principal that issues new keys fails by issuing keys improperly. This is an instance of a "common mutual exclusion" – a design can make the reliability of a system high, but only at the cost of system availability (and *vice versa*).

Spreading the Revocation

Notification of a key certificate revocation must be spread to all those who might potentially hold it, and as rapidly as possible.

There are but two means of spreading information (i.e., a key revocation) in a distributed system: either the information is "pushed" to users from a central point (or points), or else it is "pulled" from a central point(or points) by the end users.

Pushing the information is the simplest solution, in that a message is sent to all participants. However, there is no way of knowing whether all participants will actually *receive* the message. If the number of participants is large, and some of their physical or network distances are great, then the probability of complete success (which is, in ideal circumstances, required for system security) will be rather low. In a partly updated state, the system is particularly vulnerable to "denial of service" attacks as security has been breached, and a vulnerability window will continue to exist as long as some users have not "gotten the word". Put another way, pushing certificate revocation messages is neither easy to secure, nor very reliable.

The alternative to pushing is pulling. In the extreme, all certificates contain all the keys needed to verify that the public key of interest (i.e., the one belonging to the user to whom one wishes to send a message, or whose signature is to be checked) is still valid. In this case, at least some use of the system will be blocked if a user cannot reach the verification service (i.e., one of the systems that can establish the current validity of another user's key). Again, such a system design can be made as reliable as one wishes, at the cost of lowering security – the more servers to check for the possibility of a key revocation, the longer the window of vulnerability.

Another trade-off is to use a somewhat less reliable, but more secure, verification service, but to include an expiration date for each of the verification sources. How long this "timeout" should be is a decision that requires a trade-off between availability and security that will have to be decided in advance, at the time of system design.

Recovery from a Leaked Key

Assume that the principal authorized to revoke a key has decided that a certain key must be revoked. In most cases, this happens after the fact – for instance, it becomes known that at some time in the past an event occurred that endangered a private key. Let us denote the time at which it is decided that the compromise occurred as T.

Such a compromise has two implications. First, messages encrypted with the matching public key (now or in the past) can no longer be assumed to be secret. One solution to avoid this problem is to use a protocol that has perfect forward secrecy. Second, signatures made with the *no-longer-trust-*

ed-to-be-actually-private key after time T can no longer be assumed to be authentic without additional information (i.e., who, where, when, etc.) about the events leading up to the digital signature. These will not always be available, and so all such digital signatures will be less than credible. A solution to reduce the impact of leaking a private key of a signature scheme is to use timestamps.

Loss of secrecy and/or authenticity, even for a single user, has system-wide security implications, and a strategy for recovery must thus be established. Such a strategy will determine who has authority to, and under what conditions one must, revoke a public key certificate. One must also decide how to spread the revocation, and ideally, how to deal with all messages signed with the key since time T (which will rarely be known precisely). Messages sent to that user (which require the proper – now compromised – private key to decrypt) must be considered compromised as well, no matter when they were sent.

Examples

Examples of Well-regarded Asymmetric Key Techniques for Varied Purposes Include:

- Diffie–Hellman key exchange protocol
- DSS (Digital Signature Standard), which incorporates the Digital Signature Algorithm
- ElGamal
- Various elliptic curve techniques
- Various password-authenticated key agreement techniques
- Paillier cryptosystem
- RSA encryption algorithm (PKCS#1)
- Cramer–Shoup cryptosystem
- YAK authenticated key agreement protocol

Examples of Asymmetric Key Algorithms not Widely Adopted Include:

- NTRUEncrypt cryptosystem
- McEliece cryptosystem

Examples of Notable – Yet Insecure – Asymmetric Key Algorithms Include:

- Merkle–Hellman knapsack cryptosystem

Examples of Protocols using Asymmetric Key Algorithms Include:

- S/MIME
- GPG, an implementation of OpenPGP
- Internet Key Exchange

- PGP

- ZRTP, a secure VoIP protocol

- Secure Socket Layer, now codified as the IETF standard Transport Layer Security (TLS)

- SILC

- SSH

- Bitcoin

- Off-the-Record Messaging

Cryptanalysis

Close-up of the rotors in a Fialka cipher machine

Cryptanalysis (from the Greek *kryptós*, "hidden", and *analýein*, "to loosen" or "to untie") is the study of analyzing information systems in order to study the hidden aspects of the systems. Cryptanalysis is used to breach cryptographic security systems and gain access to the contents of encrypted messages, even if the cryptographic key is unknown.

In addition to mathematical analysis of cryptographic algorithms, cryptanalysis includes the study of side-channel attacks that do not target weaknesses in the cryptographic algorithms themselves, but instead exploit weaknesses in their implementation.

Even though the goal has been the same, the methods and techniques of cryptanalysis have changed drastically through the history of cryptography, adapting to increasing cryptographic complexity, ranging from the pen-and-paper methods of the past, through machines like the British Bombes and Colossus computers at Bletchley Park in World War II, to the mathematically advanced computerized schemes of the present. Methods for breaking modern cryptosystems often involve solving carefully constructed problems in pure mathematics, the best-known being integer factorization.

Overview

Given some encrypted data (*"ciphertext"*), the goal of the *cryptanalyst* is to gain as much information as possible about the original, unencrypted data (*"plaintext"*).

Amount of Information Available to the Attacker

Attacks can be classified based on what type of information the attacker has available. As a basic starting point it is normally assumed that, for the purposes of analysis, the general algorithm is known; this is Shannon's Maxim "the enemy knows the system"—in its turn, equivalent to Kerckhoffs' principle. This is a reasonable assumption in practice — throughout history, there are countless examples of secret algorithms falling into wider knowledge, variously through espionage, betrayal and reverse engineering. (And on occasion, ciphers have been reconstructed through pure deduction; for example, the German Lorenz cipher and the Japanese Purple code, and a variety of classical schemes):

- *Ciphertext-only*: the cryptanalyst has access only to a collection of ciphertexts or codetexts.

- *Known-plaintext*: the attacker has a set of ciphertexts to which he knows the corresponding plaintext.

- *Chosen-plaintext* (*chosen-ciphertext*): the attacker can obtain the ciphertexts (plaintexts) corresponding to an arbitrary set of plaintexts (ciphertexts) of his own choosing.

- *Adaptive chosen-plaintext*: like a chosen-plaintext attack, except the attacker can choose subsequent plaintexts based on information learned from previous encryptions. Similarly *Adaptive chosen ciphertext attack*.

- *Related-key attack*: Like a chosen-plaintext attack, except the attacker can obtain ciphertexts encrypted under two different keys. The keys are unknown, but the relationship between them is known; for example, two keys that differ in the one bit.

Computational Resources Required

Attacks can also be characterised by the resources they require. Those resources include:

- Time — the number of *computation steps* (e.g., test encryptions) which must be performed.

- Memory — the amount of *storage* required to perform the attack.

- Data — the quantity and type of *plaintexts and ciphertexts* required for a particular approach.

It's sometimes difficult to predict these quantities precisely, especially when the attack isn't practical to actually implement for testing. But academic cryptanalysts tend to provide at least the estimated *order of magnitude* of their attacks' difficulty, saying, for example, "SHA-1 collisions now 2^{52}."

Bruce Schneier notes that even computationally impractical attacks can be considered breaks: "Breaking a cipher simply means finding a weakness in the cipher that can be exploited with a complexity less than brute force. Never mind that brute-force might require 2^{128} encryptions; an attack requiring 2^{110} encryptions would be considered a break...simply put, a break can just be a certificational weakness: evidence that the cipher does not perform as advertised."

Partial Breaks

The results of cryptanalysis can also vary in usefulness. For example, cryptographer Lars Knudsen (1998) classified various types of attack on block ciphers according to the amount and quality of secret information that was discovered:

- *Total break* — the attacker deduces the secret key.

- *Global deduction* — the attacker discovers a functionally equivalent algorithm for encryption and decryption, but without learning the key.

- *Instance (local) deduction* — the attacker discovers additional plaintexts (or ciphertexts) not previously known.

- *Information deduction* — the attacker gains some Shannon information about plaintexts (or ciphertexts) not previously known.

- *Distinguishing algorithm* — the attacker can distinguish the cipher from a random permutation.

Academic attacks are often against weakened versions of a cryptosystem, such as a block cipher or hash function with some rounds removed. Many, but not all, attacks become exponentially more difficult to execute as rounds are added to a cryptosystem, so it's possible for the full cryptosystem to be strong even though reduced-round variants are weak. Nonetheless, partial breaks that come close to breaking the original cryptosystem may mean that a full break will follow; the successful attacks on DES, MD5, and SHA-1 were all preceded by attacks on weakened versions.

In academic cryptography, a *weakness* or a *break* in a scheme is usually defined quite conservatively: it might require impractical amounts of time, memory, or known plaintexts. It also might require the attacker be able to do things many real-world attackers can't: for example, the attacker may need to choose particular plaintexts to be encrypted or even to ask for plaintexts to be encrypted using several keys related to the secret key. Furthermore, it might only reveal a small amount of information, enough to prove the cryptosystem imperfect but too little to be useful to real-world attackers. Finally, an attack might only apply to a weakened version of cryptographic tools, like a reduced-round block cipher, as a step towards breaking of the full system.

History

Cryptanalysis has coevolved together with cryptography, and the contest can be traced through the history of cryptography—new ciphers being designed to replace old broken designs, and new cryptanalytic techniques invented to crack the improved schemes. In practice, they are viewed as two sides of the same coin: in order to create secure cryptography, you have to design against possible cryptanalysis.

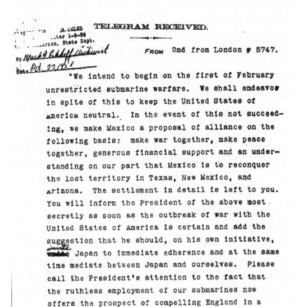

The decrypted Zimmermann Telegram.

Successful cryptanalysis has undoubtedly influenced history; the ability to read the presumed-secret thoughts and plans of others can be a decisive advantage. For example, in England in 1587, Mary, Queen of Scots was tried and executed for treason as a result of her involvement in three plots to assassinate Elizabeth I of England. The plans came to light after her coded correspondence with fellow conspirators was deciphered by Thomas Phelippes.

In World War I, the breaking of the Zimmermann Telegram was instrumental in bringing the United States into the war. In World War II, the Allies benefitted enormously from their joint success cryptanalysis of the German ciphers — including the Enigma machine and the Lorenz cipher — and Japanese ciphers, particularly 'Purple' and JN-25. 'Ultra' intelligence has been credited with everything between shortening the end of the European war by up to two years, to determining the eventual result. The war in the Pacific was similarly helped by 'Magic' intelligence.

Governments have long recognized the potential benefits of cryptanalysis for intelligence, both military and diplomatic, and established dedicated organizations devoted to breaking the codes and ciphers of other nations, for example, GCHQ and the NSA, organizations which are still very active today. In 2004, it was reported that the United States had broken Iranian ciphers. (It is unknown, however, whether this was pure cryptanalysis, or whether other factors were involved:).

Classical Ciphers

Although the actual word "*cryptanalysis*" is relatively recent (it was coined by William Friedman in 1920), methods for breaking codes and ciphers are much older. The first known recorded explanation of cryptanalysis was given by 9th-century Arabian polymath, Al-Kindi (also known as "Alkindus" in Europe), in *A Manuscript on Deciphering Cryptographic Messages*. This treatise includes a description of the method of frequency analysis (Ibrahim Al-Kadi, 1992- ref-3). Italian scholar Giambattista della Porta was author of a seminal work on cryptanalysis *"De Furtivis Literarum Notis"*.

First page of Al-Kindi's 9th century *Manuscript on Deciphering Cryptographic Messages*

Frequency analysis is the basic tool for breaking most classical ciphers. In natural languages, certain letters of the alphabet appear more frequently than others; in English, "E" is likely to be the most common letter in any sample of plaintext. Similarly, the digraph "TH" is the most likely pair of letters in English, and so on. Frequency analysis relies on a cipher failing to hide these statistics. For example, in a simple substitution cipher (where each letter is simply replaced with another), the most frequent letter in the ciphertext would be a likely candidate for "E". Frequency analysis of such a cipher is therefore relatively easy, provided that the ciphertext is long enough to give a reasonably representative count of the letters of the alphabet that it contains.

In Europe during the 15th and 16th centuries, the idea of a polyalphabetic substitution cipher was developed, among others by the French diplomat Blaise de Vigenère (1523–96). For some three centuries, the Vigenère cipher, which uses a repeating key to select different encryption alphabets in rotation, was considered to be completely secure (*le chiffre indéchiffrable*—"the indecipherable cipher"). Nevertheless, Charles Babbage (1791–1871) and later, independently, Friedrich Kasiski (1805–81) succeeded in breaking this cipher. During World War I, inventors in several countries developed rotor cipher machines such as Arthur Scherbius' Enigma, in an attempt to minimise the repetition that had been exploited to break the Vigenère system.

Ciphers from World War I and World War II

Cryptanalysis of enemy messages played a significant part in the Allied victory in World War II. F. W. Winterbotham, quoted the western Supreme Allied Commander, Dwight D. Eisenhower, at the war's end as describing Ultra intelligence as having been "decisive" to Allied victory. Sir Harry Hinsley, official historian of British Intelligence in World War II, made a similar assessment about Ultra, saying that it shortened the war "by not less than two years and probably by four years"; moreover, he said that in the absence of Ultra, it is uncertain how the war would have ended.

In practice, frequency analysis relies as much on linguistic knowledge as it does on statistics, but as ciphers became more complex, mathematics became more important in cryptanalysis. This change was particularly evident before and during World War II, where efforts to crack Axis ciphers required new levels of mathematical sophistication. Moreover, automation was first applied to cryptanalysis in that era with the Polish Bomba device, the British Bombe, the use of punched card equipment, and in the Colossus computers — the first electronic digital computers to be controlled by a program.

Indicator

With reciprocal machine ciphers such as the Lorenz cipher and the Enigma machine used by Nazi Germany during World War II, each message had its own key. Usually, the transmitting operator informed the receiving operator of this message key by transmitting some plaintext and/or ciphertext before the enciphered message. This is termed the *indicator*, as it indicates to the receiving operator how to set his machine to decipher the message.

Poorly designed and implemented indicator systems allowed first the Poles and then the British at Bletchley Park to break the Enigma cipher system. Similar poor indicator systems allowed the British to identify *depths* that led to the diagnosis of the Lorenz SZ40/42 cipher system, and the comprehensive breaking of its messages without the cryptanalysts seeing the cipher machine.

Depth

Sending two or more messages with the same key is an insecure process. To a cryptanalyst the messages are then said to be *"in depth."* This may be detected by the messages having the same *indicator* by which the sending operator informs the receiving operator about the key generator initial settings for the message.

Generally, the cryptanalyst may benefit from lining up identical enciphering operations among a set of messages. For example, the Vernam cipher enciphers by bit-for-bit combining plaintext with a long key using the "exclusive or" operator, which is also known as "modulo-2 addition" (symbolized by $\oplus$):

$$\text{Plaintext} \oplus \text{Key} = \text{Ciphertext}$$

Deciphering combines the same key bits with the ciphertext to reconstruct the plaintext:

$$\text{Ciphertext} \oplus \text{Key} = \text{Plaintext}$$

(In modulo-2 arithmetic, addition is the same as subtraction.) When two such ciphertexts are aligned in depth, combining them eliminates the common key, leaving just a combination of the two plaintexts:

$$\text{Ciphertext1} \oplus \text{Ciphertext2} = \text{Plaintext1} \oplus \text{Plaintext2}$$

The individual plaintexts can then be worked out linguistically by trying *probable words* (or phrases), also known as *"cribs,"* at various locations; a correct guess, when combined with the merged plaintext stream, produces intelligible text from the other plaintext component:

$$(\text{Plaintext1} \oplus \text{Plaintext2}) \oplus \text{Plaintext1} = \text{Plaintext2}$$

The recovered fragment of the second plaintext can often be extended in one or both directions, and the extra characters can be combined with the merged plaintext stream to extend the first plaintext. Working back and forth between the two plaintexts, using the intelligibility criterion to check guesses, the analyst may recover much or all of the original plaintexts. (With only two plaintexts in depth, the analyst may not know which one corresponds to which ciphertext, but in practice this is not a large problem.) When a recovered plaintext is then combined with its ciphertext, the key is revealed:

$$\text{Plaintext1} \oplus \text{Ciphertext1} = \text{Key}$$

Knowledge of a key of course allows the analyst to read other messages encrypted with the same key, and knowledge of a set of related keys may allow cryptanalysts to diagnose the system used for constructing them.

Development of Modern Cryptography

The Bombe replicated the action of several Enigma machines wired together. Each of the rapidly rotating drums, pictured above in a Bletchley Park museum mockup, simulated the action of an Enigma rotor.

Even though computation was used to great effect in Cryptanalysis of the Lorenz cipher and other systems during World War II, it also made possible new methods of cryptography orders of magnitude more complex than ever before. Taken as a whole, modern cryptography has become much more impervious to cryptanalysis than the pen-and-paper systems of the past, and now seems to have the upper hand against pure cryptanalysis. The historian David Kahn notes:

Many are the cryptosystems offered by the hundreds of commercial vendors today that cannot be broken by any known methods of cryptanalysis. Indeed, in such systems even a chosen plaintext attack, in which a selected plaintext is matched against its ciphertext, cannot yield the key that unlock[s] other messages. In a sense, then, cryptanalysis is dead. But that is not the end of the story. Cryptanalysis may be dead, but there is - to mix my metaphors - more than one way to skin a cat.

Kahn goes on to mention increased opportunities for interception, bugging, side channel attacks, and quantum computers as replacements for the traditional means of cryptanalysis. In 2010, former NSA technical director Brian Snow said that both academic and government cryptographers are "moving very slowly forward in a mature field."

However, any postmortems for cryptanalysis may be premature. While the effectiveness of cryptanalytic methods employed by intelligence agencies remains unknown, many serious attacks against both academic and practical cryptographic primitives have been published in the modern era of computer cryptography:

- The block cipher Madryga, proposed in 1984 but not widely used, was found to be susceptible to ciphertext-only attacks in 1998.

- FEAL-4, proposed as a replacement for the DES standard encryption algorithm but not widely used, was demolished by a spate of attacks from the academic community, many of which are entirely practical.

- The A5/1, A5/2, CMEA, and DECT systems used in mobile and wireless phone technology can all be broken in hours, minutes or even in real-time using widely available computing equipment.

- Brute-force keyspace search has broken some real-world ciphers and applications, including single-DES, 40-bit "export-strength" cryptography, and the DVD Content Scrambling System.

- In 2001, Wired Equivalent Privacy (WEP), a protocol used to secure Wi-Fi wireless networks, was shown to be breakable in practice because of a weakness in the RC4 cipher and aspects of the WEP design that made related-key attacks practical. WEP was later replaced by Wi-Fi Protected Access.

- In 2008, researchers conducted a proof-of-concept break of SSL using weaknesses in the MD5 hash function and certificate issuer practices that made it possible to exploit collision attacks on hash functions. The certificate issuers involved changed their practices to prevent the attack from being repeated.

Thus, while the best modern ciphers may be far more resistant to cryptanalysis than the Enigma, cryptanalysis and the broader field of information security remain quite active.

Symmetric Ciphers

- Boomerang attack
- Brute force attack
- Davies' attack
- Differential cryptanalysis
- Impossible differential cryptanalysis
- Improbable differential cryptanalysis
- Integral cryptanalysis
- Linear cryptanalysis
- Meet-in-the-middle attack

- Mod-n cryptanalysis

- Related-key attack

- Sandwich attack

- Slide attack

- XSL attack

Asymmetric Ciphers

Asymmetric cryptography (or public key cryptography) is cryptography that relies on using two (mathematically related) keys; one private, and one public. Such ciphers invariably rely on "hard" mathematical problems as the basis of their security, so an obvious point of attack is to develop methods for solving the problem. The security of two-key cryptography depends on mathematical questions in a way that single-key cryptography generally does not, and conversely links cryptanalysis to wider mathematical research in a new way.

Asymmetric schemes are designed around the (conjectured) difficulty of solving various mathematical problems. If an improved algorithm can be found to solve the problem, then the system is weakened. For example, the security of the Diffie-Hellman key exchange scheme depends on the difficulty of calculating the discrete logarithm. In 1983, Don Coppersmith found a faster way to find discrete logarithms (in certain groups), and thereby requiring cryptographers to use larger groups (or different types of groups). RSA's security depends (in part) upon the difficulty of integer factorization — a breakthrough in factoring would impact the security of RSA.

In 1980, one could factor a difficult 50-digit number at an expense of 10^{12} elementary computer operations. By 1984 the state of the art in factoring algorithms had advanced to a point where a 75-digit number could be factored in 10^{12} operations. Advances in computing technology also meant that the operations could be performed much faster, too. Moore's law predicts that computer speeds will continue to increase. Factoring techniques may continue to do so as well, but will most likely depend on mathematical insight and creativity, neither of which has ever been successfully predictable. 150-digit numbers of the kind once used in RSA have been factored. The effort was greater than above, but was not unreasonable on fast modern computers. By the start of the 21st century, 150-digit numbers were no longer considered a large enough key size for RSA. Numbers with several hundred digits were still considered too hard to factor in 2005, though methods will probably continue to improve over time, requiring key size to keep pace or other methods such as elliptic curve cryptography to be used.

Another distinguishing feature of asymmetric schemes is that, unlike attacks on symmetric cryptosystems, any cryptanalysis has the opportunity to make use of knowledge gained from the public key.

Attacking Cryptographic Hash Systems

- Birthday attack

- Rainbow table

Side-channel Attacks

- Black-bag cryptanalysis

- Man-in-the-middle attack

- Power analysis

- Replay attack

- Rubber-hose cryptanalysis

- Timing analysis

Quantum Computing Applications for Cryptanalysis

Quantum computers, which are still in the early phases of research, have potential use in cryptanalysis. For example, Shor's Algorithm could factor large numbers in polynomial time, in effect breaking some commonly used forms of public-key encryption.

By using Grover's algorithm on a quantum computer, brute-force key search can be made quadratically faster. However, this could be countered by doubling the key length.

Strong Cryptography

Strong cryptography or cryptographically strong are general terms applied to cryptographic systems or components that are considered highly resistant to cryptanalysis.

Demonstrating the resistance of any cryptographic scheme to attack is a complex matter, requiring extensive testing and reviews, preferably in a public forum. Good algorithms and protocols are required, and good system design and implementation is needed as well. For instance, the operating system on which the crypto software runs should be as carefully secured as possible. Users may handle passwords insecurely, or trust 'service' personnel overly much, or simply misuse the software. "Strong' thus is an imprecise term and may not apply in particular situations.

Background

The use of computers changed the process of cryptanalysis, famously with Bletchley Park's Colossus. But just as the development of digital computers and electronics helped in cryptanalysis, it also made possible much more complex ciphers. It is typically the case that use of a quality cipher is very efficient, while breaking it requires an effort many orders of magnitude larger - making cryptanalysis so inefficient and impractical as to be effectively impossible.

Since the publication of Data Encryption Standard, the Diffie-Hellman and RSA algorithm in the 1970s, cryptography has had deep connections with abstract mathematics and become a widely used tool in communications, computer networks, and computer security generally.

Cryptographically Strong Algorithms

This term "cryptographically strong" is often used to describe an encryption algorithm, and implies, in comparison to some other algorithm (which is thus cryptographically weak), greater resistance to attack. But it can also be used to describe hashing and unique identifier and filename creation algorithms. NET runtime library function Path. Get Random File Name. In this usage, the term means "difficult to guess".

An encryption algorithm is intended to be unbreakable (in which case it is as strong as it can ever be), but might be breakable (in which case it is as weak as it can ever be) so there is not, in principle, a continuum of strength as the idiom would seem to imply: Algorithm A is stronger than Algorithm B which is stronger than Algorithm C, and so on. The situation is made more complex, and less subsumable into a single strength metric, by the fact that there are many types of cryptanalytic attack and that any given algorithm is likely to force the attacker to do more work to break it when using one attack than another.

There is only one known unbreakable cryptographic system, the one-time pad, this is not generally possible to use because of the difficulties involved in exchanging one-time pads without their being compromised. So any encryption algorithm can be compared to the perfect algorithm, the one-time pad.

The usual sense in which this term is (loosely) used, is in reference to a particular attack, brute force key search — especially in explanations for newcomers to the field. Indeed, with this attack (always assuming keys to have been randomly chosen), there is a continuum of resistance depending on the length of the key used. But even so there are two major problems: many algorithms allow use of different length keys at different times, and any algorithm can forgo use of the full key length possible. Thus, Blowfish and RC5 are block cipher algorithms whose design specifically allowed for several key lengths, and who cannot therefore be said to have any particular strength with respect to brute force key search. Furthermore, US export regulations restrict key length for exportable crypto products and in several cases in the 1980s and 1990s (e.g., famously in the case of Lotus Notes' export approval) only partial keys were used, decreasing 'strength' against brute force attack for those (export) versions. More or less the same thing happened outside the US as well, as for example in the case of more than one of the crypto algorithms in the GSM cellular telephone standard.

The term is commonly used to convey that some algorithm is suitable for some task in cryptography or information security, but also resists cryptanalysis and has no, or fewer, security weaknesses. Tasks are varied, and might include:

- generating randomness

- encrypting data

- providing a method to ensure data integrity

Cryptographically strong would seem to mean that the described method has some kind of maturity, perhaps even approved for use against different kinds of systematic attacks in theory and/or practice. Indeed, that the method may resist those attacks long enough to protect the information carried (and what stands behind the information) for a useful length of time. But due to the complexity and subtlety of the field, neither is almost ever the case. Since such assurances are not actually available in real practice, sleight of hand in language which implies that they are will generally be misleading.

There will always be uncertainty as advances (e.g., in cryptanalytic theory or merely affordable computer capacity) may reduce the effort needed to successfully use some attack method against an algorithm.

In addition, actual use of cryptographic algorithms requires their encapsulation in a cryptosystem, and doing so often introduces vulnerabilities which are not due to faults in an algorithm. For example, essentially all algorithms require random choice of keys, and any cryptosystem which does not provide such keys will be subject to attack regardless of any attack resistant qualities of the encryption algorithm(s) used.

Legal Issues

Since use of strong cryptography makes the job of intelligence agencies more difficult, many countries have enacted law or regulation restricting or simply banning the non-official use of strong crypto. For instance, the United States has defined cryptographic products as munitions since World War II and has prohibited export of cryptography beyond a certain 'strength' (measured in part by key size), and Russia banned its use by private individuals in 1995. It is not clear if the Russian ban is still in effect. France had quite strict regulations in this field, but has relaxed them in recent years.

Examples

- PGP is generally considered an example of strong cryptography, with versions running under most popular operating systems and on various hardware platforms. The open source standard for PGP operations is OpenPGP, and GnuPG is an implementation of that standard from the FSF.

- The AES algorithm is considered strong after being selected in a lengthy selection process that was open and involved numerous tests.

Examples that are not considered cryptographically strong include:

- The DES, whose 56-bit keys allow attacks via exhaustive search.

- Wired Equivalent Privacy which is subject to a number of attacks due to flaws in its design.

- The Clipper Chip, a failed initiative of the U.S. government that included key escrow provisions, allowing the government to gain access to the keys.

- Almost all classical ciphers.

The latest version of TLS protocol (version 1.2), used to secure Internet transactions, is generally considered strong. Several vulnerabilities exist in previous versions, including demonstrated attacks such as POODLE. Worse, some cipher-suites are deliberately weakened to use a 40-bit effective key to allow export under pre-1996 U.S. regulations.

Data Security

Data security means protecting data, such as a database, from destructive forces and from the unwanted actions of unauthorized users.

Data Security Technologies

Disk Encryption

Disk encryption refers to encryption technology that encrypts data on a hard disk drive. Disk encryption typically takes form in either software or hardware. Disk encryption is often referred to as on-the-fly encryption (OTFE) or transparent encryption.

Software Versus Hardware-based Mechanisms for Protecting Data

Software-based security solutions encrypt the data to protect it from theft. However, a malicious program or a hacker could corrupt the data in order to make it unrecoverable, making the system unusable. Hardware-based security solutions can prevent read and write access to data and hence offer very strong protection against tampering and unauthorized access.

Hardware based security or assisted computer security offers an alternative to software-only computer security. Security tokens such as those using PKCS#11 may be more secure due to the physical access required in order to be compromised. Access is enabled only when the token is connected and correct PIN is entered. However, dongles can be used by anyone who can gain physical access to it. Newer technologies in hardware-based security solves this problem offering full proof security for data.

Working of hardware-based security: A hardware device allows a user to log in, log out and set different privilege levels by doing manual actions. The device uses biometric technology to prevent malicious users from logging in, logging out, and changing privilege levels. The current state of a user of the device is read by controllers in peripheral devices such as hard disks. Illegal access by a malicious user or a malicious program is interrupted based on the current state of a user by hard disk and DVD controllers making illegal access to data impossible. Hardware-based access control is more secure than protection provided by the operating systems as operating systems are vulnerable to malicious attacks by viruses and hackers. The data on hard disks can be corrupted after a malicious access is obtained. With hardware-based protection, software cannot manipulate the user privilege levels. It is impossible for a hacker or a malicious program to gain access to secure data protected by hardware or perform unauthorized privileged operations. This assumption is broken only if the hardware itself is malicious or contains a backdoor. The hardware protects the operating system image and file system privileges from being tampered. Therefore, a completely secure system can be created using a combination of hardware-based security and secure system administration policies.

Backups

Backups are used to ensure data which is lost can be recovered from another source. It is considered essential to keep a backup of any data in most industries and the process is recommended for any files of importance to a user.

Data Masking

Data masking of structured data is the process of obscuring (masking) specific data within a database table or cell to ensure that data security is maintained and sensitive information is not exposed to unauthorized personnel. This may include masking the data from users (for example so banking customer representatives can only see the last 4 digits of a customers national identity number), developers (who need real production data to test new software releases but should not be able to see sensitive financial data), outsourcing vendors, etc.

Data Erasure

Data erasure is a method of software-based overwriting that completely destroys all electronic data residing on a hard drive or other digital media to ensure that no sensitive data is leaked when an asset is retired or reused...

International Laws and Standards

International Laws

In the UK, the Data Protection Act is used to ensure that personal data is accessible to those whom it concerns, and provides redress to individuals if there are inaccuracies. This is particularly important to ensure individuals are treated fairly, for example for credit checking purposes. The Data Protection Act states that only individuals and companies with legitimate and lawful reasons can process personal information and cannot be shared. Data Privacy Day is an international holiday started by the Council of Europe that occurs every January 28.

International Standards

The international standard ISO/IEC 17799 covers data security under the topic of information security, and one of its cardinal principles is that all stored information, i.e. data, should be owned so that it is clear whose responsibility it is to protect and control access to that data.

The Trusted Computing Group is an organization that helps standardize computing security technologies.

The Payment Card Industry Data Security Standard is a proprietary international information security standard for organizations that handle cardholder information for the major debit, credit, prepaid, e-purse, ATM and POS cards.

Industry and Software

There are several data security software available to be used by consumers and one of the most used data security software with a U.S issued patent is Folder Lock.

Network Security Services

In computing, Network Security Services (NSS) comprises a set of libraries designed to support cross-platform development of security-enabled client and server applications with optional support for hardware TLS/SSL acceleration on the server side and hardware smart cards on the client side. NSS provides a complete open-source implementation of cryptographic libraries supporting Transport Layer Security (TLS) / Secure Sockets Layer (SSL) and S/MIME. Previously tri-licensed under the Mozilla Public License 1.1, the GNU General Public License, and the GNU Lesser General-al Public License, NSS upgraded to GPL-compatible MPL 2.0 with release 3.14.

History

NSS originated from the libraries developed when Netscape invented the SSL security protocol.

FIPS 140 Validation and NISCC Testing

The NSS software crypto module has been validated five times (1997, 1999, 2002, 2007, and 2010) for conformance to FIPS 140 at Security Levels 1 and 2. NSS was the first open source cryptographic library to receive FIPS 140 validation. The NSS libraries passed the NISCC TLS/SSL and S/MIME test suites (1.6 million test cases of invalid input data).

Applications that use NSS

AOL, Red Hat, Sun Microsystems/Oracle Corporation, Google and other companies and individual contributors have co-developed NSS. Mozilla provides the source code repository, bug tracking system, and infrastructure for mailing lists and discussion groups. They and others named below use NSS in a variety of products, including the following:

- Mozilla client products, including Firefox, Thunderbird, SeaMonkey, and Firefox for mobile (Fennec).

- AOL Communicator and AOL Instant Messenger (AIM)

- Google Chrome and Chromium except for Android / OS X, and Opera

- Open source client applications such as Evolution, Pidgin, OpenOffice.org 2.0 and later, and Apache OpenOffice.

- Server products from Red Hat: Red Hat Directory Server, Red Hat Certificate System, and the mod nss SSL module for the Apache web server.

- Sun server products from the Sun Java Enterprise System, including Sun Java System Web Server, Sun Java System Directory Server, Sun Java System Portal Server, Sun Java System Messaging Server, and Sun Java System Application Server, open source version of Directory Server OpenDS.

- Libreswan IKE/IPsec requires NSS. It is a fork of Openswan which could optionally use NSS.

Architecture

NSS includes a framework to which developers and OEMs can contribute patches, such as assembly code, to optimize performance on their platforms. Mozilla has certified NSS 3.x on 18 platforms. NSS makes use of Netscape Portable Runtime (NSPR), a platform-neutral open-source API for system functions designed to facilitate cross-platform development. Like NSS, NSPR has been used heavily in multiple products.

Software Development Kit

In addition to libraries and APIs, NSS provides security tools required for debugging, diagnostics, certificate and key management, cryptography-module management, and other development tasks. NSS comes with an extensive and growing set of documentation, including introductory material, API references, man pages for command-line tools, and sample code.

Programmers can utilize NSS as source and as shared (dynamic) libraries. Every NSS release is backward-compatible with previous releases, allowing NSS users to upgrade to new NSS shared libraries without recompiling or relinking their applications.

Interoperability and Open Standards

NSS supports a range of security standards, including the following:

- TLS 1.0 (RFC 2246), 1.1 (RFC 4346), and 1.2 (RFC 5246). The Transport Layer Security (TLS) protocol from the IETF supersedes SSL v3.0 while remaining backward-compatible with SSL v3 implementations.

- SSL 2.0 and 3.0. The Secure Sockets Layer (SSL) protocol allows mutual authentication between a client and server and the establishment of an authenticated and encrypted connection.

- DTLS 1.0 (RFC 4347) and 1.2 (RFC 6347).

- DTLS-SRTP (RFC 5764).

- The following PKCS standards:

    o PKCS #1. RSA standard that governs implementation of public-key cryptography based on the RSA algorithm.

    o PKCS #3. RSA standard that governs implementation of Diffie–Hellman key agreement.

    o PKCS #5. RSA standard that governs password-based cryptography, for example to encrypt private keys for storage.

    o PKCS #7. RSA standard that governs the application of cryptography to data, for example digital signatures and digital envelopes.

    o PKCS #8. RSA standard that governs the storage and encryption of private keys.

    o PKCS #9. RSA standard that governs selected attribute types, including those used with PKCS #7, PKCS #8, and PKCS #10.

   o   PKCS #10. RSA standard that governs the syntax for certificate requests.

   o   PKCS #11. RSA standard that governs communication with cryptographic tokens (such as hardware accelerators and smart cards) and permits application independence from specific algorithms and implementations.

   o   PKCS #12. RSA standard that governs the format used to store or transport private keys, certificates, and other secret material.

- Cryptographic Message Syntax, used in S/MIME (RFC 2311 and RFC 2633). IETF message specification (based on the popular Internet MIME standard) that provides a consistent way to send and receive signed and encrypted MIME data.

- X.509 v3. ITU standard that governs the format of certificates used for authentication in public-key cryptography.

- OCSP (RFC 2560). The Online Certificate Status Protocol (OCSP) governs real-time confirmation of certificate validity.

- PKIX Certificate and CRL Profile (RFC 3280). The first part of the four-part standard under development by the Public-Key Infrastructure (X.509) working group of the IETF (known as PKIX) for a public-key infrastructure for the Internet.

- RSA, DSA, ECDSA, Diffie–Hellman, EC Diffie–Hellman, AES, Triple DES, Camellia, IDEA, SEED, DES, RC2, RC4, SHA-1, SHA-256, SHA-384, SHA-512, MD2, MD5, HMAC: Common cryptographic algorithms used in public-key and symmetric-key cryptography.

- FIPS 186-2 pseudorandom number generator.

Hardware Support

NSS supports the PKCS #11 interface for access to cryptographic hardware like SSL accelerators, HSM-s and smart cards. Since most hardware vendors such as SafeNet Inc. and Thales also support this interface, NSS-enabled applications can work with high-speed crypto hardware and use private keys residing on various smart cards, if vendors provide the necessary middleware. NSS version 3.13 and above support the Advanced Encryption Standard New Instructions (AES-NI).

Java Support

Network Security Services for Java (JSS) consists of a Java interface to NSS. It supports most of the security standards and encryption technologies supported by NSS. JSS also provides a pure Java interface for ASN.1 types and BER/DER encoding. The Mozilla CVS tree makes source code for a Java interface to NSS available.

References

- Smith, Hubbert (2012). Data Center Storage: Cost-Effective Strategies, Implementation, and Management. CRC Press. ISBN 9781466507814. Retrieved 2012-11-15.

- Goodstein, Laurie (2002-06-27). "Albany Diocese Settled Abuse Case for Almost $1 Million". The New York

Times. ISSN 0362-4331. Retrieved 2016-03-21.

- "Confidentiality in Settlement Agreements Is Bad for Clients, Bad for Lawyers, Bad for Justice". www.americanbar.org. Retrieved 2016-03-20.

- ""Quality, Not Quantity: An Analysis of Confidential Settlements and Lit" by Alison Lothes". scholarship.law.upenn.edu. Retrieved 2016-03-20.

- Ahi, Kiarash (May 26, 2016). "Advanced terahertz techniques for quality control and counterfeit detection". Proc. SPIE 9856, Terahertz Physics, Devices, and Systems X: Advanced Applications in Industry and Defense, 98560G. doi:10.1117/12.2228684. Retrieved May 26, 2016.

- Yupu Zhang, Abhishek Rajimwale, Andrea C. Arpaci-Dusseau, Remzi H. Arpaci-Dusseau. "End-to-end Data Integrity for File Systems: A ZFS Case Study" (PDF). Computer Sciences Department, University of Wisconsin. Retrieved 2014-01-02.

- Eliasson, C; Matousek (2007). "Noninvasive Authentication of Pharmaceutical Products through Packaging Using Spatially Offset Raman Spectroscopy". Analytical Chemistry 79 (4): 1696–1701. doi:10.1021/ac062223z. PMID 17297975. Retrieved 9 Nov 2014.

- Li, Ling (March 2013). "Technology designed to combat fakes in the global supply chain". Business Horizons 56 (2): 167–177. doi:10.1016/j.bushor.2012.11.010. Retrieved 9 Nov 2014.

- Boritz, J. "IS Practitioners' Views on Core Concepts of Information Integrity". International Journal of Accounting Information Systems. Elsevier. Retrieved 12 August 2011.

Permissions

Index